ARCHIVES OF ARCHITECTURE

PAOLO PORTOGHESI

THE HAND OF PALLADIO

PHOTOGRAPHS BY
LORENZO CAPELLINI

UMBERTO ALLEMANDI & C.
TURIN ~ LONDON ~ VENICE ~ NEW YORK

Concept by Lorenzo Capellini,
Text and layout by Paolo Portoghesi

Translation by Erika G. Young

Contents

7 PREFACE

9 INTRODUCTION

CHAPTER ONE
17 Reason and Sentiment

CHAPTER TWO
89 The Loggia

CHAPTER THREE
113 Intersections. Spaces within Spaces

CHAPTER FOUR
145 Bareness and Horror Vacui

CHAPTER FIVE
177 Numbers, Music, the Absolute

CHAPTER SIX
201 The Joys of the Worksite

CHAPTER SEVEN
225 The Palladian Landscape

257 BIBLIOGRAPHY

263 INDEX OF NAMES

265 INDEX OF PLACES

Preface

This book was born from a mysterious affinity. The affinity between Palladio and Borromini first came to me only through their shared profession as stonemasons, but then I saw it existed in other fields: in particular in their uninhibited and creative relationship with Classical Antiquity, in the transparency in their works, in the drawings of their creative and design process, in the contrast between the importance of form produced by the hand of man and the marketable value of materials, in their complete mastery of a craft intimately related to an ethical commitment and loyalty. The strong link between Borromini and Palladio proves that although architects, distant in time and space, might have different theoretical approaches, this does not stop them from building on common ideas to create a deep and meaningful relationship.

Borromini's interest in the maestro from Vicenza was certainly influenced by his reading of *The Four Books of Architecture*, one of many in his prestigious library. Suffice it to compare the two courtyards of the House of the Filippini and that of Palazzo Iseppo da Porto, study the ceiling of the Vallicelliana Library and the project for the restoration of St. Paul's outside the Walls, a replica of the layout of Villa Trissino with its concave wings opening as if in an embrace. Other Palladian influences can be found in Borromini's decorative style, for instance in the small continuous arches depicted in the xylograph of the Malcontenta that he used in San Carlino, Palazzo Falconieri and Sant'Ivo.

A possible clue to whether or not the Lombard architect had hands-on knowledge of Palladio's work could lie in a strange coincidence: the star in an oculus in Villa Cornaro enlarged and highlighted in the oval windows of the attic in the façade of Sant'Ivo alla Sapienza. However despite the uncertainties about its Palladian origin, the problem can be solved by turning to Longhena's interpretation of the alleged Palladian motif in Santa Maria della Salute, yet another sign of this dialogue that overcame time and ideologies and transversally enriches and permeates the history of universal architecture.

I should also recall their shared interest for heretical solutions, for instance in the Lateran Basilica: a leafy socle over a traditional base to make the shaft of the column taller. Palladio illustrates this Roman example in the *Four Books* and adopts a similar solution in the internal façade of San Giorgio, while Borromini cites it in his *Opus Architectonicum* and exploits this stratagem in order to use an old column in the House of the Filippini.

However, to turn my interest into a genuine critical contribution, I needed to have first-hand knowledge of Palladio's works. Having lived in Venice for ten years and having become in recent years something of a "Venetian" architect, coupled with the fact that some of my works were part of an exhibition held in the Basilica of Vicenza, this rekindled my interest and turned it into a debt to be paid. So much so that I became convinced I should pay an albeit perhaps superfluous, but none the less intense and passionate homage to an architect who is indeed one of the most acclaimed and imitated in the history of architecture, but also often one of the misunderstood and misconstrued.

Detailed and comprehensive iconographic material was no less important. This problem was successfully solved by my friend Lorenzo Capellini, a great photographer to whom we owe so many unforgettable images of human faces. In 2007 he took over 5000 photos and gave us a new vision of Palladio's works - a vision that is neither pedantic nor measured, but spontaneous and candid. This is how this little book came into being. It reflects my thoughts and readings, but above all, it testifies to the joy of having discovered, through Palladio's writings, drawings and works, one of the persons responsible for improving the reputation and prestige of architects. How did he achieve this? By emphasising the intellectual value of reified thought as well as of the more practical importance of matter, properly organised to be useful, enjoyable and lasting.

Architecture all over the world is undergoing a period of intense vitality and dynamism, based on the belief that innovation doesn't need roots or continuity. This means that my considerations about Palladio's works are controversial yet topical. It also encourages me to state clearly why I wrote this book, something I can explain by citing the lines written by Eliot in the second of his *Four Quartets*, *East Coker*, in the now distant year 1947:

> ... And what there is to conquer
> By strength and submission, has already been discovered
> Once or twice, or several times, by men whom one cannot hope
> To emulate ⁄ but there is no competition ⁄.
> There is only the fight to recover what has been lost
> And found and lost again and again
> For us there is only the trying.

Remember that in the preface to the first of the *Four Books* Palladio speaks of "those who come after us" with a note of hope. As the title of the book suggests, my objective is to discover the hand of Palladio, to identify the most representative traits of his style, his preferences, tics, manias, work method and the different stages of his education and periods of creativity. Faced with such a broad mandate, I thought it best to lead the reader to the threshold of a kingdom which will require he engage his mind and open his heart if he wishes to enter. To do this I have drawn on the immense corpus of work written and completed by scholars, above all starting in the 1950s when the Centre for the Study of Architecture "Andrea Palladio" was founded in Vicenza. Therefore, my sincere thanks go to all those who have contributed to shedding light on Palladio's architecture, in particular, Rudolf Wittkower and Giulio Carlo Argan, my teachers, James S. Ackerman, Manfredo Tafuri, Howard Burns, Lionello Puppi, Tonci Foscari, Antonio M. Dalla Pozza, Rosario Assunto, Guglielmo De Angelis d'Ossat, Franco Barbieri, Renato Cevese, Camillo Semenzato, Licisco Magagnato, Marcello Fagiolo, Christoph Luitpold and Sabine Frommel.

Special thanks to Maria Ercadi for her invaluable editorial support.

I would like to dedicate this book to Dino De Poli who in 1999 asked me in to build the Latin District in Treviso, thereby rekindling my love for Venetian traditions and Palladio's work.

Introduction

"Such an affable and gentle disposition"
GIORGIO VASARI

"There is something divine in his designs,
much like a great poet
who from truth and fiction creates a third reality,
captivating in its fictitious existence."
JOHANN WOLFGANG GOETHE

The task I set myself was to discover what sets Palladio apart from all other architects, to examine his personal "signature touch" and, as a result, his style. This relieves me of following the rules that normally govern a comprehensive monograph and accurate review of the history of critique. Here and there I shall touch on some issues of "designation" and the problematic questions posed by critics, but my main ambition is to lead the reader along a meandering and intriguing path. I want to make him feel I am giving him inside information about the workings of Palladio's mind and his buildings. To do this, I shall review the issues and problems that fired his imagination and inspired him in his studies. However, to provide reliable signage to the open itinerary I propose, I'll start by providing a concise biography of the architect since this will help to understand the man who could and did bequeathed such an important legacy.

Andrea was born in Padua on November 8, 1508. His mother, Martha, was known as "Zota", the lame one, and his father, a miller, was called Pietro, son of a gardener known as "della Gondola" because he used to transport his own grains by water. When he was thirteen, his father, probably on the advice of the boy's godfather Vincenzo Grandi who worked in the construction business, sent him to Bartolomeo Cavazza's *bottega* in Padua. During his five-year apprenticeship his salary was to be one ducat a year; he was to be fed and given clothes (but not shirts) and receive a final payment of 6 ducats. Yet after just two years Andrea left and returned home to his father in Vicenza. When Cavazza arrived in Vicenza he convinced his father to send him back and forced him to work for him for another three years. Recent studies have shown that in Cavazza's *bottega*, *lapicida e architettore* of works of excellence, the young apprentice probably learned not only specific techniques, but also developed a particular interest in architecture. However, in 1524 before finishing his apprenticeship, Andrea returned to Vicenza and enrolled in the fraternity of the stonemasons and marble masons, secretly helped in this endeavour by Giovanni di Giacomo da Porlezza, a member of the Pedemuro *bottega* with whom he began to work. For a short period in 1530 Andrea rented one of the *bottega* in the old *Palazzo della Ragione* and a few years later married Allegradonna who was to give him four children: Leonida, Marcantonio, Silla and Zenobia. These names leave no doubt as to the precocious interest of their father for ancient history and its monuments. In particular, the name Silla (Sulla in English) can be explained by her father's enthusiasm for the sanctuary of Fortuna Primigenia in Palestrina, dating back to the Sullan period, which was to inspire some of his greatest works.

We know very little about Allegradonna, except that she worked for the noblewoman Angela Poiana who respected and befriended her, so much so that when she married Palladio, Angela paid her dowry. Her husband, Bonifacio, asked Palladio to build their villa at Poiana Maggiore: his first great masterpiece.

There are no documents testifying to his work in the Pedemuro *bottega* and scholars disagree on the different theories that have been put forward. He probably did take part in the design of the main doors of Santa Maria dei Servi and the altar of the Cathedral shaped like a triumphal Roman arch. What we do know, however, is that working in this *bottega* (named after the Pedemuro district in Vicenza) allowed him to gradually come into contact with many influential people. His neighbour Alberto Monza introduced him to Giacomo and Antenore Pagello, Ludovico Godi and Taddeo Gazzotti (his first clients) and Rizzardo Alidosio who on numerous occasions helped him to enlarge his circle of acquaintances. In 1532, Andrea worked as a stonemason in the convent of San Michele. In 1537 - the year in which Marcolini, the Venetian editor, published the fourth treatise written by Sebastiano Serlio - Andrea built Villa Godi at Lonedo. Documents initially describe him as a stonemason and then, in 1540, as *messer Andrea architetto*. It is likely that in 1539, together with his friend, the poet and painter Gian Battista Maganza known as Magagnò, Andrea was present at the inauguration of the temporary theatre built by Sebastiano Serlio in Palazzo Colleoni Porto (Vicenza) where he probably met Serlio and had the opportunity to discuss Vitruvius and Roman antiquities with him. This social event was written up by contemporary reporters as being an extremely important gathering. Lucrezio Beccanuvoli, who most probably arrived with Serlio, wrote that "in a few days" the event had made Vicenza "holier than Rome, nobler than Naples, grander than Bologna my sweet native land, lovelier than Florence, haughtier than Genoa, more virtuous than Athens, bigger than Milan and finally richer than Vinegia her lord and master."

In 1540, Andrea designed Palazzo Civena. This was a time in his apprenticeship that was definitely influenced by Sanmicheli who was in touch with the Pedemuro *bottega* and who Andrea was to meet in 1544 when they were both involved in the surveying of Monte Berico. While working on the building site of Villa Cricoli he met Giangiorgio Trissino who immediately became his patron and friend. It was with Trissino that he made his first trip to Rome in 1545. In his biography, Gualdo writes that in order to develop Andrea's talent, Trissino personally explained Vitruvius and took him to Rome three times. Andrea probably acquired the name Palladio when he was co-opted into Trissino's academy and became associated with a character, the angel Palladio, who in the play entitled *Italy freed by the Goths*, descends from the heavens with "two huge wings above his arms / and two smaller ones on his heels," (a sort of Mercury) to defend an ideal building. Perhaps he needed to take a pen name because there was another Andrea in Vicenza, a stonemason from the Ticino region. Between 1538 and 1540, Trissino moved to Padua. It was probably around this time that Palladio met Alvise Cornaro, supporter of "holy agriculture," a real nonconformist, to whom he was to pay homage in the prologue of the first of the *Four Books*.[1] Cornaro was certainly influential in the pragmatic aspects of Andrea's cultural education, even if the generic amateurism in the few pages of his treatise which summarily examines the issue of columns divided by a wall is a far cry from Palladio's culture and sensibilities. His partnership with Trissino, which ended only in 1550 when the writer died, was cemented by their common belief that classical tradition was a saving grace. But Trissino also had a political reason for his belief: he was pro-Imperialist and anti-Venetian. The verses from *Italia Liberata* pronounced by the angel Palladio in which he extols the virtues of modularity - something that well befits Palladio's style - can be considered as rather bizarre proof of this partial affinity.

> And the courtyard is surrounded
> By wide loggias, with round columns,
> As tall as the floor is wide
> And thick an eighth of the width.
> And more than the height;
> And they have on top silver capitals
> As high as the column is thick;
> And underneath they have metal volutes, which are
> Half the size of capital at the top.

It's surprising to see how much these lines are like modern Italian. This is thanks to Trissino's efforts to create a simple language, without local inflexion: a goal very similar to certain aspects of Palladio's studies.

From 1541 to 1545, between his first and second visit to Rome, Palladio's workload increased. During this period he designed Villa Valmarana at Vigardolo, Villa Gazzotti at Bertesina, Villa Pisani at Bagnolo, Villa Saraceno at Caldogno and Villa Thiene at Quinto Vicentino. In 1542, Palladio is recorded as present on the building site of Palazzo Thiene, recently attributed to Giulio Romano based on an old piece of gossip by Scamozzi who indirectly called the author of the *Four Books* a forger (since Palladio had included it amongst his own works). Undoubtedly Giulio, who Andrea met in 1542, influenced him, however this actually contributed to Palladio's defeat in the competition for Palazzo della Ragione. The idea that he worked with Raphael's brilliant pupil should not be taken into consideration, as we will see later (p. 21), based on a question of style. In 1543, Palladio was tasked with masterminding the decorations for the solemn entrance procession of the new Bishop, Ridolfi. Andrea travelled for the first time to Rome in 1541 and then again in 1545 with Trissino and Marco Thiene. The third time, in 1546, Palladio also went to Tivoli and Palestrina where he saw and studied classical monuments and began to put together a series of ideas for his first books: *The Antiquities of Rome* and *Descriptions of the Churches of Rome*, both published in 1554 by the editor Vincenzo Lucrino and destined to be runaway bestsellers. From 1545 to 1547, when Giangiorgio Trissino lived in Rome, Palladio stayed with him in his house in Campo Marzio near the Pantheon "where the crème de la crème of Roman society gathered."[2] During this period Palladio came into contact with the architects of the schools of Bramante, Peruzzi and Sangallo. He also met Michelangelo who Trissino describes as "the gentle spirit who honours the city of Rome, an example of the goodness of common sense and the virtue of value, a genius greater than Praxiteles as a sculpture, Apelles as a painter and Tetrarch as a poet, the incomparable man who he loved greatly and who he held dear in his heart above all others." Even Palladio, who called Michelangelo *divinissimo* in his small publication on *The Antiquities of Rome*, fell under the spell of Michelangelo's myth - an influence very evident in his later works.

Palladio built two ciboria in Rome, one in Santo Spirito in Sassia and the other (still visible) in the centre of two small rooms in the Santo Spirito hospital. In his biography Gualdo writes of the intention of Pope Paul III Farnese to summon the architect to Rome and ask him to complete St. Peter's, an intention thwarted by the death of the Pope in 1549.

Once back in Vicenza in 1546, while working on Palazzo Iseppo da Porto and on Villa Thiene at Quinto Vicentino, he embarked on his greatest adventure: the building of Palazzo della Ragione. For this project he had consulted Sansovino in 1535, Serlio in 1539, Sanmicheli in 1541 and Giulio Romano in 1542. In March 1546, together with Giovanni da Porlezza, Palladio presented a project - well received because it was "economical" (*sic!*) - and was authorised to build an almost full-scale model of a span. Later on, in 1548, he was asked to study four different solutions which he was to use to build a *modellum ligneum*, this time without Giovanni's help. In the spring of 1549, the *Consiglio dei Cento* chose between three designs: a *designum sive modellus vetus* (which had become outdated), the one submitted by Giulio Romano who proposed a compromise solution which lowered the level of the main square and raised that of Piazza delle Erbe, and finally Palladio's model. The result of the vote was overwhelming: 99 to 17. This resounding victory by Palladio, who was named "proto" of the Basilica on May 1, 1549, testifies to the alliance formed by the architect's noble clients who decided to support the restructuring of the city based on this new Roman style. In fact, from the very first his supporters included the Chiericati, Godi and Valmarana families. Between 1548 and 1551, he designed and partially built Villa Poiana at Poiana Maggiore, Villa Saraceno and Palazzo Chiericati.

In the meantime his fame began to spread across Italy and he started to travel more and more: in 1548 he was in Venice where he returned again and again; in 1550 he went to Brescia and Sirmione; 1552 saw him in Trento and Innsbruck and 1562 again in Brescia. In 1566 he went to Piedmont and Provence (France) summoned by Emanuele Filiberto of Savoy to whom he dedicated the third of the *Four Books*.

Giangiorgo Trissino died in 1550; it's not difficult to imagine what effect this had on Palladio. However, around this time he met Daniele Barbaro who offered him his friendship and with whom he developed an intense cultural relationship. Barbaro was a much more learned humanist and less solitary and individualistic as a person. His friendship with the patriarch of Aquileia (of Venetian origin and with an Aristotelian education) was decisive for his studies - Barbaro asked Palladio to draw "the more important figures" of his translation of Vitruvius published in 1566 - and for his future fortunes in Venice.

During the fifth decade of that century, his social relations and travels became more intense. He went to Bassano, Venice, Brescia, Trento and Innsbruck summoned by Cardinal Madruzzo who wanted to exploit his creative genius.

Between 1551 and 1560, Palladio worked on Palazzo Dalla Torre in Verona, on Villa Pisani at Montagnana, Villa Cornaro at Piombino Dese and Palazzo Antonini in Udine, three buildings which were almost finished and where Palladio designed a temple loggia with two superimposed orders ⁄ the classical equivalent of a Venetian building model. Instead he designed a single storey temple loggia for Villa Ragona (never actually built), for Villa Chiericati at Vancimuglio, for Villa Badoer at Fratta Polesine and Villa Foscari (La Malcontenta) ⁄ the most perfect of his villas which, in the xylograph of the treatise, appears surrounded by gardens with a exquisite crenu⁄ lated fence. The design for the villa belonging to Daniele and Marcantonio Barbaro at Maser, as well as Villa Repeta (destroyed by fire) is instead unique. In the design of this latter villa, the architect tried to follow the equalitarian ideology of the Anabaptists embraced by its heretical owner: he did not distinguish between the master's house and the *barchesse* for the agricultural work. In the *Four Books* (II, 15, p. 52), Palladio writes: "as much as that looses in grandeur, for not being more eminent than this, so much this of the villa increases in its prop⁄ er ornament and dignity, by being made equal to that of the master, which adds beauty to the whole work." For Villa Reputa, Palladio also designed a special wing for guests where each person found the virtues to which they were most inclined:

> On the flank, opposite to the stables, there are rooms, of which, some are still dedicated to continency, others to justice, and others to other virtues, with elogiums and paintings, adapted to the subject [...] This was done, that this gentleman, who very courteously receives all those who go and see him, may lodge his visitors and friends in the rooms inscribed to that virtue to which he thinks them mostly inclined.

In the sixties, the finances of the Palladio family were still fairly precarious despite his many professional commitments. For instance, apart from participating in the competition for the post of *proto del sal*, in 1563 Andrea claimed his Padua birthright to enrol his son Silla in a college for young children born in Padua; in 1564, he found it difficult to scrap together 400 ducats to ensure a dowry for his daughter Zenobia who was to marry the jeweller Giambattista Dalla Fede.

The early stages of his involvement with Venice was anything but positive: he was not awarded the Office *del sal*, and in 1555 Sansovino won the competition for the Golden Staircase of Palazzo Ducale. Again, for the Rialto bridge, which he worked on from 1554 to 1565, his design was passed over in favour of the one by Sansovino. It was from the sixties onwards that his friend⁄ ship with the Barbaro brothers gradually opened even the doors of Venice. Apart from Villa Pisani, his only assignment had been the façade of San Pietro di Castello, the Venetian cathedral, for which he prepared a wooden model in 1558: unfortunately, the model was later radically altered by the builders. In 1560, the Lateran Canons entrusted him with the design and construction of the Covent of Charity. Palladio used this design to present himself in Venice as a courageous champion ready to import Roman grandeur ⁄ totally disregarding local taste. Goethe in his *Travels in Italy* considered this design as Palladio's best work and defined it "the most beautiful staircase in the world." In 1560, he began to build the refectory of the convent of San Giorgio and in 1564⁄65 he built the church of Santa Lucia, later destroyed by fire in 1864. Only when Sansovino died in 1570 did Palladio effectively become, albeit unofficially, the *proto* of the architects of the Serenissima.

During the fifties, construction was ongoing on the loggias of the Basilica in Vicenza. In 1561 the nine spans of the first order along Piazza Maggiore had been completed and in 1564 con⁄ struction on the upper loggias finally got underway. Four were finished in 1570. In the meantime, Palladio was involved with Palazzo Trissino, Palazzo Poiana and perhaps Casa Cogollo, for centuries considered his family home. In 1555, he was a founding member of the *Accademia Olimpica* and in 1558 began to build his first cupola: the cupola of the cathedral.

The sixties were crucial for Andrea: it was a time when new and in some ways unexpected developments were taking place in his creative activities, especially in two fields: spatiality and decoration. In July 1560 he took part in the launching ceremony of a galleon, perhaps one he himself designed. This idea of Palladio working on non-architectural designs is not as far-fetched as it seems if you consider that (as reported by Lionello Puppi)[3] Giuseppe Ceredi in his book *Three ways of raising water* describes a machine designed by Palladio to "get water from low-lying areas." In 1562, he went to Brescia as a consultant for the Town Council. In 1563 he was involved in the construction of Villa Valmarana at Lisiera (a design that was to be changed many times), as well as the side door of the Basilica in Vicenza for Canon Almerico. Between 1562 and 1570, Palladio often worked in the Verona area for the Serego family who had launched an ambitious water reclamation and channelling programme. Palladio built them a villa (unfinished and later destroyed) in Miega at Cologna Veneta, the *barchesse* of a villa in Cucca (now Veronella) and part of a project described in the *Four Books* for the villa of Santa Sofia at Pedemonte. Between 1564 and 1566, he built Villa Emo Capodilista at Fanzolo, Palazzo Pretorio at Cividale, Villa Zeno at Donegal, La Rotonda, the Bassano bridge, Palazzo Valmarana, Palazzo Barbaran(o), Palazzo Schio and the Loggia del Capitanio in Vicenza. Apart from these works which were at least partially built, we should also recall his contemporary projects illustrated in the treatise but never executed: Palazzo Angarano, Villa Mocenigo on the Brenta, Villa Valmarana Braga and the enormous Villa Trissino at Maledo.

In June 1566, Palladio met Emanuele Filiberto of Savoy in Vicenza. He dedicated the third of the *Four Books* to him and was invited by the later to Piedmont, probably to receive a mandate which, however, never materialised. Palladio took advantage of this journey to go to Provence (France) and study the Roman monuments in Nîmes, helped by his son Orazio who had just graduated in law at Padua university.

In May 1566 Palladio met Giorgio Vasari in Venice. In the second edition of his book, *Lives of the Artists* (1568) in an appendix on the life of Sansovino, Vasari published a short but extremely comprehensive note on his works, ending it with the flattering words:

> [...] I shall say no more about him; because this is enough for him to become known as the excellent architect he is by anyone who sees his wonderful works; since he is young and is continuing his studies, we can hope he will go on to even better things in the future. I shan't deny that so much talent is accompanied by a pleasant and affable nature which endears him to all; this has gained him the privilege of being accepted amongst the academics of Florentine draughtsmen.

In 1570 the *Four Books* was published in Venice by the editor Domenico de' Franceschi, first in two separate volumes, but after a few months in just one. Presumably he started work on it in the fifties since Doni in his *Seconda Libraria* (1555) talks about a Palladian treatise, still without a title, but definable as "Norms of real architecture." The work was much more ambitious than that and included a manuscript on Terms, already drafted in 1580 and in the hands of Jacopo Contarini with whom Palladio lived during his final years.

In the meantime, Palladio was grappling with a number of setbacks. On May 22, 1560, his salary for the work on the Basilica was withdrawn due to his many absences from the worksite. He had to wait two months before the problem was solved in his favour. In 1565 he complained in a letter to Vincenzo Arnaldi about the endless difficulties he had encountered when trying to build a temporary wooden theatre in the courtyard of Palazzo Foscari in Santa Croce for the *Compagnia della Calza*. In October 1567, together with Magagnò, he was at the bedside of his dying friend Francesco Pisani in the villa he had built for him in Montagnana; in 1569, during an argument over women at a party, his son Leonida stabbed and killed the host Alessandro Camera. Almost certainly thanks to his father Leonida was later pardoned by the podestà, adding to his unhappiness. In 1570 Daniele Barbaro died. When dedicating the first book of the treatise to count Giacomo Angarano, Palladio complains of "many great concerns that oppress my mind and my spirit" and

Introduction 13

speaks of "serious infirmities", early signs of the first "ailments" of encroaching old age. In 1571, his son Orazio was investigated and then released by the Sant'Uffizio. The following year two of his sons, Leonida and Orazio, died in rapid succession. His wife Allegradonna fell seriously ill and was "close to death", causing Palladio "enormous concern". His first-born Leonida and Orazio helped him prepare the drawings for the book *De Bello Gallico* which was to come out in 1575, published by the same publisher of the *Four Books*, De' Franceschi.

In the preface, after having explained how Trissino had introduced him to the study of the "order and discipline of ancient militia," Palladio first talks about his sons' interest in his work and then goes on to lament their deaths in such sorrowful terms that it is worth citing this "unique" autobiographic fragment:

> So I started to read all the ancient authors and historians who dealt with this issue, and having for years and years toiled and studied these things, when I thought I had acquired sufficient knowledge, I decided to also introduce my very dear sons Leonida and Orazio, young (and if I may say) gifted with beautiful manners and intelligence: and so very quickly I taught them the basics of the subject, which as soon as they had learnt, decided to follow in the footsteps that I, on the path of this science had walked and had shown them; and this they did so that, fascinated by the sweetness of such beautiful and strange studies, in agreement and unanimously they wanted to illustrate all the barracks of the armies, the roads around cities, problems of weapons and everything that Caesar had written about and described in his writings. However they were not able to finish this worthy endeavour because death, envious of human happiness and glory, stepped in to stop their intentions, to my profound and bitter sorrow, in just two and a half months, I was deprived of my dear children leaving me dejected and miserable. After their death, I found several pieces of paper in which they had, with words and drawings, started their labours so well, I thought that this (still immature and foreign effort) was an opportunity to execute the idea I had much earlier, encouraged also by a father's love: because I decided this powerful means could at least serve to portray their honourable desire for glory, to which they both aspired. And so, looking at what little they had done and I had found, and adding what I believed necessary to finish it, I decided to make it apparent to the eyes of man, to honour the memory of my sons, but also to follow my natural inclination, to give the world what little I can to make it better. Nor do I want to deny that our labours are not without error, all men have some imperfections, and I too have been born with this same condition, nor do I consider myself above others: I say that, if the defects of men are worthy of pardon, then those of two young men should be who perhaps more than any other started this honourable labour, and that of an afflicted and disconsolate father who, defeated and subjected by that serious and tedious passion that others can also feel when they loose dear and important things, was unable to provide all those advices that experience teaches to help finish this important and remarkable endeavour in noteworthy and perfect terms.[4]

In the 1570s the Veneto region went through a period of economic recession that slowed down or halted the building frenzy of earlier years. Work on the Basilica stopped for ten years and was to be completed only in 1617. In 1571, Palladio probably began Palazzo Porto-Breganze (of which only a spectacular fragment remains) and became a consultant for Venice for the Celestine convent. In 1572 and later in 1578 and 1579, he was in Bologna as a consultant for the façade of San Petronio (which came to nothing) and in 1574 was tasked with designing the triumphal arch in honour of the arrival of Henry III of France. The following year, an untiring Palladio even managed to design an ebony writing desk in the shape of a triumphal arch. In 1575 and for the whole of 1576 the pest raged in Venice, so Palladio fled to Vicenza and managed to survive. In 1575, he went to Brescia to be consulted about the loggia and became interested in the restoration of Palazzo Ducale after the fire of December 1577. His proposal for Palazzo Ducale was that the façade be demolished. In 1576 he designed the Valmarana funeral chapel in the church of Santa Corona, the arch of the Scalette at the foot of Mount Berico and was asked to design the votive temple of Il Redentore at the Giudecca, inaugurated only in 1592. In 1578, the year in which it is thought his wife Allegradonna died, he designed the last of his works in Vicenza, the church of Santa Maria Nova, and in the autumn returned to Bologna. In 1579 he designed the cloister of the Cypresses on the island of San Giorgio and went to Belluno in March where he was humiliated when his advice for the construction of a bridge over the river Piave was rejected. He died on August 19, 1580, perhaps while working on the worksite of the small temple next to Villa Barbaro at Maser. He was buried in the church of Santa Corona where his son Silla had bought a place for the family tomb.

Anyone wanting to mentally recreate Palladio's legacy on the day he died would be forced to paint a dramatic and disturbing picture. Only a few of the many buildings he began were actually completed and none of these were his more famous masterpieces. Neither the Basilica, which was only completed in the seventeenth century, nor La Rotonda, of which only one of the four loggias still remained, nor the church of San Giorgio, which didn't have a façade, nor Il Redentore, which was to be inaugurated only in 1592, nor the Convent of Charity, only partially built and ravaged by fire in 1630, nor the Loggia del Capitanio, which was still as Palladio had left it, nor the houses in Vicenza, precious fragments of much bigger and more complex buildings either designed or still on the drawing board and recorded in all their ideal grandeur in the tables of his treatise. And what can we say about his written works? Only a vague outline of the ambitious project of the preface of the *Four Books* remains, mainly because the parts that were already written were senselessly scattered. His relationship with his clients, considered in recent decades as one of the strong points of his professional career, was not as idyllic as it might have seemed. If in the printed edition of the *Four Books*, this relationship is described in glowing terms, in the draft manuscript it is portrayed in a totally different light. On the issue of the "division of rooms", he wrote:

> It is convenient that I rightly excuse myself with my readers, because an architect is very much obliged to conform more to the will of those who pay, than to that which ought to be done, in order to respect the wishes of the clients who, partly to preserve the old fabricks, partly because of other requests and desires, obliged me to depart from what I have written and should be observed and would have done, although I have always tried to be as correct as I could.

This excerpt brings to mind the affectionate observation made by Goethe in his *Travels in Italy* for October 6, 1776:

> In those works which Palladio actually terminated, especially in the churches, I have found both wonderful inventions but also some I disagree with, so reflecting on how right or wrong I could be compared to such a brilliant man, I felt he was standing next to me and said: I did this and that against my will, but nevertheless, I did it, because this was the only way, given the circumstances, that I could come as close as possible to my idea of perfection.

Palladio has always been considered a successful architect, but we should remember that this success arrived late in life and was only briefly enjoyed while he was still alive. The generation that came after him didn't recognise his genius: the legend of Palladio was created by a generation which not only had never met him personally, but felt him to be distant, like someone who came from "antiquity." Suffice it to recall that the first biography on Palladio was written in 1617, that his son, Silla ⁄ who had the right to finish his works ⁄ was only employed to finish the Teatro Olimpico, and that Scamozzi (who was meant to preserve his legacy and continue his works) had such an inferiority complex that he often avoided pronouncing his name and even started to spread rumours and malignant gossip about him.

[1] All quotes from the *Four Books* are taken from the 1965 edition published by Dover Publications, In., New York. Page numbers refer to this edition. All the references to drawings and tables (either pages or figures) are taken from the *Quattro Libri dell'Architettura* published by Il Polifilo in 1980 edited by Licisco Magagnato and Paola Marini.
[2] GIANGIORGIO ZORZI, *I disegni dell'Antichità di Andrea Palladio*, Venice 1959, p. 20.
[3] LIONELLO PUPPI, *Palladio. Introduzione alle architetture e al pensiero teorico*, San Giovanni Lupatoto 2005, p. 13.
[4] ANDREA PALLADIO, *Scritti sull'architettura (1554-1579)*.

1. Reason and Sentiment

"Palladio was a sensual artist, as proficient in the alchemy of vision as any other contemporary Venetian artist... He liked to balance light, and introduced completely new colouristic and surface values into architecture... it was indeed this combination of sensual and intellectual elements that endeared Palladio to so many generations..."
JAMES S. ACKERMAN

Palladian architecture has always been admired by two kinds of critics; those who appreciate his loyalty to an ideal of rationality and regularity and those who are "unsettled", who recognise, as Piovene rightly put it, "the unexpected, the fluidity, the mystery and the sudden combustion of his visions." Palladio was part of a cultural environment that witnessed the blossoming of the pictorial vision of Titian, Veronese and the Bassano brothers: this should alert those who would prefer to secrete his penchant for a sensual and hedonistic manner of expression. Likewise, his ongoing and successful attempts to give a didactic dimension to his choices should be a warning for those who underestimate his ambition to reconcile reason and sentiment – his one true goal.

Palladian rationalism is expressed primarily through two different indirect systems of control over aesthetic and distributive qualities: "typology" and classical orders. In both cases, Vitruvius' treatise is his starting point. His early villas reflect the traditional Venetian idea of a home: a prismatic block with a roof and load-bearing walls that complete the outer envelope and correspond to the standard measurements then used for beams. Initially Palladio simply imposed on this elementary model a symmetrical, three or five part partition orthogonal to the entrance façade, giving additional width to the central part which coincided with a loggia. Examples of this design are villas built for the Godi, Gazzotti, Saraceno, Caldogno, Angarano families and Villa Thiene at Quinto Vicentino.

Only in Villa Poiana does the system illustrated by Wittkower in his famous comparative table start to appear. It involves five parallel fascia of different widths: the central one (normally the loggia) is wider, while the two adjacent fascia (normally for the stairs) are narrower and the side fascia is intermediate in width. Palladio's *ars combinatoria* is at its best in this flexible framework: it allows the centre rooms to be either square, round, cross or T-shaped, the stairs to be symmetrically arranged dividing the house into two sets of rooms, and the loggias to characterise the façades with their spatial permeability. The 11 villas indicated by Wittkower belong to this second type: Villa Thiene at Cicogna, Villa Sarego at Miega, Villa Poiana at Poiana Maggiore, Villa Badoer at Fratta Polesine, Villa Zeno at Cessalto, Villa Cornaro at Piombino Dese, Villa Pisani at Montagnana, Villa Emo Capodilista at Fanzolo, Villa Foscari at Malcontenta, Villa Pisani at Bagnolo and La Rotonda. In actual fact, La Rotonda, together with Villa Trissino, Villa Mocenigo and Villa Thiene at Cicogna are a third type with two axes of orthogonal symmetry. When considering the position of the *barchesse*, another three types emerge: with concave wings (Villa Badoer, Villa Trissino, Villa Mocenigo and Villa Thiene at Cicogna); with rectilinear porticoes that act as wings (Villa Mocenigo at Marocco, Villa Emo Capodilista and Villa Barbaro), and the "C" configuration where the villa is surrounded by porticoes on all three sides. These include Villa Poiana at Poiana Maggiore, Villa Sarego at Santa Sofia, Villa Pisani at Bagnolo, Villa Saraceno at Finale di Agugliaro, Villa Repeta at Campiglia dei Berici, Villa Ragona at Ghizzole di Montegaldella and Villa Angarano at Bassano del Grappa. The latter has a *barchesse* system that can be enlarged using a herringbone pattern. The courtyard type is present in Villa Serego at Santa Sofia (partially built), and in Villa Mocenigo at Dolo, which no longer exists. An intermediate type, a cross between a villa and a building but without agricultural outhouses, would include: Palazzo Antonini at Udine, Villa Garzadori at Vicenza, Villa Sarego at Miega, Villa della Torre at Verona, Villa Cornaro at Piombino Dese, Villa Pisani at Montagnana and Villa Foscari (La Malcontenta).

Palladian critics are unanimous in emphasising the specifics of his typological philosophy, yet they are divided when it comes to iconology. Some consider it foreign to Palladio's sensibilities and therefore relative only to the plastic and pictorial dec\orations of his villas, while others (Fagiolo, Corboz, Lewis and Rupprecht) deem it an important element that influenced all his choices, above all, those regarding his most important masterpieces. The villas were always meant to be linked to the revival and development of agriculture thanks to the direct involvement

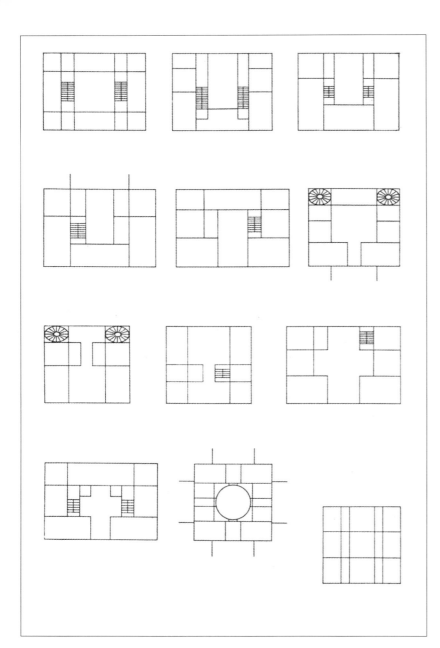

Fig. 1. Schematic layout of eleven Palladian villas (Rudolf Wittkower, *Architectural Principles in the Age of Humanism*, London 1962).

of the owners in the economics of the estate at a time when cultivated land was enjoying a new season of popularity. This agenda was believed either to reflect and support early forms of capitalism or, on the contrary, to be an attempt to defend feudal pacts and parasitic revenue, in opposition to the central authority of Venice. The Palladian model successfully combined the owner's residence with the agricultural buildings (the *barchesse*, the attics used as hay lofts and the cellars as service areas), but it also gave many villas a overall "unfinished" air. These two characteristics have sparked a debate which has not yet led to any credible conclusions. Despite all this, from an iconological point of view there are parallels between this agenda and Palladio's efforts (both in the fields of architecture and decoration) to develop the villa as a self-sufficient microcosm in which to honour virtue and its fruits - peace, concord, tranquillity and the pleasure of living totally immersed in a natural landscape. Rupprecht cites an excerpt from Gallo[1] in which he speaks of Adam being driven from Eden: "There where - even if he deserved to be driven out - he remained through divine mercy, and with him sweet Agriculture as a companion so that, apart from nourishment, there be cool shade and enjoyment during grave and bitter calamities [...] being this art the oldest, most righteous and useful of them all." Whatever the reason and whatever the economic yield from this adulation and sacralisation of agriculture, it is an element common to architecture and plastic decoration. Villa Emo was one of Palladio's few projects to be built "as designed" and one in which production (renewed production of corn) is important and meaningful. Here, the goddess Ceres stands over the entrance, while in the centre room, Zelotti painted two frescoes featuring scenes from Roman history exalting virtue: Virginia killed by her father to save her from Appio's desire and Scipio renouncing the female slave owed to him as booty. In the same villa, the frescoes of mythological scenes involving the punishment of passion are located above the doors: this is "the typological and Christian synthesis of narration. *Noli me tangere* contrasts the *cupiditas* of Nessus; the tears of a repentant Venus stands across from a "penitent St. Jerome"; Christ as *Ecce Homo* counters a slain Argo."[2] The main ethics of this iconology appears to allude to a terrestrial condition of happiness and a non-religious trust in justice on earth. When Palladio talks of happiness in his treatise, he's always a little sceptic. For example when he talks about leisure pursuits while at the villa:

> But perhaps he will not reap much less utility and consolation from the country house; where the remaining part of the time will be passed in feeling and adorning his own possessions, and by industry, and the art of agriculture, improving his estate; where also by the exercise of which in a villa is commonly taken, on foot and on horseback, the body will more easily preserve its strength and health; and finally, where the mind, fatigued by the agitations of the city, will be greatly restored and comforted, and be able quietly to attend the studies of letters, and contemplation. Hence it was the ancient sages, commonly used to retire to such like places; where being oftentimes visited by their virtuous friends and relations, have houses, gardens, fountains, and such like pleasant places, and above all, their virtue, they could easily attain to as much happiness as be can attained *here below* (II, 12, p. 46).

The same expression "here below" can be found in the preface in Book One when Palladio cites Vitruvius' dream about the birth of architecture and society as being the consequence of discovering the pleasure of sitting with other people and warming oneself

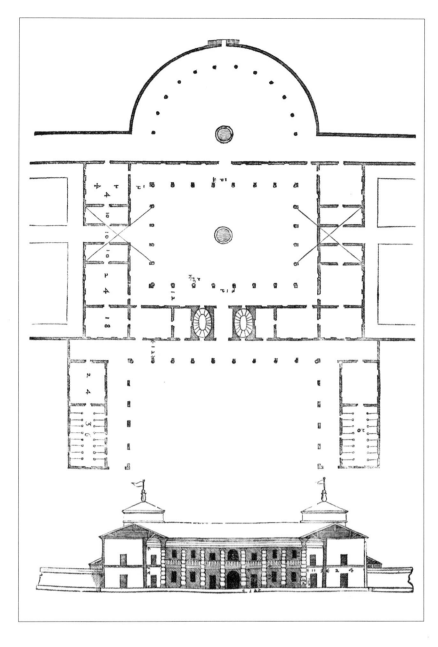

Fig. 2. Villa Serego at Santa Sofia di Pedemonte (*Four Books*, II, 15).

in front of the fire. Palladio writes: "it being very probable, that man lived formerly by himself; but afterwards, he felt he required the affection of other men, to obtain those things that might make him happy, (if any happiness is to be found here below)." So despite the fact that his villas paid tribute to an entirely earthly way of "living in harmony" with nature, Palladio never hid his religious nature and his faith in transcendence. Perhaps this is the key to understanding his title pages: it was not his intention to desecrate but consecrate the home and therefore the family (despite his sceptic aristocratic clientele). So much so that in Villa Almerico, he identified it as being the "custodian" of the true Christian temple which, according to St. Paul (also cited by Serlio), is not a building, but man himself as a living temple. Contrary to what one would expect (given the obvious separation of the master's house from the *barchesse*), in Palladio's villas this separation is not exclusive because often pathways and functions merge and the part reserved for the owners are located above the service quarters of the ground floor and under the attic used to store grain. In Villa Badoer at Fratta Polesine, this stratification is emphasised by Palladio who uses words that reveal the importance of his symbolic choice:

The granaries are above, and the kitchen, cellars, and other places, belonging to its convenience, are below. The columns of the loggias of the master's house, are of the Ionic order. The cornice, like a crown, encompasses the whole house. The frontispiece, over the loggias, forms a beautiful sight, because it makes the middle part higher than the sides. Lower on the plane are found the places for the steward, bailiff or farmer, stables, and other suitables for a villa (II, 14, p. 48).

The satisfaction of the creator vis-à-vis his creation is not based only on the use of a flexible and eloquent architectural style, but also on the ability to apply aesthetics to the quality of individual life within an orderly system of relationships. André Corboz[3] wrote: "so, grain under the roof, wine in the cellar. But function has nothing to do with this: whether it's wheat or corn, it could well be stocked only in the attic of the *barchesse* and wine in special cellars not located in the main building." Corboz offers two possible iconographic interpretations: "The grain is in the upper part of the main building, behind the pediment; it's obvious it's a *solar* product [...] To this solar, dry and zenithal element corresponds a symmetrical terrestrial element, liquid and *nadir* in nature - wine - that anchors the house to the ground. It endorses the owner's relationship with the economics of his property. The master of the house lives on the mezzanine between the heavens and hell." After the cosmological explanation he provides a religious one as well: "In fact the owner doesn't live in just any old nation or age, but in a catholic country. He finds himself between grain and drink, in short between bread and wine, in other words, between the two kinds of Eucharist." Regarding La Rotonda, we will see how Palladian critics, above all in recent decades, have focused on decoding a form which, because it is absolute, appears to have been designed to unleash the relentless, mesmerizing dance of interpretative *fury*.

With regard to his buildings, there are only three examples in the treatise in which he elaborates the ideal typology of the isolated volume lit on all four sides: Palazzo Thiene, only partially built, and the projects (only on paper) of Palazzo Trissino and Palazzo Angarano. All the other provide examples of how the architect creatively "adapted to the sites," to lots with two or three blind

Reason and Sentiment 19

Elevations and plans of several villas:
Fig. 3. Villa Thiene at Quinto Vicentino (*Four Books*, II, 14), with the inner courtyard.
Fig. 4. Villa Mocenigo at Marocco (*Four Books*, II, 14).
Fig. 5. Villa Thiene at Cicogna (*Four Books*, II, 14).
Fig. 6. Autographical drawing of Villa Mocenigo on the Brenta (Riba, X, 2, detail).

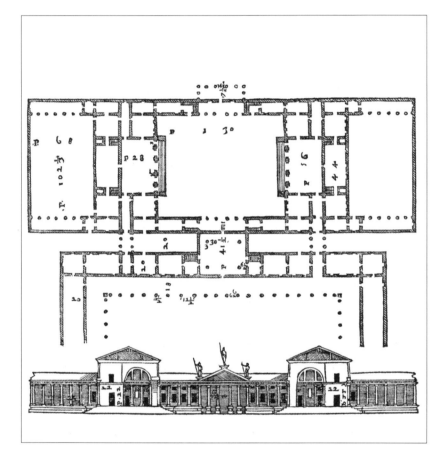

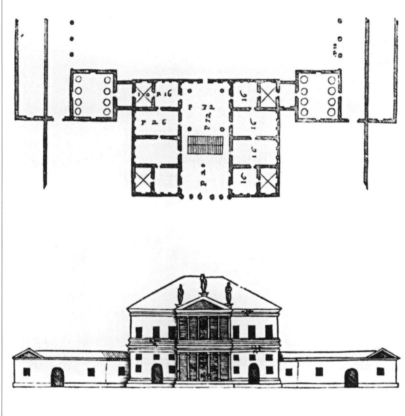

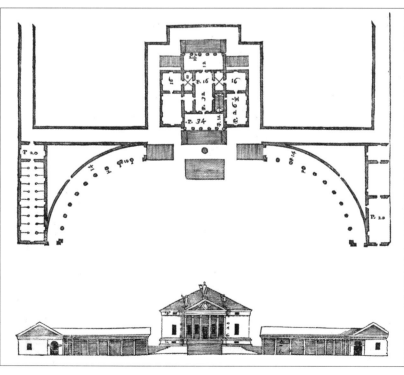

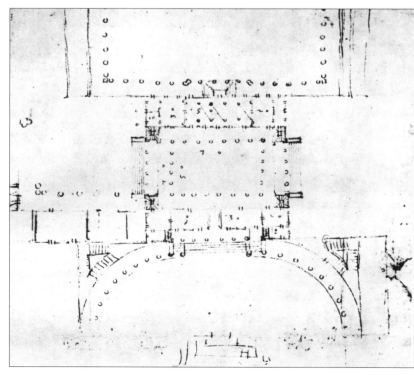

20 Reason and Sentiment

sides where he could not design windows. This applies to most of the houses he designed (i.e., for the Iseppo da Porto, Valmarana and Barbarano families), but also to those that were never built: the house in Vicenza for the Capra family, the one in Venice on a pyramidal lot and another with a grand oval staircase, a prototype of the one Mascherino was to build in Palazzo Quirinale in Rome. Another typology had one blind and three relatively open sides ⁄ Palazzo Chiericati and another (more difficult to classify), Palazzo Bonin Thiene. Palladio considered planning difficulties as a challenge. This is obvious from the broad range of solutions he proposed, his ability to find distributive stratagems to solve the problematic shape of sites and the spatial opulence of his buildings. When designing façades, his main aim was to master the Roman model: drawings in the collection of the Royal Institute of British Architects (RIBA) show how in his studies for Palazzo Iseppo da Porto he elegantly recalls Raphael's house designed by Bramante, while inside the courtyard (never actually built) he introduces a variation on the theme of the giant order. This variation has an impressive and powerful plasticity with a trabeation eroded by small brick bridges making the columns look like statues placed side by side. It's true that the introduction of terracotta in a stone environment was inspired by the Balbi crypt seen in a drawing housed in the RIBA collection in London (XI, 2), but Palladio's design turns an irrelevant technical detail into an opportunity for him to express his scientific and also highly expressive sensibilities.

In Palazzo Thiene, the ideas he took from Giulio Romano, for example the ashlar windows, are placed inside a solid monumental frame (inspired by others) and emphasised by the corner towers directly reminiscent of the Bramantesque archetype of Palazzo dei Tribunali in Via Giulia. Giulio Romano's muse, regrettably referred to based on nasty gossip spread by Scamozzi, always ready to propose cuts and alliterations to the compositional plan, would never have inspired such a poised and imposing concept, gently enriched by the elegant, restrained vibrations of the farmhouse ⁄ if anything, closer in style to the one used by Sanmicheli. If it's easy to see Giulio's influence in the structure of the entrance hall, but it's less obvious in the large courtyard with its gentle pattern of Corinthian pilasters intended by Palladio to be crowned with statues standing out against the sky. The large space around Palazzo Chiericati allowed Palladio to achieve a Vitruvian dream: Piazza dei Latini surrounded by colonnades as illustrated in the *Four Books* (III, 18, p. 74); to the ground floor portico resting on a stylobate like a temple Palladio added two loggias next to the only part of the façade closed off by a wall. The triple bay portico with its double row of columns and superbly decorated coffered ceiling was inspired directly by Vitruvius, but it does create a space that is not at all archaeological and enhances the great regional style of the portico recessed to welcome the traveller. In Palazzo Barbaran(o), Palladio repeats the superimposed orders of Palazzo Chiericati and merges the two façades by making the columns intersect, but is unable to respect standard intercolumniation. So he experiments, as he did in the Loggia del Capitanio, using decorations to see if this can offset the closure effect of the wall. However, in the first order, the slight, graceless plasticity of the reliefs certainly introduces discordant vibrations into the balanced structure through the use of the scrolls so fiercely criticised in the *Four Books*. In the fragment of Palazzo Porto⁄Breganze (terribly Michelangiolesque and full of unusual and novel typologies), the order has a 2:1 intercolumniation, very similar to the *eustylos*. Ultimately it drastically reduces the luminosity of the windows and marks Palladio's refusal to balance *utilitas* and *venustas* which had appeared to be a key issue in his studies. In the Venetian buildings included in his treatise, Palladio disregards the local model (with lots of windows in the centre area) and proposes ⁄ using a decidedly non⁄Venetian style ⁄ superimposed orders and walled façades crowned by a central tympanum. It's no wonder that all these proposals never got off the drawing⁄board.

The first time Palladio had to tackle the design of an ecclesiastical building was in 1565 when he was asked to develop a project for the Benedictine convent of San Giorgio Maggiore.

Fig. 7. Preparatory drawing for the xylograph of the *Four Books*, showing Palazzo Iseppo da Porto at Vicenza (RIBA, XVII, 3).

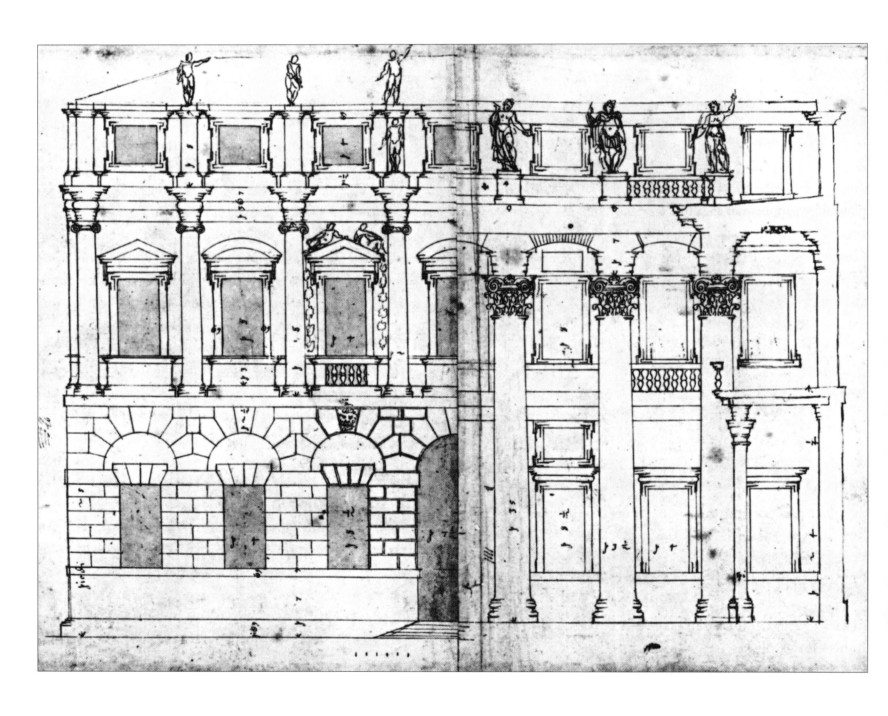

Palladio was almost sixty: the Council of Trent (participated by Daniele Barbaro) had concluded its work two years earlier. The Council decrees make no mention of the shape of new churches, a topic which was to be dealt with in detail in the book written by St. Carlo Borromeo and published seven years after the *Four Books*.[4] In his treatise, Palladio shows he fully espouses the trends sanctioned by the Council, even if he was still fascinated by the platonic symbolism of the circle and convinced of the independence of architecture and its symbolic codes. With regard to San Giorgio Maggiore, after praising how well round forms are suited to churches, also because "many people may there be able to assist at divine office," he adds,

> Those churches are also very laudable, that are made in the form of a cross, which have their entrance in the part representing the foot of the cross, and opposite to which should be the principal altar, and the choir; and in the two branches, that are extended from either in the form of the cross, they represent to the eyes of the beholders that wood from which depended our salvation (IV, 2, p. 82).

When asked for his opinion on church design, one of the ideas that Palladio continually expresses is the visibility of the altar and the priest celebrating mass. In his comments on the Cathedral in Brescia written in 1567, he recommends "that when priests celebrate mass, they should be visible from all areas of the church." Questioned by Martino Bassi on the position of the new choir in the Cathedral in Milan, he again suggests placing it under the tribune "so that divine offices can be heard all over the church." In his treatise, his key views on Christina basilicas culminate in a view that that altar should be in a dominant position.

> But we, by omitting the porticoes round the temples, build them very like basilicas, in which, as it has been said, porticoes were made in the part within, as we now do in temples. Which happened, because the first who, enlightened by truth, gave themselves up to our religion, were accustomed, for fear of the gentiles, to assemble in the basilicas of private men; whence feeling that this form succeeded very well, because the altar was places with great dignity, in the place of the tribunal, and the choir stood very conveniently round the altar, and the remaining part was free for the people, it has not been altered since (IV, 5, p. 86).

This excerpt gives us a clear idea about Palladio's religious beliefs. His instinctive religiosity, like that of many others, made Palladio almost immune to the heretic ideas[5] of the numerous Vicentine nobles who had turned him into a successful professional. Yet he was receptive to the ferments of the catholic reform begun even before Luther wrote and published his manifesto. Proof of this sensibility comes, on the one hand, from his mention of Queen Virtus, placed as a symbol of the treatise in the middle of the only broken tympanum designed by Palladio and already present (in just as eminent a position) in Barbaro's 1565 edition of Vitruvius, and, on the other, from persistent emphasis on the visibility of priests and liturgical recitals which require personal, subjective involvement, very similar ⁄ it could be said ⁄ to modern sensibilities.

Typologically speaking, Palladio was faithful to his convictions and to his vocation for *ars combinatoria*; he designed and in part created the two models of a cruciform plan and centrality. He tried to merge them and even go further in the last of his designs, if one includes the unusual project of Santa Maria Nova in Vicenza amongst his autobiographical experiences. In San Giorgio, the cruciform plan has a domed space and the transept, with its apses, recalls a theatrically "represented" centrality, even if it is not fully developed. Looking at the central nave from the entrance, one is immediately aware of Palladio's instinctive tendency towards lateral dilation of vision. The onlooker is drawn not only to the axial vision centred on the presbytery and the altar (culminating in the splendid drum with plain niches and rectangular windows), but also to the amplification created by turning one's gaze and exploring the theatrical wings created by the double pilasters supporting the arches dividing the nave. Another duality captures the onlooker's attention: the contrast of scale and position between the two orders, the minor order resting directly on the floor and the major order on the towering pedestals that are far taller than a man and therefore juxtapose two kingdoms, two different spatial qualities corresponding to two different levels of luminosity.

Reason and Sentiment 23

FIGS. 8-10. AN ENGRAVING WITH THE PLAN OF SAN GIORGIO MAGGIORE IN VENICE AND, BELOW, THE PLAN OF IL REDENTORE IN VENICE (FRANCESCO ANTONIO MUTTONI, *ARCHITETTURA DI ANDREA PALLADIO... CON LE OSSERVAZIONI DELL'ARCHITETTO N.N.*, VENICE 1740-1748). RIGHT, CENTRAL-PLAN CHURCH, PERHAPS DESIGNED BY PALLADIO AS A POSSIBLE SOLUTION FOR IL REDENTORE (RIBA, XIV, 16).

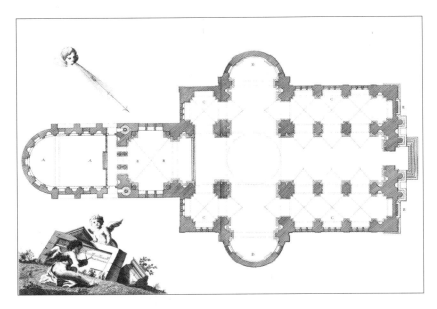

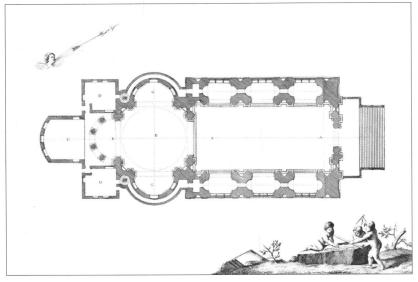

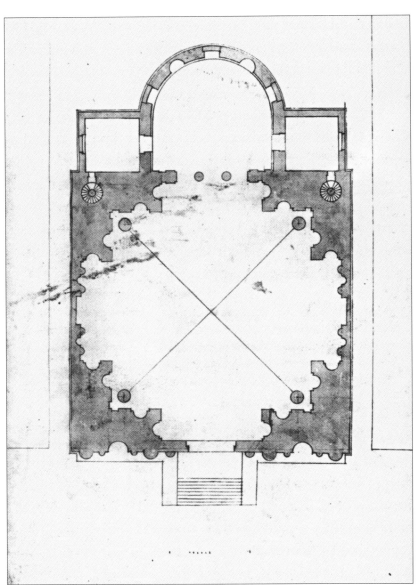

We do not know for certain whether it was Palladio who designed the presbytery with the transenna dividing the choir. He certainly was instrumental in the decision to avoid putting the choir between the faithful and the altar based on his deep-rooted conviction that the faithful should be fully involved. However the two orders of the transenna do not play the same syntactic role in other crucial intersecting parts. The solution studied for Il Redentore is much better. Although visually separate, between the church and choir he has inserted a much needed and pure image of the transparent light-filled niche. A different apostolic agenda and cultural tradition existed between the Benedictine order (which commissioned San Giorgio) and the Capuchins (that the Republic of Venice wanted to be the custodians of the votive temple of Il Redentore). On the one hand, an awareness of their social role and, on the other, the Franciscan rule of humility and poverty. The two choirs truly reflect this difference; the one dedicated to Benedictine privacy was elegant and graceful to the point of ostentation, with its masterly rhythm of interconnected openings, while the choir of the Capuchins was bare to the point of being deliberately plain, with a small cornice

24 Reason and Sentiment

FIGS. 11 AND 12. ELEVATION AND PLAN OF THE RIALTO BRIDGE, FIRST SOLUTION (CIVIC MUSEUM, VICENZA).

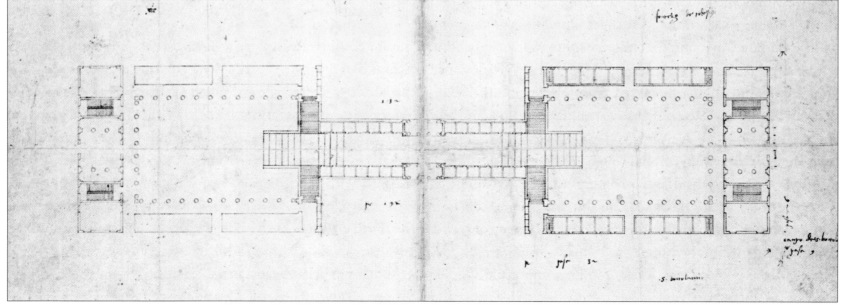

Reason and Sentiment 25

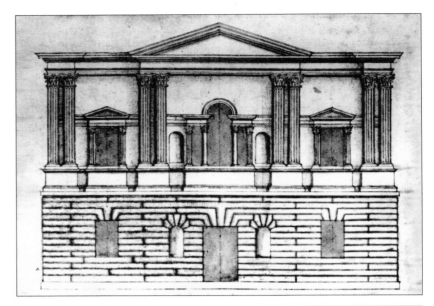

marking the start of the ceiling. If however in San Giorgio there is continuity between the choir and the church, on the contrary in Il Redentore the humility of the custodians is juxtaposed against the majesty of a public work, above all a temple erected to give thanks for the rapid end of the pest which ravaged Venice in 1574. Like the biblical altar built by David, Il Redentore is a legendary moment in the history of the city. A celebration was planned immediately and was to be repeated every year, the first Sunday in July. It highlighted and "spectacularised" the contrast between the real rhythm of daily life and a "sacred time" that does not inexorably pass, but can be repeated ad infinitum, just as it is in the ceremony of the Eucharist.

It's clear in the design for San Giorgio that Palladio was already concerned about providing space for public ceremonies in which the faithful could participate and every social class fulfil its role. Space became processional because of its eschatological axiality and the presence of corridors parallel to the nave. In Il Redentore - once the attempt to develop a central plan proposed by Marcantonio Barbaro had failed - the processional aspect is represented in the series of spaces recalling the rules Aristotle suggested for tragedies. Tripartition, Vitruvian *taxis*, is achieved not only frontally in the division of the façade and naves, but also in the spatial movement of the three next areas: the threshold of the churchyard raised above the huge flight of steps; the monumental design of the nave, and the end of the three-chamber naos in which a sort of *apotheosis* is achieved through the revelation of a virtual centrality jointly intersected with the longitudinal axis. This marks the final step in what we could call the (exclusively architectural) "Palladian reform": in other words, the transition from a perspective vision emphasising continuity and the homogeneity of space, to perspective discontinuity, to the possibility of using (as in the theatre) intervals, breaks, contraction, dilation, transfer, so that space can be divided, doubled, compenetrated and accompany and embrace a human being or else be detached, ascend, distance itself, until it implies the idea of infinity. Without this reform we would never have had the

Baroque, the creative neoclassicism of Boullée, Ledoux, Schinkel or the spatial breakdown of the modern movement. On the façade of Il Redentore, Palladio celebrates the joint unitary nature of the interior and exterior. The distant viewpoint of the Zattere and the small square inspired him to design a telescopic criteria of association between interpenetrating aedicules which, depending on the light, are either distinct or merge in an opaque and compact wall. The static system of flying buttresses reveals the internal pattern of the side chapels, while the dome and the small towers can be seen from the side; this increases the perceived height of the façade up to the lantern designed as a base for the great votive statue of Il Redentore.

Figs. 13-16. Three drawings by Palladio for the façade of Palazzo da Monte and an initial design for Palazzo Civena at Vicenza (RIBA, XVII, 19, 23, 26 and XIII, 10).

The concept of an aristocratic chapel and even of a funerary mausoleum is important in the design of the chapel at Maser, undoubtedly developed by the architect together with Marcantonio Barbaro in honour of his friend Daniele who died in 1570. Mention has often been made of the model of the Pantheon and the archaeological aspects of this design. In this case, Palladio takes the Temple of Romulus as his model, combining centrality with the cross shape suggested by Carlo Borromeo. In a natural setting he designs a building with a very decisive character, a strong wall mass that the temple portico turns, on an axis to the entrance path, into a vibrant chiaroscuro, contrasting the nearby villa with a different, contracted rather than dilated frontality.

The design for the Rialto bridge (one of his most daring attempts at innovation) reflects Palladio's typological concept that includes exchanges, combinations and interpolations. The first project documented by a set of four drawings in the Civic Museum in Vicenza[6] is an excellent example of conciseness. A small temple, similar to the one at the source of the river Clitunno (for which he made a series of very accurate studies) stands between two big walls that curve to the side next to two huge flights of stairs. The bridge that supports this design has three round arches all the same height and two smaller depressed arches near the flight of steps. At the bottom of the steps there are two squares surrounded by shops: these create the spatial link with its urban surroundings undoubtedly violated by this type of double insert yet at the same time revived by a structure that gives trade great institutional prestige, based on justice and other virtues which, in the form of statues above the small temple, look out over the whole area and dialogue with the four figures in the big aedicules crowned with river deities. Donatella Calabi and Paolo Morachiello, in their important monograph on the Rialto bridge,[7] identify a harmonic progression in the relationship between the elements, confirming and corroborating Wittkower's theory. They write: "numbers are not needed in the drawing to indicate all the new measurements: proportions are enough. He then divides the length into 5 parts to obtain a similar number of supports, as taught to us by nature, corresponding to three central arches and two outer arches, smaller in size, to achieve easy access. [...] Between the diameters of the arches he establishes a 2:3 ratio, equivalent to an interval of a fifth; between the diameter of the smaller arches and the width of the pilasters, 1:2, an eighth; between the latter and the diameter of the larger ones, 1:3, in other words, a ratio made up of the first two 1:2:3, a fifth and an eighth together!"

The second project, illustrated in two tables of the treatise, is an assembly of parts each with its own "history" and typological independence. The bridge itself was inspired directly by the Rimini model, illustrated a few pages earlier, with the aedicules

Reason and Sentiment 27

resting on breakwater pylons. The central loggias are similar to the ones in Villa Cornaro, while the small side loggias, destined for merchants, look like *barchesse* facing the road. Two loggias, as tall as the central loggias, enhance the two entrances from the city through three flights of steep steps, making the building look like an urban acropolis. Like the Loggia del Capitanio, to the sides of these loggias there is a triumphal arch motif (almost forcefully inserted) with an independent order the same height as the commercial porticoes. What should we make of this acropolis of trade rising above the Grand Canal like a majestic belvedere similar to the one designed by Palladio for the solemn arrival of Henry III of France? Some people consider this project as a precursor of that academic, bombastic and acrobatic classicism that filled the most important nineteenth-century cities with useless monuments. However, perhaps it's better (when assessing how important it was) to portray it as Canaletto did in his paintings, as a homage to the uniqueness of Venice: a city "which is one of the greatest and most noble in Italy, the metropolis of many other cities, where there is extensive trade from all over the world." For this "extensive trade" Palladio designed three parallel roads from the two porticoed areas which he imagined as packed with a noisy crowd "to serve the grandeur and dignity of the city and increase its already huge revenue": a gesture of love for the *genius loci* of the mercantile city par excellence, a gesture that Venice rejected, maintaining only a shadow of the original design in the picturesque bridge of Rialto.

During his many visits to Rome, Palladio made an in-depth and analytical study of architectural orders to solve the obvious contradictions between the rules established by Vitruvius and the concrete phenomenology of Roman buildings. The most famous and well-known part of his contribution as a scholar and restorer of antiquity was the improvement of what we could call classical grammar. In other words, he established the rules governing the basic elements of the architectural language of the ancients, i.e., the architectural orders considered as a set of elements (the pedestal, the base, the column, the trabeation and the frontispiece), bound by an inalterable law of superimposition and modularity. However his greatest innovative and creative contribution was his study of the syntax of classical style, i.e., the combination of important grammatical elements and the creation of the architectural equivalent of sentences and logical propositions. It makes sense to ask ourselves whether or not they have any meaning. Indeed, his patient and inspired *ars combinatoria* was instrumental in developing a logic which for three centuries inspired the studies of all kinds of architects, each with their own creative sensibilities - Bernini, Schinkel, Borromini, Gibbs, Muttoni, Jones, Wren, Kent, Valadier, Soane and Semper. To understand the importance of his work, I shall analyse certain characteristics of Palladio's grammar and above all his syntax, in particular the column, his tendency to project it on a frontal plane, the rhythmic elements of the cornice, the use of rustic elements and the corner joint. During Palladio's later years, his use of these elements reveal the quality, scope and depth of his studies and his efforts to experiment with, and improve, the expressive possibilities of classical style.

Palladio considered the column as the quintessence of architectural art. The rationally and emotionally charged element brimming with expressive virtuality, because the column implies order, laws of rhythmic iteration, superimposition and modularity. But it also has another emotional potential linked to its plastic and luminous configuration insofar as it is shaped by the swelling of *entasis* that Barbaro, in his comments on Vitruvius, defines with literary finesse "the swelling in the middle of the column so that it becomes sweet and tender and appears gentle." It is this swelling, that Palladio also uses for the pilasters, which when struck or caressed by the light determines an extremely nuanced chiaroscuro effect that fades gradually and in a myriad of different ways, day after day, hour after hour, from shade to shade of intense or pale light. After citing the *Hypnerotomachia Poliphili* and *Eupalino* by Valery, in their very unique book three Dutch architects[8] write this about classical style:

FIGS. 17-19. THREE DETAILED DRAWINGS IN THE CIVIC MUSEUM IN VICENZA BY PALLADIO. THE FIRST SHOWS THE JOINT BETWEEN THE BASE AND THE COLUMN IN THE ARCH OF CONSTANTINE, WITH THE CHARACTERISTIC CURVILINEAR JOINT PREFERRED BY PALLADIO; THE SECOND PORTRAYS THE INTERNAL FAÇADE OF SAN FRANCESCO DELLA VIGNA WITH THE ALLEGORICAL FIGURE OF FAITH ABOVE AN ELEGANT, GRACEFUL SARCOFAGHUS; THE THIRD IS PART OF A DRAWING OF PORTA AUREA AT RAVENNA SHOWING AN OLD EXAMPLE OF THE SHIFT FROM TRADITIONAL MOULDINGS TO SIMPLIFIED FASCIA, A SOLUTION SYSTEMATICALLY ADOPTED BY PALLADIO.

Reason and Sentiment   29

FIGS. 20 AND 21. TWO SKETCHES SHOWING THE PREPARATORYY WORK INVOLVED IN DRAWING ANCIENT MONUMENTS.
THE FIRST (RIBA, VIII, 14*v*) IS A FIELD SKETCH OF A PEDESTAL AND BASE OF THE IONIC ORDER OF THE COLOSSEUM SHOWING THE CURVILINEAR JOINT PREFERRED BY PALLADIO; THE SECOND (RIBA, IX, 18*v*) IS A METICULOUSLY ACCURATE DRAWING OF THE TRABEATION OF A ROMAN TOMB NEAR SPOLETO, A FAIR COPY READY FOR PRINTING.
NOTE THE DIFFERENCE IN THE HATCHING: THE FIRST SKETCH EMPHASISES THE PLASTICITY OF THE FORMS WHILE THE SECOND ACCENTUATES SHADOWS AND REFLECTIONS.

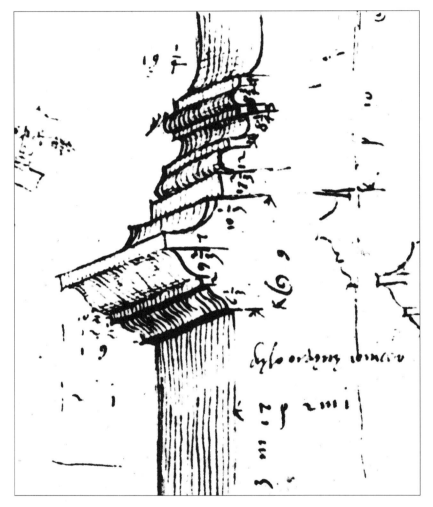

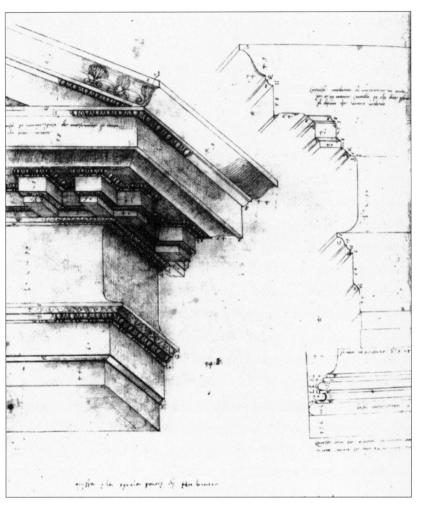

[...] the erotic pleasure of classicism is implied by the curvature of the cyma, by the swelling and contraction of the small waves of matter that quiver like flesh, the slightly grooved shafts of the columns, the gently curved scotia, the shell, the torus, the ring, the astragal, the cavetto that arches as if to impart a tender caress. It is a way to give a female or male identity to the bodily form of the building. In fact, if you lean against a column on a warm summer afternoon, your heart skips a beat, your skin becomes taut, your breathing quickens, your cheeks redden. But there are those who are indifferent to classicism...

Perhaps the reader will consider this excerpt as extreme and embarrassing, but when you look at some of Palladio's mouldings in Palazzo Chiericati, in Villa Foscari or the tapered pilasters in the church of San Giorgio, you are seduced by something beyond the rational interpretation of proportions and grammar, something that recalls the emotional force of certain pieces of music like the *Sonata to Kreutzer* that Tolstoy accused of being diabolically sensual.

Le Corbusier wrote, *à la modanature on reconnait le plasticien*, but in Palladio's case, sculptural and pictorial sensibilities are one and the same and moulding is always a game of plasticity and luminosity in the search for an organic whole expressed through the complex continuity of the line and matching chiaroscuro vibration. All you have to do is look at the tables illustrating the orders of the treatise and his signature works. What stands out is his fondness for certain parts, for example the modillions which, one could say, mark time in the Ionic and Corinthian cornices, creating a very visible rhythmic break at the corners, or the pedestals that in church façades, and even inside San Giorgio, strongly emphasise the relationship between man and God, inspiring a sense of elevation towards transcendence. When defining the plastic value of pedestals, Palladio distances himself from all the other theorists, affirming his own different idea of moulding. A comparison between the tables of the *Four Books* on this subject (I, 15, p. 41, 49, 57, 63) and the ones by Vignola reveal a very different approach which doesn't involve setting groups of mouldings against one another by using breaks, but making them thicker and linking them to an organic whole. On this issue Howard Burns wrote that in Palladio "mouldings are not distinct as in classical architecture, but each element merges into the overall form."[9] To give greater plasticity to the point where the column rests on the pedestal, Palladio borrows the upwards-inflected plinth from the Colosseum or the Gavi arch in Verona, softly linking it with the protruding dripstone. He proposes this motif in all four orders. The comparative table of architectural orders shows how there is a coherent progression from the Doric to the composite which, with varying degrees of complexity and refinement, reaffirms the same principle of harmonious continuity and organic relationship, as if this were the profile of a human face to be drawn again and again until the draftsman captures the divine secret of beauty.

He applies the same method to his study of the trabeations of the different orders, starting with the Tuscan order. Together with the simple version with its wooden architrave, in the treatise Palladio illustrates the combined version in which the arch is decorated with soft, fluid mouldings contrasting with the rustic frieze. The same tendency in the pedestals is present in other orders - interlinking lines, minimum breaks, extremely slender listels and soft dilated curves. To stress its resistance to weight, the frieze in both the Ionic and the Composite swells (an architect would say expands) as often happens in constructed works both in the trabeations and in the doors and windows or in the outline of the sarcophagi or other such structures, for instance, the wash-basin of the refectory of San Giorgio (p. 58) or Brunoro Volpe's funerary arch in the church of San Lorenzo in Vicenza.

First and foremost, orders create rhythm and Palladio, from the very start of his professional career (Villa Gazzotti, Villa Pisani and Palazzo Cilena) employs them in the flat form of the pilasters, distancing them (as the Romans did) just enough so that he could use them with arches. At the same time he tried to introduce the rustic order (Villa Pisani at Bagnolo) as well as radically simplifying the arch without orders (Villa Caldogno and Villa Poiana). Even in Palazzo Iseppo da Porto, it is the sequence of arches on the ground floor that determines the spaced-out rhythm of the columns with the windows in-between. However, it is in the Basilica and Palazzo Chiericati that the order takes on a new rhythmic force. In the Basilica, the column is grafted onto the wall in the major orders and is doubled and free-standing in the minor orders. The Roman syntagma (the arch between half-columns), typical of the Colosseum, is disassembled and reassembled; for this he exploits the solution used by Sansovino in the Marciana Library but with a radically different commitment and passion. The arch no longer intersects with the major order. When freed from this link, it reappears duplicated and free-standing in the Palladian windows that create an unusually thick wall which, when seen horizontally, looks like a series of attractive theatre wings. The multiplication of the columns and the dialogue between the free-standing columns and those imprisoned in the wall inaugurated a fertile season of research which was to last at least up until Bernini's first project for the Louvre. After previous attempts at intercolumniation where it varied between the 5.8 modules in Palazzo Cilena and the 4.5 modules in Palazzo da Porto, for the first time the intercolumniation in Palazzo Chiericati was never more than the three diameters established by Vitruvius. In *De Architectura*, for the Tuscan order alone, intercolumniation (*aerostylos*) is designed to be more than 3 modules. In other cases, based on the height of the column, the recommended values are 1¼ for the *pycnostyle*, 2 for the *sistylos*, 2¼ for the *eustylos* and 3 for the *diastylos*.

The consequence of adopting a standard intercolumniation is extremely important: it becomes the defining trait of a generation given that between 1550 and 1555 Vignola was to design a sim-

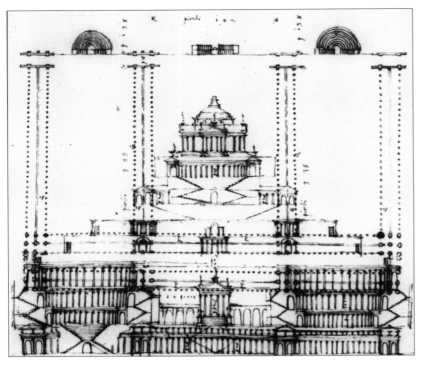
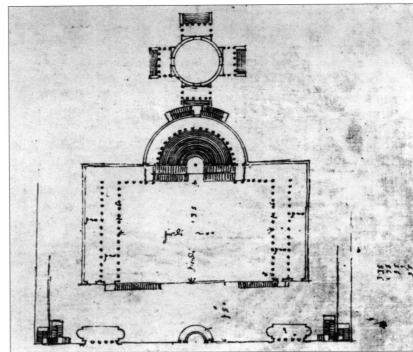
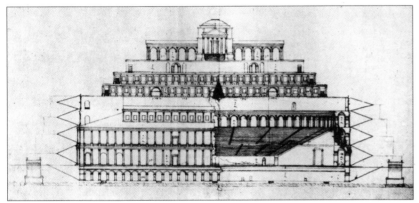
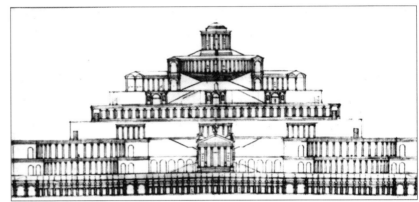

ilar colonnade with intercolumniation in Villa Giulia in Rome. Standard intercolumniation allowed Palladio to retrieve from the temple system not only the tympanum, but the entire syntactic organism which he was to experiment with in Villa Cornaro (2,4), Villa Pisani at Montagnana (2,7), Villa Chiericati at Vancimuglio (2,4), Palazzo Antonini at Udine (3,3), Villa Badoer (2,3), Villa Foscari (2,5), Villa Emo (2,7), Palazzo Valmarana (3), the Loggia del Capitanio (3,2) and La Rotonda (2). The genesis of these loggias comes from the renewed use of old values and tastes long forgotten - loggias recognisable from a distance, loggias that herald, like the intense features of faces standing out in a crowd, places of delight and serenity, loggias scattered in the landscape that conjure up old and new desires: to live in a villa, to be close to nature, to personally take care of one's lands and control its revenue, to give the house back its original, sacred and long forgotten nature.

In Palladian grammar, the corner is one of the key parts of a design. In fact, in the system of the orders, it is the corner that provides an endless number of combinations, of "joints" that make it possible to insert continuity, discontinuity and all the in-between nuances into the relationship of two orthogonal and intersecting planes. In the Doric order, the problem of the corner involves the age-old problem of "angular conflict." Since the frieze of the trabeation is cadenced by metopes and triglyphs, and triglyphs have to coincide with the axis of the column, the corner column forces the designer to change the series or else abandon correspondence with the triglyph. Palladio doesn't seem to worry about this problem which he solves by having the right-sized metope curl around the sides of the triglyph in order not to change the vertical relationship between order and trabeation. This realistic approach reflects the virtuoso nature of his corner joints where he experiments with coupling the pilaster and the column - typical of a temple in *autis* - always using combinations with a strong plastic effect. In the convex corner joints of his temple porticoes the Ionic order requires changes in the capital with its own privileged frontality. With casuistic gusto, in Villa Foscari at Malcontenta Palladio uses the capital of the temple of Portunus with an angular volute placed diagonally. Instead in Villa Serego at Santa Sofia, the capital is sectioned and turned upside-down so that when viewed from inside it looks symmetrical to the diagonal plane. In Palazzo Chiericati and Palazzo Barbaran(o), Palladio borrows one of the most novel ideas used in the small Roman home of the Farnesina ai Baullari. The intersection of two columns that interpenetrate on a diagonal axis. In the portico of Palazzo Chiericati, this joint is an example of virtuoso design. In many cases, the corner joint is combined with

Figs. 22-25. Four drawings in which Palladio creatively combines survey, philological reconstruction and arbitrary imaginative solutions. Drawings 22, 23 and 25 depict the Temple of Fortuna Primigenia along the Via Prenestina. The temple above the spectacular design is a foretaste of the double axiality of Villa Almerico called "La Rotonda" at Vicenza (RIBA, IX, 7; IX, 8 and IX, 6). The drawing in fig. 24 is a reconstruction of the Roman theatre in Verona (RIBA, IX, 10).

Fig. 26. Trabeation of the Arch of Constantine. Final drawing probably used in the *Book of Arches* that Palladio intended to attach to the *Four Books* (Civic Museum, Vicenza).

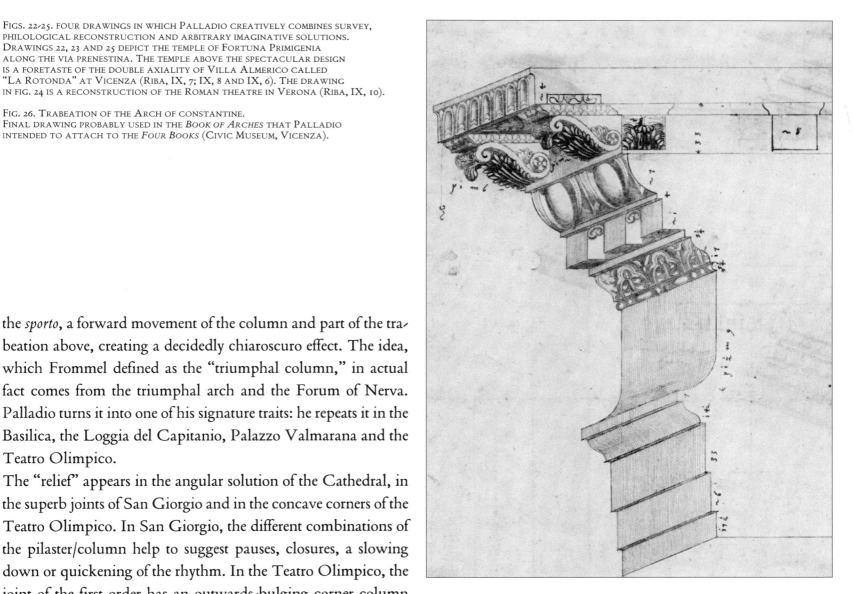

the *sporto*, a forward movement of the column and part of the trabeation above, creating a decidedly chiaroscuro effect. The idea, which Frommel defined as the "triumphal column," in actual fact comes from the triumphal arch and the Forum of Nerva. Palladio turns it into one of his signature traits: he repeats it in the Basilica, the Loggia del Capitanio, Palazzo Valmarana and the Teatro Olimpico.

The "relief" appears in the angular solution of the Cathedral, in the superb joints of San Giorgio and in the concave corners of the Teatro Olimpico. In San Giorgio, the different combinations of the pilaster/column help to suggest pauses, closures, a slowing down or quickening of the rhythm. In the Teatro Olimpico, the joint of the first order has an outwards-bulging corner column mirrored on the walls by two matching pilasters. The latter lay the groundwork for a spectacular plastic decoration on the upper floor: two half-columns facing each other, with pilasters to the side and, in the middle, a deep area of shadow in which other frames are half hidden. The protruding trabeations of the two half-columns intersect at the top, while a slender festoon links the two capitals. The way in which the order is declined is impeccable - the work of a genius: it is difficult to attribute it to others even if it was probably built by his beloved son Silla Palladio.

The *fascia* is one of Palladio's favourite forms. He uses it to achieve simplicity - one of the key traits of his style. It is an element with a rectangular section that juts out slightly from the surface of the wall to become a point of reference. For this reason it is often considered as a "stringcourse," but Palladio studies other ways in which its potential can be expressed. In late sixteenth-century and early seventeenth-century architecture, a sort of "fascia order" began to be used to replace the entire structure of classical orders with both a vertical and horizontal framework. Palladio only rarely uses it as a vertical element to replace the pilaster or pier (Villa Poiana, Palazzo Chiericati, etc.), but when he does he couples it with a similarly-designed arch. Instead, he often uses it as a horizontal element to replace the trabeation or parts of it (Villa Pisani at Montagnana, Villa Cornaro, Villa Badoer, Villa Emo) and produce intriguing results. He uses the concise nature of the fascia to contrast the superfluous plasticity of the trabeations and replaces all or each of the parts into which the trabeation is divided: architrave, frieze and cornice. In Villa Foscari, for example, the trabeation of the temple portico changes radically when it embraces the prismatic volume. While the architrave continues with its reliefs and the same happens with the frieze, the protruding cornice becomes flatter, a simple fascia crowned only by a straight cyma and listel. The cornice reappears in all its plastic force in the tympanum above the protruding structure of the rear façade. The effect of this metamorphosis is the perceived perfect clarity of the volume, the "linking" effect of the fascia and the relationship it creates with the surroundings. If you imagine the cornice as an uninterrupted crowning, you can understand how far removed Palladio was from the academic involutions of classicism.

Another recurrent detail in Palladio's grammar is the outward fold of the window frame above the sill. Normally, the frame of classical windows is shaped like the architrave which often curls around the frame above like the Greek letter *tau*.

A similar design for the base is extremely rare in Roman architecture. It is present and more visible in the so-called Temple of Vesta in Tivoli which Palladio studied very carefully, refusing, however,

Reason and Sentiment 33

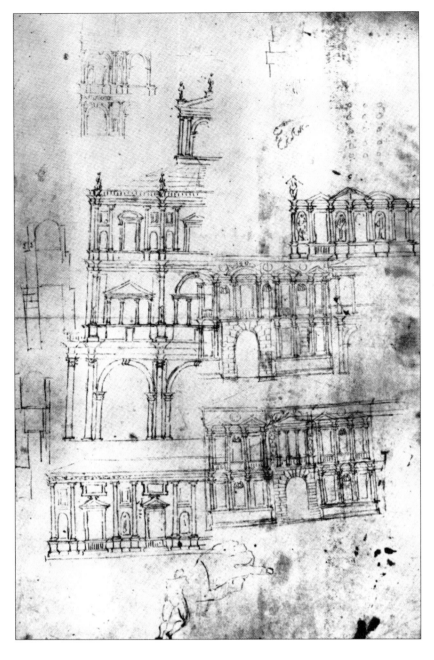

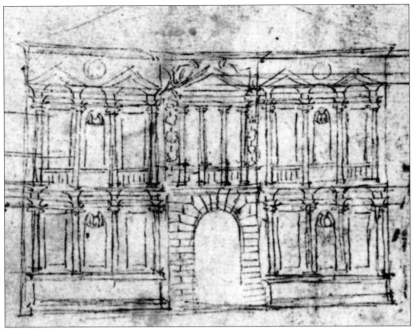

to accept its unusually-shaped Corinthian capital. Bramante's pupils, from Sangallo to Peruzzi, noted this anomaly in the drawings, but did not use it in their works. Instead Palladio exploited it in Palazzo Iseppo da Porto, Palazzo Valmarana, Palazzo Barbaran(o) and Palazzo Porto-Breganze. Consequently, Scamozzi also used it quite frequently. This can be explained by his ambition to make city buildings more elegant and by his passion for the reciprocal link between lexical elements and classicism. His fondness for this element probably influenced his design for the inner windowsills of Villa Poiana (p. 209): one of the best examples of Palladio's poetic sensibility towards everyday objects. Another interesting and novel trait in Palladio is his use of a "pause" (in other words, a way to eliminate the tensions introduced in the wall surface by the plastic elements of the order) to achieve a "break", a moment of silence. This ruse was already adopted in Villa Pisani at Bagnolo where between the towers and the loggia the wall recedes a few centimetres so that when it meets the tympanum the protruding trabeation doesn't interrupt the vertical line of the corners. In Palazzo Thiene, a narrow gap separates the protruding bases of the pilasters from those of the windows - a pause worthy of a great orchestra director. In Villa Poiana, the gap of a few centimetres between the fascia of the Palladian window and the other windows avoids tangency (often used by Michelangelo) between the compositional elements. Instead, Palladio uses them in Palazzo Valmarana and in San Francesco della Vigna where, amongst other things, we can admire one of the most subtle pauses in his repertoire - a vertical pause that separates the fragments of the tympanum from the wings of the central building of the façade. The same solution is used in the façade of San Pietro di Castello: the subtle variants remind us that, at least here, Palladio's drawings were scrupulously respected and implemented.

One of his more general compositional strategies is "bilateral symmetry", a strategy present in all Palladio's practical and theoretical works: it became a way of using cosmic harmony to assess reality. The rationale behind this choice came from tectonics, as explained in the treatise:

> The rooms ought to be distributed on each side of the entry and hall; and it is to be observed, that those on the right correspond with those on the left, that so the fabrick may be the same in one place as in the other, and

34 Reason and Sentiment

FIGS. 27-29. THREE OF THE MOST BEAUTIFUL DRAWINGS BY PALLADIO (ONE COMPLETE AND TWO DETAILS) (RIBA, X, 15R). ONE SKETCH SHOWS THE TOWN HALL IN BRESCIA FOR WHICH PALLADIO IMAGINED A FANTASTIC ROOFTOP LOGGIA RAISED ON A FLIGHT OF STEPS; THE DETAILS SHOWS HIS STUDIES FOR A TOWN HOUSE WITH A CENTRAL THREE-LIGHT WINDOW REMINISCENT OF PALAZZO DI ANTONIO GIOVANNI CAPRA ALONG CORSO PALLADIO AT THE CORNER OF PIAZZA DEL CASTELLO IN VICENZA.

that the walls may equally bear the burden of the roof, because if the rooms are large in one part, and small in the other, the latter will be more fit to resist the weight, by reason of the nearness of the walls, and the former more weak, which will produce in time great inconveniences, and ruin the whole work (I, 21, p. 27).

Undoubtedly, the static principle is valid in particular for small structures built on even ground. But Palladio, an admirer of nature and an passionate believer in organicity, turned it into a universal rule, a rule he applied very strictly in his design for La Rotonda (even if the different widths of the two intersecting corridors constitutes an exception to biaxial symmetry). Palladio almost always remained faithful to this principle which, after theorisation by Durand, was to become one of the cornerstones of the teachings of the *École des Beaux-Arts* in Paris and was to lead to that maniacal cult of symmetry which made it easy to invalidate traditional codes, something crucial and essential for the development of the Modern Movement.

Perhaps mindful of the freedom Aristotle accorded poets, when Palladio (the most learned and elegant theorist of the order) actually used it, he often implemented bold and daring changes. This shows how confident he had become over the years thanks to his studies of the works of the ancients which often contradicted not only Vitruvius' theories, but any and every general rule. For example the trabeation, for which the treatise envisages hard and fast rules, was then freely interpreted based on technical and aesthetic requirements. The same can be said for the superimposition of the orders. If a list was made of all Palladio's exceptions to various rules, we would be amazed to see how many and how daring they were, even if regular use of the neologism "anticlassical" in modern critiques would certainly make Palladio smile. He considered classicism as a moment of freedom not a limitation and innovative variations as a way to enhance the value and flexibility inherent in the legacy of the ancients. Certain "abbreviations" of the trabeation were used in the schools of Bramante and Raphael (for instance the elimination of the frieze), but Palladio mastered even overhangs with great freedom, turning them into flat fascia depending on the light. One particular model of Villa Cornaro at Piombino Dese (p. 73) - which I believe he made, because in July 1554 the chief foreman "Bartolomeo the bricklayer" was sent to Venice to consult *messer Andrea Palladio* - is an excellent opportunity to study his linguistic sensibilities and daring. The detail is the "bend" of the cornice of the first order. From the deep shadows of the gallery there is a shift to the lateral closure wall, pierced by an arch, inspired by the portico of Octavia, typical of Palladian loggias. The lateral shift in the wall, based on the Roman model, determines a doubling of the convex dihedral. But Palladio decided, as often he did when designing his architectures, to simplify the classical cornice along the side wall, eliminating the overhang of the dripstone and replacing it with a flat fascia. However, Palladio thought it crucial that the front view retain the full plastic force of its corner doubling and invented a partial "bend" that to all effects and purposes is an exception ironically made "to respect the rules." This syntactic mediation obliged the architect to force the issue a little: he created a break along the frieze. This meant creating a protruding pedestal above the cornice. Vision rather than abstract rule or elaboration of the rule to the point of paradox? Fully aware of the expressive need to accentuate the joint, I prefer the first option - vision rather than abstract rule.

The problem of the "rustic" order is extremely important in Palladio's stylistic choices. He first identified the problem in a series of Roman buildings from the Claudian period: from the portico of the Celio to the so-called Porta Maggiore. The latter were studied by many Renaissance architects: Palladio himself in his studies of classical buildings dedicated several sheets to these two monuments and to the theatres in Pola and Verona, built in part using irregular stones. During his entire career, he often used rustic stones, especially for the bases of villas and buildings. He first experimented with this style in his design for Palazzo Thiene in which many elements reveal his intention (certainly shared by his clients) to experiment this "rustic" style, pioneered by the great Giulio Romano in both his Roman designs as well as those

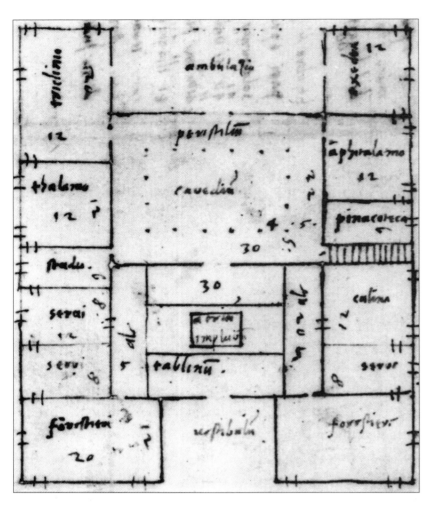
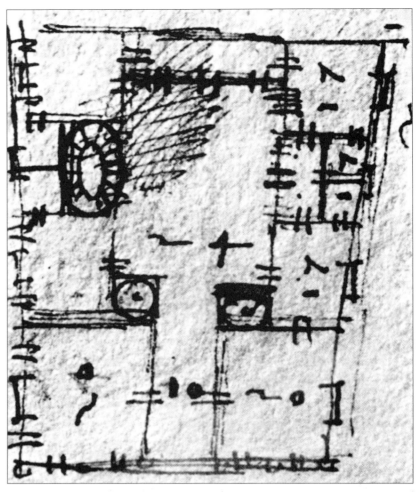
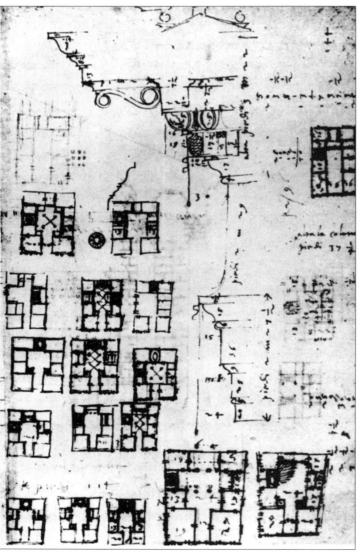
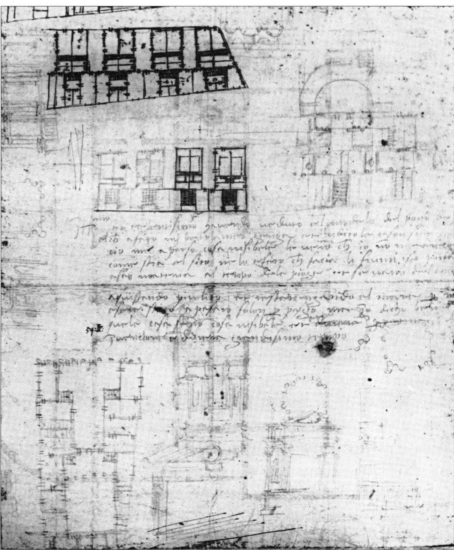

FIGS. 30 AND 31. A VITRUVIAN PLAN, ATTRIBUTED BY LEWIS TO GIANGIORGIO TRISSINO (RIBA, CASTIGLIONE MANUSCRIPT 8, VOL. III, DRAWING D) AND A HASTY SKETCH BY PALLADIO OF THE PLAN OF A BUILDING (RIBA XI, 22*v*, DETAIL). NOTE THE STENOGRAPHIC NATURE OF THE DRAWINGS IN WHICH CONVENTIONAL SIGNS ARE USED TO INDICATE THE DOORS AND WINDOWS AND THE WIDTH OF THE WALLS IS BARELY SHOWN.

FIGS. 32 AND 33. TWO DRAWINGS OF PLANIMETRIC IDEAS. THE FIRST (RIBA, XI, 22*v*, RIGHT, HALF OF THE PAGE) SHOWS PALLADIO'S *ARS COMBINATORIA* IN WHICH THE ARCHITECT COMPARES SEVERAL SOLUTIONS TO THE SAME PROBLEM; ON THE SECOND (RIBA, XVI, 9*v*) THERE IS THE PLAN OF A BUILDING AND A LETTER ABOUT THE PORT OF PESARO AS WELL AS THE DESIGNS FOR A SERIES OF MODEST ROW HOUSES ON AN IRREGULAR-SHAPED LOT, PROBABLY IN VENICE.

in Mantua. However, they did not affect the overall concept which was (as we have seen) completely devoid of the irregularities, complications and showiness typical of Giulio who was constantly concerned about surprising and unsettling the observer with his "refined vulgarities": this was a far cry from Palladio's vision especially early on in his career. On the other hand, Palazzo Thiene clearly reveals the premises of his personal interpretation of the "rustic" order, in particular in the bases of the buildings. In Palazzo Civena, the lower portal introduces the irregular structure, more similar to the one used by Serlio than by Giulio Romano. But the key to understand how he so elegantly and vigorously used this motif is evident in the loggia in Villa Caldogno and later in Villa Serego at Santa Sofia where the availability of Lessinia stone (Serego owned the quarries) encouraged Palladio, in what was perhaps his last villa, to enhance the plastic power of stone as a metaphor of military art - one of his passions. In other designs - Villa Pisani, Villa Caldogno, Palazzo Antonini, Palazzo Valmarana, Palazzo Cividale, Palazzo Schio - he uses stone very sparingly, often to visually reinforce the corners, leaving irregular plaster surfaces in the middle, surfaces which introduce an irregular element even in his most balanced and subtle compositions such as Palazzo Valmarana.

The most direct proof of the hand of Palladio naturally comes from the countless drawings that have survived to the present day, similar in number (another coincidence) to the monumental *corpus* of drawings by Borromini housed in the Albertina in Vienna. Most of Palladio's graphic works were bought in the eighteenth century by Lord Burlington and are today in the collection of the Royal Institute of British Architects. The publication of the London *corpus* has yet to see the light of day, but will undoubtedly constitute a milestone in Palladian studies. The catalogue of the exhibition of Palladio's drawings held in Washington in 1981 (an improved reprint was published in 2000) is also of great importance. Another important group of Palladio's drawings, housed in the Civic Museum in Vicenza, was published by Lionello Puppi in 1989.

Most of the drawings portray Roman monuments, including some based on survey drawings by other architects. It's difficult to tell the difference between Palladio's drawings of classical monuments and the ones he did for his projects because there are sketches of some of his design ideas in his survey drawings. When drawing a monument either in ruins or half-submerged by earth and debris, Palladio often "designed" the rest using philology: when this was not enough to visualize the hidden or lost parts, he let his imagination take over. What he theorised was based purely and simply on his own creativity. One example is the breath-taking reconstruction of a temple that could be the Temple of Hercules in Tivoli, but which looks more like the rural complex in Palestrina. Here Palladio creates a coping that anticipates the cruciform structure of Villa Almerico. He places it on a base with two concave porticoes and superimposed loggias: a fascinating example of how he sculpted a space only hinted at by archaeological reality.

One very personal trait, found in both his archaeological and design drawings, is Palladio's tendency to draw just the outline of the mouldings of the classical order and only sketch the ends of the horizontal divisions. Being a talented "grammarian", Palladio identified and classified mouldings into important groups, separating the architrave, frieze and cornice in the trabeation and the base, shaft and capital in the column. Instead, he indicated only parts of the horizontal divisions of the other mouldings: although these abbreviations tend to simplify the drawing, I believe that this was an almost didactic requirement, a way to clarify his ideas, something very similar to what in literary terms we would call logical analysis.

To a certain extent this methodological distinction helps to identify his early drawings from those he did later in life. In the former, apart from the calligraphic data of the captions, for example the letter *Y* used as a letter *E*, his most personal trait is his crisscross hatching. Palladio drew with a very sharp pencil point; this allowed him to draw shadows like an engraver who works copper with short well-distanced strokes. Palladio used this tech-

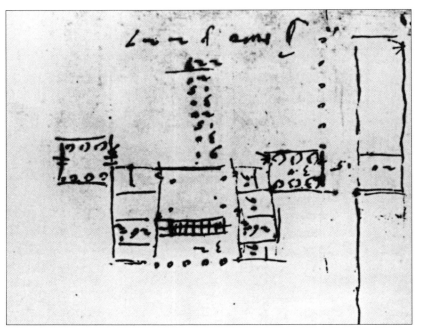
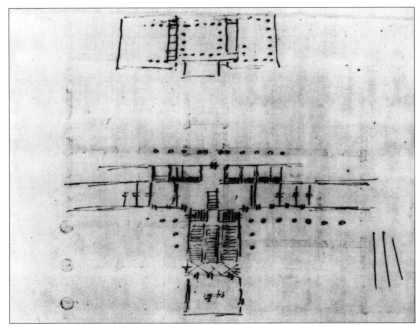
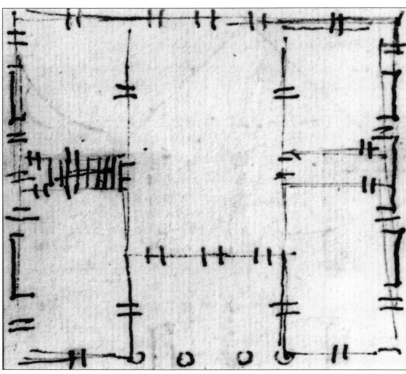
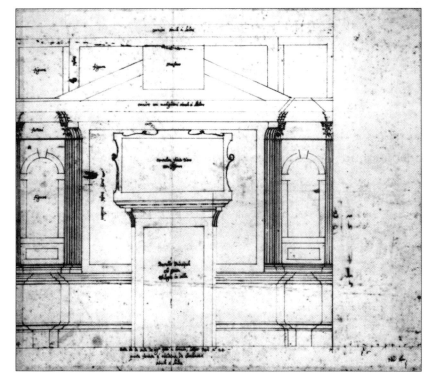

nique in his 'good' drawings of ancient monuments as well as in his designs. One example is the superb table of the trabeation of the Temple of Serapidis on the Quirinale Hill in which the hatching, with virtuoso bravura, follows the parallel lines of the cyma recta. Another example is on the reverse side of the same page (RIBA, IX, 18) showing his outstanding drawing of the ashlars of the *Torre Sacello* in Spoleto using two different types of ink. In comparison, the set of drawings that Douglas Lewis identifies as Palazzo Da Monte (RIBA, XVII, 26, 23 and 19), are much less elaborate, with a mixed technique in which criss-cross hatching is used only for the transparent shadows that gradually fade away while the brush-strokes help to underline the darkest parts of the shadows. In the drawings Palladio did later in life, starting with those for Palazzo Da Porto and Palazzo Chiericati, the criss-cross hatching disappears, replaced by a smooth brush-stroke background emphasising the doors and windows, while the sectioned parts are visible in the layouts.

Only in the extremely detailed and precise drawings Palladio gave to his clients did he use shadows, for example, in the three sheets for the first project of the Rialto bridge, in the drawing for the building on the water (fig. 79), in the drawing of the *Scuola grande della Misericordia* and in the drawing of the internal façade of San Francesco della Vigna. All these drawings are currently housed in the Civic Museum in Vicenza (from nos. 44 to 50 in the Puppi catalogue). The same style is visible in a drawing which once belonged to Giorgio Vasari, probably the Nicolini chapel in Santa Croce, and now in the Museum of Beaux-Arts in Budapest. A caption was added in the eighteenth century, indicating Veronese as the author of the figurative parts. We know that Palladio was quite capable of executing good drawing of statues thanks to several autographical drawings; however, he probably didn't like to waste time on this type of detail and often left this task to carefully chosen collaborators like Bernardino India, Federico Zuccari and Paolo Veronese. There

38 Reason and Sentiment

FIGS. 34-36. THREE HASTY SKETCHES BY PALLADIO OF VILLA MOCENIGO AT MAROCCO (HOWARD BURNS ET AL., *ANDREA PALLADIO 1508-1580: THE PORTICO AND THE FARMYARD*, LONDON 1975, P. 223, N. 392), VILLA BARBARO AT MASER (RIBA XVI, 5*v*) AND VILLA CALDOGNO AT CALDOGNO (RIBA, XVI, 20A*v*).

FIG. 37. A DRAWING WITH AUTOGRAPHICAL CAPTIONS FOR THE DECORATIONS OF THE LIVING ROOM IN VILLA GODI AT LONEDO, SHOWING HOW PALLADIO TOOK A KEEN INTEREST IN THE ILLUSORY ARCHITECTURES FRESCOED BY HIS COLLABORATORS (RIBA, DEVONSHIRE COLLECTIONS, CHISWICK, 37).

are many examples, especially during the last ten years of his life, that he increasingly availed himself of collaborators and their services, especially Francesco Zamberlan who helped him when he was consulted about the Town Hall in Brescia. However, when they worked together on the restoration of Palazzo Ducale, Zamberlan proposed different solutions to those of his *maestro*. We shouldn't forget that in later life Palladio was also helped by his sons and one of his nephews. He worked mainly with Leonida and Orazio on the publication of the *Commentaries of Caesar*, published in 1574, while Marcantonio and Silla helped him and probably worked with him in a different capacity. For instance, Marcantonio sculpted several keystones of the Basilica and collaborated in the restoration of Palazzo Ducale. Thanks to the handwriting of the captions, he is also credited with the dynamic drawing of the Teatro Olimpico (RIBA, XIII, 5) in which the sharp overhang of the mouldings of the architraves show he was no amateur when it came to the rules governing architecture. We know that Silla was mandated by the Teatro Olimpico to execute his father's design and that after Palladio died he tried to convince the Academy to publish more books of the treatise. However, the most explicit and genuine proof of the hand of Palladio lies not in his accurate and detailed drawings, executed using contemporary tools - tools described in minute detail by Scamozzi in his treatise[11] - but in the sketches he hastily drew in the margins of other drawings, often without even leaning on a table, but possibly just by resting the sheet on his knees or on part of the scaffolding. Perhaps his habit of drawing ancient monuments (which requires rapid sketches in the field to be finished later on) was what made Palladio so concise. Only very few of these sketches - compared to the many thousands that were lost - have survived - and quite by accident. However they give us an idea of the speed and incisiveness of his visual philosophy. In one drawing (RIBA, X, 15 - fig. 26), the sheet is covered in these sketches: they refer to several designs and are sketched with a stenographic technique using conventional marks to indicate structures, capitals and decorations. The sketches seem to be left unfinished, superimposed as if in a cinematographic fade-out, yet each maintains its own unique nature (a trait emphasised by the different lines that converge at the top). The drawings make us feel as if we are "entering" not only his own personal workshop, but his mind, where the forms, the elements of classical grammar exist not as monads but as self-organised adjacent parts that merge and intertwine as the result of an agreement or harmony, a reciprocal feeling of friendship that the architect only has to encourage and reveal in all its glory.

The style used to sketch these plans, at times executed with an almost violent incisiveness, looks almost like shorthand. Take, for example, the drawings in figures 30 and 31. The first is an interpretation of Vitruvian rules by Giangiorgio Trissino, the second is probably the plan of Villa Chiericati at Vancimuglio and the third is a study of a plan for Palazzo Barbaran(o). The two drawings were done years apart, yet the graphic signs are the same and were already used in the amateur drawing by Trissino: two parallel dashes mark the windows and doors, and the width of the walls is either not shown or shown only slightly. Only the pencil mark changes: in the last two, executed at the end of the 1560s, it becomes darker and bolder.

Many drawings highlight another of Palladio's characteristic traits: his habit of drawing different solutions side by side or comparing models by analogy. In the drawing in figure 32 (RIBA, XI, 22*v*), next to a sketch of the Temple of Mars Ultor, there are twenty different solutions for a building which could in some ways refer to Palazzo Barbaran(o), like the one already shown to in figure 31. While the solutions drawn inside a trapezoidal figure seem to concern problems regarding the irregular site of Palazzo Barbaran(o) (in which the orthogonal geometric plan became oblique), the other sketches seem to refer to a more common shape - a rectangle - in which the variables are the position of the stairs and the design of the hall with one or more cross-vaults. The drawing (RIBA, XVI, 9*v*) reproduced by Zorzi,[12] is no less interesting. Apart from the pencilled draft of a letter and a series of beautiful drawings of plants and elevations, including an axial sequence of enlarged and compressed space, there are two layouts of row houses at the top of the sheet. This is proof of Palladio's rather unusual and astonishing interest in a completely different and not at all aristocratic construction type probably designed for an irregular lot in Venice. However, the most hastily and rapidly executed drawing by Palladio is the one in figure 35 (RIBA, XVI, 5v). It probably refers to the first project for Villa Barbaro: at the top there is a building with three courtyards, at the bottom, a staircase with three parallel flights of steps in a building set in the middle of three porticoes. Palladio studied all types of staircases and stairs, their spectacularity and potential: it appears he came close to imagining the double staircase that was to triumph during the baroque. His strong, concise pencil marks betrays his enthusiastic desire to draw all the possible options and variations of this spatial model.

[1] AGOSTINO GALLO, *Le vinti giornate dell'agricoltura e dei piaceri della villa*, Venice 1572.
[2] ANDRÉ CORBOZ, *Per un'analisi psicologica della villa palladiana*, in "Bollettino del Centro Internazionale di Studi di Architettura Andrea Palladio", XV, 1973, p. 253.
[3] For the iconography of the villas, see BERNARD RUPRECHT, *L'iconologia nella villa veneta*, in "Bollettino del Centro Internazionale di Studi di Architettura Andrea Palladio", X, 1968, p. 229.
[4] CARLO BORROMEO, *Instructiones Fabricae et supellectilis Ecclesiasticae*, Milan 1577.
[5] The fact Palladio did not adhere to the ideas of the Lutheran reform is obvious given the importance he attributes to indulgences in his *Descrizione de le Chiese, Stationi, Indulgenze e reliquie de Corpi Santi, che sono in la Città de Roma*, Rome 1554.
[6] Cfr. LIONELLO PUPPI (edited by), *Palladio, Corpus dei disegni del Museo Civico di Vicenza*, Milan 1989, pgs. 44-47 and 110-111.
[7] DONATELLA CALABI and PAOLO MORACHIELLO, *Rialto. Le fabbriche e il Ponte*, Turin 1987.
[8] ALEXANDER TZONIS, LIANE LEFAIVRE and DENIS BILODEAU, *Le classicisme en architecture, La poétique de l'ordre*, Paris 1985, p. 45.
[9] HOWARD BURNS, *Le antichità di Verona e l'architettura del Rinascimento*, in *Palladio e Verona*, exhibition catalogue, Venice 1980, p. 114.
[10] Cfr. DOUGLAS LEWIS, *The Drawings of Andrea Palladio*, New Orleans 2000. See also: HOWARD BURNS, *I disegni di Palladio*, in "Bollettino del Centro Internazionale di Studi di Architettura Andrea Palladio", XV, 1973, p. 169; LIONELLO PUPPI, *Palladio. Introduzione alle Architetture e al Pensiero teorico*, Venice 2005, the chapter *La lunga e incompiuta fatica per un trattato sull'Architettura e i disegni*, which analyses the dispersion of Palladio's graphic legacy.
[11] BERTOTTI SCAMOZZI, OTTAVIO, *Le terme dei Romani disegnate da Andrea Palladio: e ripubblicate con la giunta di alcune osservazioni di Ottavio Bertotti Scamozzi, giusta l'esemplare del lord co. Di Burlington impresso in Londra l'anno 1732*, Vicenza 1785, vol. I, 15, pgs. 49-52.
[12] Cfr. GIANGIORGIO ZORZI, *Le opere pubbliche e i palazzi di Andrea Palladio*, Venice 1964, tab. 31.

Giovan Battista Maganza, "Portrait of Andrea Palladio", 1576 (detail).
Villa Valmarana ai Nani at Vicenza.

Reason and Sentiment 41

From left to right, top to bottom: Villa Saraceno at Finale di Agugliaro, Villa Poiana at Poiana Maggiore, Villa Godi at Lonedo, Villa Pisani at Bagnolo, Villa Valmarana at Vigardolo and Villa Gazzotti at Bertesina.

Reason and Sentiment Villas

From left to right, top to bottom: Villa Badoer at Fratta Polesine, Villa Chiericati at Vancimuglio, Villa Caldogno at Caldogno, the part actually built of Villa Trissino at Meledo, the rear façade of Villa Foscari and the inner façade of Villa Cornaro at Piombino Dese.

Villas Reason and Sentiment

Top: Rear façade of Villa Pisani a Bagnolo and Villa Caldogno at Caldogno.
Bottom: Front and rear façades. Villa Thiene, Quinto Vicentino.

44 Reason and Sentiment   Villas

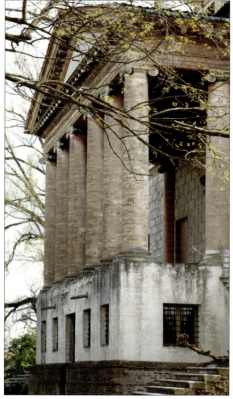  

From left to right, top to bottom: Villa Foscari alla Malcontenta, Villa Pisani at Montagnana, Villa Chiericati at Vancimuglio, side view of Villa Foscari, the other façade of Villa Pisani at Montagnana and Villa Serego at Santa Sofia.

From left to right, top to bottom: Villa Almerico called La Rotonda at Vicenza, Villa Barbaro at Maser, Villa Piovene at Lonedo, Villa Zeno at Cessalto, Villa Zeno at Cessalto (rear façade) and Villa Emo Capodilista at Fanzolo.

46 Reason and Sentiment   Villas

The rusticated portico of Villa Serego at Santa Sofia di Pedemonte.

Top: Barchesse of Villa Caldogno at Caldogno, Villa Barbaro at Maser;
Centre: Barchesse of Villa Badoer at Fratta Polesine;
Bottom: Barchesse of Villa Saraceno at Finale di Agugliaro and Villa Emo Capodilista at Fanzolo.

48   Reason and Sentiment   The Barchesse

Right barchessa. Villa Barbaro at Maser.

Internal façade. Villa Cornaro at Piombino Dese.

Villa Badoer at Fratta Polesine.

Rear façade and façade towards the Brenta.
Villa Foscari alla Malcontenta.

52 Reason and Sentiment   Villas: two versions of the pediment

Palazzo Cogollo, Palazzo Iseppo da Porto and Palazzo Barbaran(o) (Vicenza).

54 Reason and Sentiment   Buildings: the superimposed orders

Palazzo Thiene and Palazzo Porto-Breganze (Vicenza).

Buildings: the superimposed orders and the giant order   Reason and Sentiment

Palazzo Iseppo da Porto and Palazzo Chiericati (Vicenza).

56 Reason and Sentiment Buildings

Main façade. Palazzo Thiene (Vicenza).

Wash-basin at the entrance to the refectory of the convent of San Giorgio Maggiore in Venice and other views of the same area.

58 Reason and Sentiment   Convents

Ceiling. Refectory
of San Giorgio Maggiore (Venice).

Convents Reason and Sentiment

Courtyard. Convent of Charity (Venice).

60 Reason and Sentiment Convents

Tablinum or sacresty. Convent of Charity.

Convents Reason and Sentiment 61

San Giorgio Maggiore
and San Francesco della Vigna (Venice).

62 Reason and Sentiment Churches: the façades

San Giorgio Maggiore and Il Redentore, Venice (interiors).

64 Reason and Sentiment   Churches: the interior

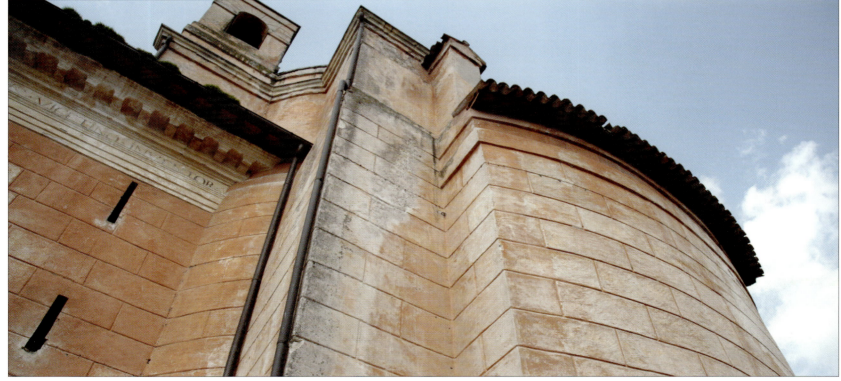

Chapel. Villa Barbaro at Maser (interior and exterior).

66   Reason and Sentiment   Churches: central-plan

Churches: central-plan Reason and Sentiment 67

Broken trabeation in Villa Foscari
alla Malcontenta
and Villa Poiana at Poiana Maggiore.

68 Reason and Sentiment   The broken trabeation

Broken trabeation in Villa Barbaro at Maser,
Villa Poiana at Poiana Maggiore
and San Francesco della Vigna in Venice.

The broken trabeation   Reason and Sentiment

Centre: Palazzo Porto-Breganze (detail);
Above: Trabeation. Loggia del Capitanio;
Left: Trabeation. Palazzo Iseppo da Porto;
Right: Trabeation. Palazzo Bonin-Thiene;
Below: Trabeation. Teatro Olimpico;
all in Vicenza.

70 Reason and Sentiment   Protrusion

Corner pilasters.
Il Redentore (Venice).

Protrusion Reason and Sentiment 71

From left to right, top to bottom:
corner solutions in Villa Serego at Santa Sofia di Pedemonte,
Villa Pisani at Bagnolo,
Palazzo Chiericati, the Teatro Olimpico,
the Basilica, on the façade of Palazzo Chiericati
and inside the loggia, all in Vicenza,
and in Villa Badoer at Fratta polesine.

Corner of the first order.
Main façade, Villa Cornaro
at Piombino Dese.

The Corner   Reason and Sentiment

Corner pilaster. Il Redentore, Venice.
Opposite page: corner solution under the cupola.
San Giorgio Maggiore (Venice).

74 Reason and Sentiment The Corner

The Corner Reason and Sentiment 75

The fringing of the cornice of the major and minor orders.
San Giorgio Maggiore (Venice).

76 Reason and Sentiment   The Corner

Centre: the pedestal and base of the column
in the Zitelle in Venice
and in the Teatro Olimpico in Vicenza;
Left: columns and pilasters with entasis
in San Giorgio Maggiore in Venice;
Right: pilaster with entasis in the Barbaro Chapel at Maser.

Top: detail of the pulvinated frieze and other swollen shapes in Villa Pisani di Lonigo, Palazzo Antonini in Udine, Palazzo Iseppo da Porto in Vicenza;
Centre: detail of the well designed by Palladio. Villa Godi at Lonedo; left and right: the corner column in Palazzo Chiericati;
Bottom: detail of Villa Caldogno at Caldogno, window sill in Villa Godi at Lonedo and the trabeation of an aedicule in the Palazzo Ducale in Venice.

DETAIL OF THE LOGGIA (INTERIOR AND EXTERIOR).
VILLA CALDOGNO AT CALDOGNO.

Reason and Sentiment   The Rustic Order

Oculi in Villa Caldogno at Caldogno,
the Valmarana Chapel at Santa Corona (Vicenza);
Oval window. Villa Caldogno.
Palladian window with oculi. Villa Valmarana at Vigardolo.

Ocular window in the tympanum.
Villa Cornaro at Piombino Dese.
Rhomboid window in the tympanum.
Villa Caldogno at Caldogno.

The Ocular Window   Reason and Sentiment

Balustrades in Palazzo Iseppo da Porto,
Villa Godi at Lonedo,
Palazzo Schio in Vicenza,
Villa Godi at Lonedo,
Villa Caldogno at Caldogno
and Villa Chiericati at Vancimuglio.

Reason and Sentiment   The Balustrade

Detail of the carved balusters.
Rear façade of Villa Godi at Lonedo.

The Balustrade Reason and Sentiment

PALLADIAN CONSOLES IN PALAZZO ISEPPO DA PORTO IN VICENZA, THE ENTRANCE TO THE REFECTORY OF THE CONVENT OF CHARITY IN VENICE, THE CATHEDRAL AND PALAZZO THIENE IN VICENZA.

Consoles. Palazzo Valmarana
Main entrance door. The Cathedral (Vicenza).

The Console   Reason and Sentiment

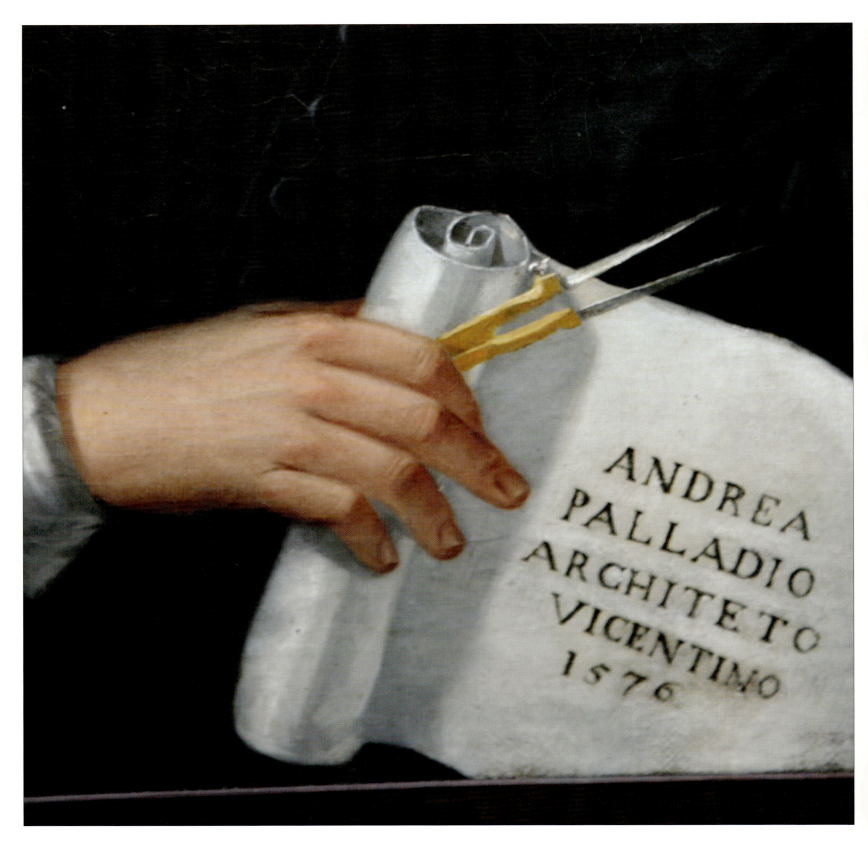

Giovan Battista Maganza, "Portrait of Andrea Palladio", 1576 (detail). Villa Valmarana ai Nani in Vicenza.

2. The Loggia

> "Palladio states his case clearly: it involves inserting a solid form, a geometric and volumetric construction, in a natural space that is always different; it means creating a harmonious relationship, indeed a relationship of perfect equivalence, between these two realities. Natural, infinite spatiality has to become tangible in the final form of the building; the latter must transcend the limit of its finiteness, entering into contact, in unison, with natural, infinite spatiality."
> GIULIO CARLO ARGAN

"These loggias serve for many uses, as to walk, eat in, and other recreations; and are either made larger or smaller, according to the needs and conveniency of the fabrick requires; but for the most part, they are not to be made less than ten foot wide, nor more than twenty." (I, 21, p. 27). This is Palladio's definition of the Loggia: a place of transition between the exterior and interior that was to allow him to radically and creatively transform the legacy of his contemporaries and the ancients. It is with the loggia that he succeeds in fully developing his distinctive use of Venetian tradition, archaeological culture and the achievements accomplished by Bramante and his pupils, to create something truly unique from this combination of styles.

Palladio started his studies on the loggia in 1537 when he designed Villa Godi at Lonedo. The traditional loggia measured 6 x 8.5 metres and was open on only one side with three arches framing the magnificent landscape: nothing more than the crystallisation of a problem that was to fascinate him and steer him towards new horizons. In Villa Forni-Cerato at Montecchio Precalcino (difficult to date even if it is attributed to Palladio despite the lack of documentary evidence), the loggia, which interprets the Palladian window concept as *aurea simplicitas*, juts outwards and appears to be crowned by a tympanum. However, even if it is open on all sides its spatiality remains compressed and rigid as it does in Villa Gazzotti at Bertesina where the tympanum is even more important. It is during the genesis of Villa Pisani at Bagnolo that the problem of the loggia becomes increasing central to his studies. This is increasingly obvious in the illustrations in the *Four Books* rather than in the house itself. For the first time a temple-shaped portico extends outwards crowned by a thermal window. The RIBA drawings show how Palladio, before arriving at this solution, had thought of creating a more complex temple pattern in the façade by inserting half of a small round temple divided by two small walls pierced by an arch. The set of four drawings is crucial to understand Palladio's research method at this point in his career, after his first visit to Rome in 1541. His interest in Bramante's nymphaeum in the Belvedere Courtyard in the Vatican is the driving force behind this idea which he develops by focusing on the dialogue and contradiction between the loggia and the wall, something that was to fascinate him all his life. If the image in Serlio's treatise (III, 119, 120) is correct, the Belvedere nymphaeum was a simple exedra. Instead, in Villa Pisani Palladio designed a concave portico with six columns and two half-columns resting against the arched walls next to the two small towers: these partition arches anticipate the loggia of Palazzo Chiericati and were to become his most popular signature element. In the first sketch (RIBA, XVII, 2v, fig. 59), the concept is summarily presented (with only four pilasters) as a hallway leading to a biapsidal room with three, three-mullioned windows similar to those found in spas. In the first geometric interpretation (RIBA, XVII, 18v, fig. 57), only two columns stand next to the Bramantesque staircase, anticipating the solution illustrated in the treatise. Only in the third solution (RIBA, XVII, 17 and XVI, 7, figs. 38 and 39) does Palladio fully develop the concept. In the general plan, in axis with the round staircase, a double staircase extends towards the river creating a sort of embarcadero. His loggia niche (perhaps discarded for financial reasons) was replaced by a Doric rusticated three-mullioned window that reflected and reinforced the motif of the ashlar base. Only the convex staircase was left to recall the beautiful conch-shaped loggia between the exterior and interior or to create a direct link between what could be seen from the loggia and the visibility of the loggia itself seen from a vessel travelling on the river.

The rusticated three-mullioned window returns in Villa Saraceno at Finale di Agugliaro, but without the architectural order: the ashlars becomes "softer" because their tips, dug out of the smooth plaster, are less pointed. Instead, in Villa Poiana, the loggia is more imposing thanks to another Bramantesque and Sangallesque element (p. 163): the completely new crown of five oculi over the door which not only strongly characterises the simplified Palladian window, but also creates a series of "correspon-

Figs. 38 and 39. Two drawings. Villa Pisani at Bagnolo (RIBA, XVII, 17 and XVI, 7).
An exception to Palladian types, the manor house faces a river and has a porticoed courtyard at the rear. The staircase was inspired by Bramante's staircase in the Belvedere Courtyard in Rome.

dences" between the exterior and the interior. In fact, the pattern is repeated three times and therefore, even if the openings in the portico are now closed, it virtually "crosses" at least three buildings linking the loggia, the main room and the façade in an extraordinary sequence of monoaxial openings (cfr. Chap. VII).

In 1546, Palladio was given an important mandate: to build the most famous and grandiose of his loggias around the old town hall in Vicenza, what was to become, by definition, the Palladian Basilica. As a rule, not much thought is given to the fact that this building was not a "palazzo", something surrounded by walls, but a ring of porticoes, an amplification, a monumentalisation, a sublimation of the concept that gave cities in the region, especially Venetian cities, a distinctive uniqueness: porticoes running along streets and roads. It was Herman Hesse who noted how the psychological significance of porticoes consists in the house being recessed on the ground floor to afford space and protection to passers-by, a sort of courtesy, of "urbanity" that gives the architecture not only warmth and a breathing space, but a sense of shared *humanitas*. One could cite as an example Palazzo della Ragione in Padua, but Palladio wanted to move beyond the interpreted model. Not many buildings in Italy are surrounded by a continuous portico; the ones that do normally have a market and, apart from the one in Padua, only one floor. The Basilica in Vicenza is the most monumental and fascinating of all because the thickness of its wall structure, with its double arches and columns, emphasises its three-dimensional nature. It is a building that provides and projects space beyond its own walls; each of the Palladian windows is a hospitable shelter, an inviting niche sculpted in space. The upper loggia is an elevated urban space, a privileged view point from which to observe the hustle and bustle of life in the square below. It is here that the dialectics between observer and observed (an aspect deliberately developed in Palazzo Chiericati), reaches its full potential. In fact, all the Palladian windows are different in size. The ones at the ends are the narrowest, while the others decrease in size from

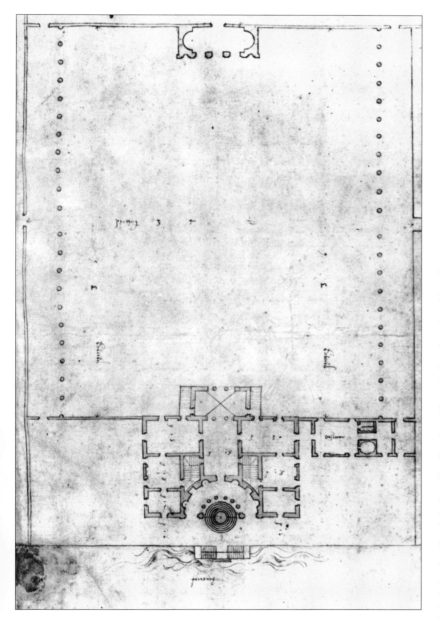

the centre outwards so that when entering from the street along the Loggia del Capitanio, the impression is of lateral perspective dilation, something that Bernini was to produce later on (p. 103).[1]

In 1551, after staying in Rome from 1547 to 1549, Palladio was asked to design Palazzo Chiericati in Piazza dell'Isola, a building where the loggia becomes the key element of the design. When he tried to plan and solve the problem of the loggia he probably remembered Vitruvius' ideas about Greek and Roman squares which involved continuous, two floor architrave loggias along the sides. The free, grouped, coupled and even compenetrated column is the crucial element in a concept that sets two different indications of depth against one another: the frontal depth and orthogonal depth along the portico on the ground floor. Apart from the arched partition walls that emphasise the concept already expressed, but never implemented, in the drawings for Villa Pisani at Bagnolo, the only other wall is located in the centre of the first floor. His work on the porticoes of the Basilica, improved by what he saw in Rome, allowed Palladio to develop a completely unique loggia. In the portico, open on three sides, the silver-shaded chiaroscuro and the very visible presence of the cylindrical Doric shafts (so close that almost touch one another like living bodies) produce an effect of intense joyful sensuality that projects an oneiric image of classical antiquity. This was very different from contemporary Roman designs even though Palladio borrows from Antonio da Sangallo or Baldassarre Peruzzi (more precisely from Palazzetto Le Roy) the idea of compenetrated shafts also interpreted as an improbable Gothic reference. The internal space of the portico on the ground floor is divided into three sections by a transparent partition created by inserting a column towards the exterior; the latter is, almost attached to the one which, doubled diagonally, allows the central corpus to be moved slightly forward. This simplified junction is repeated, towards the interior, for the pilasters. If necessity dictated that the gallery of the Basilica had to be joined to the rough wall of the fifteenth-century building, in Palazzo Chiericati the

The Loggia 91

row of free-standing columns is gracefully mirrored in the pattern of the pilasters, while the role of the coffered ceiling was to connect the two façades and characterise the three sections of the portico. The walls at the end of the superimposed loggias are here in their final form; they protrude compared to the row of columns and are slightly off axis - the hallmark, as we have already mentioned, of a strict syntactic rationale (fig. 41 and pgs. 56, 97-99 and 112).

It is in the three villas built between 1542 and 1544 (Villa Cornaro at Piombino Dese, Villa Pisani at Montagnana and Villa Chiericati at Vancimuglio) that the loggia concept is fully developed as a key element. In Vancimuglio, a small tetrastyle Ionic temple, closed between two arched walls, stands in front of a prismatic block with simple openings; in Piombino Dese, on the façade towards the garden, and in Montagnana, the temple pattern is repeated in two superimposed orders: Ionic and Corinthian in Villa Cornaro and Doric and Ionic in Villa Pisani. In the other façade of Villa Cornaro the loggia recedes in line with the façade of the building, creating a model that was to be repeated in many villas, in Palazzo Trissino, Palazzo Garzadori (illustrated in the *Four Books*, but never actually built), Palazzo Antonini in Udine and Palazzo Dalla Torre in Verona (unfinished).

In the villas built in the 1550s and 1560s, the loggia was developed even further; recessed loggias were built in Villa Badoer, Villa Mocenigo, Villa Valmarana at Lisiera and Villa Emo Capodilista at Fanzolo, while protruding loggias were designed for his masterpieces, Villa Malcontenta and La Rotonda, characterising each villa in completely different ways. In the former, the portico juts out above a base that can be reached using two flight of steps and extends outwards into the Brenta landscape, almost disconnected from the building itself. In the latter, four loggias emerge from the cube behind it, creating two hierarchically separate routes (due to the different size of the corridors): the main frontal route crosses the entrance hall and opens towards the south-east and the transversal route, creating another two view-

points towards the "theatre" of the surrounding hills. In these two designs, the tympanum above the loggia is finally and definitely consecrated by developing the concept of the "laic" tympanum only partially developed in Villa Gazzotti at Bertesina. Once and for all, it also clarifies the affinity between the house and the temple which, especially in recent decades, has been one of the most controversial and debated topics among Palladian critics. Here too, Palladio had been preceded by Pietro Lombardo in Villa Giustiniani at Roncade and was to find a companion-in-arms in Pirro Logorio. In the villa he built in 1558 for Pope Pius IV in the Vatican, there are numerous similarities with Palladio's later works with regard to the continuous vibrations of the decorations covering the bare walls.

In the *Four Books*, Palladio himself provided an explanation for this, his most important design choice.

> I have made the frontispiece in the forefront in all the fabricks for villas, and also in some for the city, in which are the principal gates; because such frontispieces show the entrance of the house, and adds very much to the grandeur and magnificence of the work. Besides, the forefront being thus made more eminent than the rest, is very commodious for placing the ensigns or arms of the owners, which are commonly put in the middle of the front. The ancients also made use of them in their fabricks, as is seen in the remains of the temples, and other public edifices; from which, as I have said in the preface to the first book, it is very likely that they took the invention, and the reasons for private edifices or houses (II, 16, p. 53).

In another part of the book (II, 14, p. 49) when writing about Villa Badoer, Palladio said: "The frontispiece over the loggias, forms a beautiful sight, because it makes the middle part higher than the sides." He provides practical explanations and asks that the architect be left free to make his own stylistic choices vis-à-vis both recent and ancient traditions, yet at the same time emphasising the need for a rationale. He was convinced that in classical antiquity the façade was not a characteristic exclusive to the temple system, a conviction expressed in Barbaro's Vitruvian edition and in the *Four Books*. So, in my opinion, his decision to use it in his villas is a sign he wanted to stress the dig-

FIG. 40. THE PALLADIAN BASILICA (ENGRAVING)
(Francesco Antonio Muttoni, *Architettura di Andrea Palladio...*
con le osservazioni dell'Architetto N.N., Venice 1740-1748, vol. I, tab. VII).

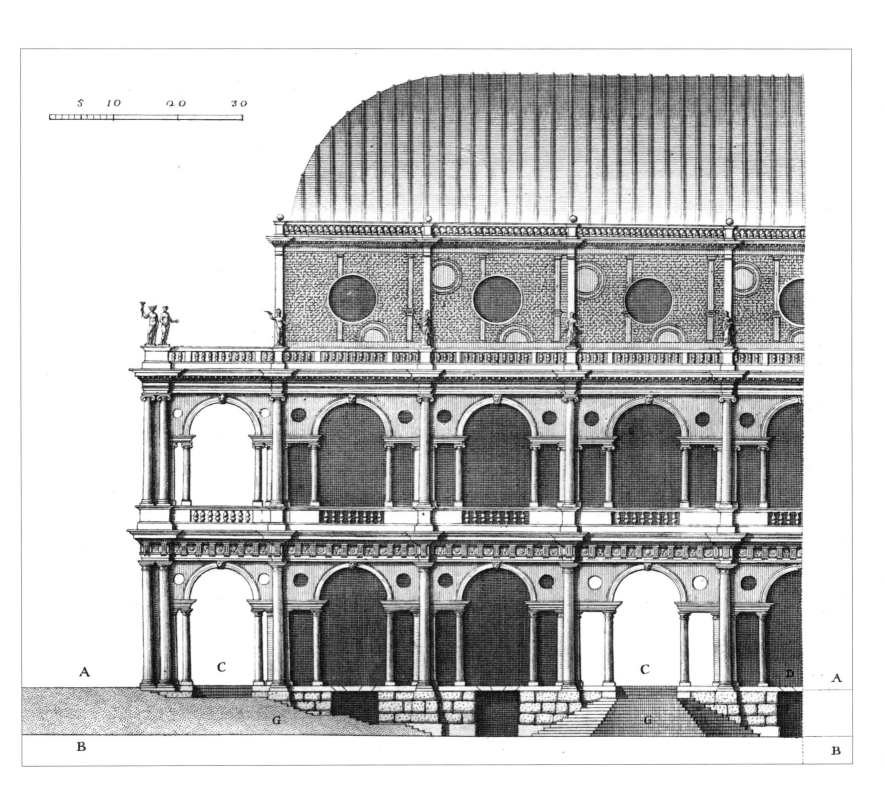

Fig. 41. Design. Palazzo Chiericati (Vicenza).
(RIBA, Burlington, Devonshire, VIII, 11).

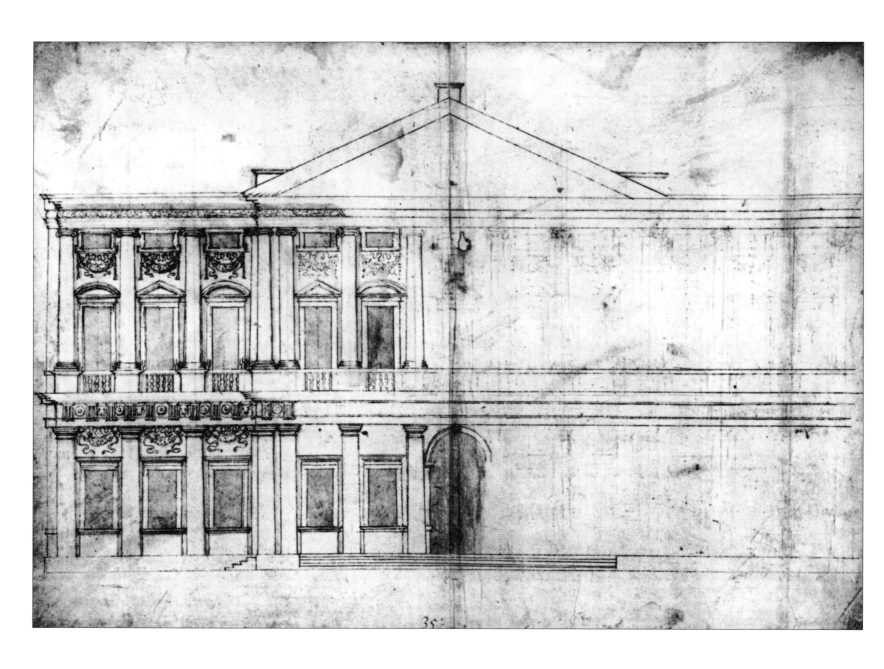

94 The Loggia

nity of civilian architecture by praising its human dimension and importance.

The house and the temple are not irreconcilable and divergent typologies. On the contrary, they have common roots based on the fact that the tympanum is created when the two surfaces of the roof are sloped to avoid damage to the building when it rains. Palladio had certainly read and appreciated Vitruvius' preface to the second book of *De Architectura* in which, in the most poetic part of his treatise, the Roman architect talks about the birth of architecture. In Barbaro's translation, the fascinating fairytale told by Vitruvius reads as follows:

> Mankind originally brought forth like the beasts of the field, in woods, dens, and groves, passed their lives in a savage manner, eating the simple food which nature afforded. A tempest, on a certain occasion, having exceedingly agitated the trees in a particular spot, the friction between some of the branches caused them to take fire; this so alarmed those in the neighbourhood of the accident, that they betook themselves to flight. Returning to the spot after the tempest had subsided, and finding the warmth which had thus been created extremely comfortable, they added fuel to the fire excited, in order to preserve the heat, and then went forth to invite others, by signs and gestures, to come and witness the discovery. In the concourse that thus took place, they testified their different opinions and expressions by different inflexions of the voice. From daily association words succeeded to these indefinite modes of speech; and these becoming by degrees the signs of certain objects, they began to join them together, and conversation became general. Thus the discovery of fire gave rise to the first assembly of mankind, to their first deliberations, and to their union in a state of society. For association with each other they were more fitted by nature than other animals, from their erect posture, which also gave them the advantage of continually viewing the stars and firmament, no less than from their being able to grasp and lift an object, and turn it about with their hands and fingers. In the assembly, therefore, which thus brought them first together, they were led to the consideration of sheltering themselves from the seasons, some by making arbours with the boughs of trees, some by excavating caves in the mountains, and others in imitation of the nests and habitations of swallows, by making dwellings of twigs interwoven and covered with mud or clay. From observation of and improvement on each others' expedients for sheltering themselves, they soon began to provide a better species of huts. It was thus that men, who are by nature of an imitative and docile turn of mind, and proud of their own inventions, gaining daily experience also by what had been previously executed, vied with each other in their progress towards perfection in building. The first attempt was the mere erection of few spars united together by means of timbers laid across horizontally, and covered the erections with reeds and boughs, for the purpose of sheltering themselves from the inclemency of the seasons. Finding, however, that flat coverings of this sort would not effectually shelter them in the winter season, they made their roofs of two inclined planes meeting each other in a ridge at the summit, the whole of which they covered with clay, and thus carried off the rain.

Vitruvius' story solemnly established that architecture, language and society were born together after the discovery of fire. He makes no mention of religion, but it's obvious that in this cosmic vision it is another result of "living together" between men who share the same fears and a common belief. In the *Four Books*, Palladio assigns to religion the role of "custodian and protector of citizens," indicating hills in the city as an ideal place on which to build. So time is the daughter of the house, in a certain sense it is a sublimation and there is no reason not to establish a certain affinity of style between the two architectural realities.

With regard to Palladio's choice, people have talked about the effects of a "zeroing" of the symbolic value of architectural elements and even - in homage to a now outdated terminology - of sacrilege. Manfredo Tafuri wrote:

> In actual fact, concepts have to be destroyed in order to freely combine a classicist vocabulary with contemporary sources: we have to break down all the syntactic links inherent in the language and typologies used as sources and, therefore, compromise all associated symbolic meanings [...] and "de-historicise" and destroy the symbolic structure of language itself.[2]

Tafuri considered Palladio's sensible and constructive antidogmatism as a revolutionary choice: a "tangible insertion of the sacred into the profane," admitting, nevertheless, that instead of talking about the desecration of the temple, when considering domestic tympana we should talk of the "sacralisation of bucolic country life". However, he judged it to be irreconcilable with the eclipse of the sacred "implicit in considering as new formal *values* the structure of architectural typologies, the repetitive nature of grammatical solutions, the verifiability of syntax and its real relationship to worldly and practical goals." However, he forgot to give a better explanation of what these elliptic statements of principle actually mean. Perhaps speaking as a layman and after having studied them carefully, Palladio just wanted to relativise symbology, typology and grammatical and syntactic rules, arranging them freely according to his needs, without loosing his confidence in architecture, a confidence deeply rooted, in my opinion, in his faith in God and in a profound ancestral feeling for sacredness, something he felt very strongly about as the son of a miller and not of a prince or intellectual.

We should also point out that in the choice of tympanum for civic buildings, there was the famous, normally ignored, solemn commitment by Leon Battista Alberti who, in his *De Re Aedificatoria* stated: "In private houses never should the design of the tympanum be such as to come close to that of the solemnity of the temple. Although the vestibule, however, can be embellished with a slightly raised front and even by a proper and dignified tympanum". Numerous precedents had already been built - Villa Poggio at Caiano, the nearby Villa Giustiniani at Roncade, noted by Boucher[3] (which preceded Palladio's tympana by at least forty years) and the building painted by Baldassarre Peruzzi and noted by Luitpold Frommel.[4] We should not forget that in the Renaissance the frontispiece crowns not only temples, but also aedicules, window frames and all types of doors, loggias and passageways. With regard to antiquity and the proliferation of tympana in complex spa buildings, this reassured Palladio that his use of the tympanum in a new style of building had no heretical overtones. In 1972, in reply to Tafuri's statements (to which Palladian critics developed much more subtle and appropriate considerations), Rosario Assunto wrote:

> What is noticeable in La Rotonda is the use of a central plan for a private building, a plan whose original sacredness, like fundamental Neo-Platonism, is not in question. The use of a central plan perhaps corresponds more to the philosophy of Palladio and his client, Monsignor Almerico, who saw it as a consecration of private architecture rather than a "desecration" of religious architecture. This is based on a theory which is justified (if we can speak of justification) only by certain modern cultural trends and the use of a terminology which is almost compulsory these days. To interpret the adoption of a central plan and the façades of classical temples for private architecture as a consecration of profane architecture corresponds to the fundamental poetics of the Palladian concept of architecture, since poetics is the ingredient which in architecture, as in all the arts, combines the sacred and the profane, insofar as it gives solemnity to what is profane and freedom from the servitude of function which is inherent in sacredness. To places which are profane and destined for daily use, it brings the light of sacredness, its role as the representative of infinite time in a finite space, in line with the lesson imparted by Cusana who saw infinity in the circle.[5]

[1] Guglielmo De Angelis d'Ossat, *Palladio rivisitato*, in "Bollettino del Centro Internazionale di Studi di Architettura Andrea Palladio", XXII, 1985, p. 9.
[2] Manfredo Tafuri, *Committenza e tipologia nelle ville palladiane*, in "Bollettino del Centro Internazionale di Studi di Architettura Andrea Palladio", XI, 1969, p. 127.
[3] Bruce Boucher, *Palladio*, Turin 1994, p. 77, fig. 68.
[4] Christoph Luitpold Frommel, *Roma e la formazione architettonica del Palladio: nuovi contributi*, Milan 1990, p. 146, fig. 29.
[5] Rosario Assunto, *Introduzione all'estetica del Palladio*, in "Bollettino del Centro Internazionale di Studi di Architettura Andrea Palladio", XIV, 1972, p. 14.

Upper loggia. Palazzo Chiericati (Vicenza).

Colonnade of the lower loggia.
Palazzo Chiericati (Vicenza).

98   The Loggia   The wall, columns and open areas

The ceiling of the upper loggia.
Palazzo Chiericati (Vicenza)
The vault of the central loggia.
Villa Pisani at Bagnolo.

The wall, columns and open areas The Loggia 99

The loggia of Villa Pisani at Bagnolo.

100 The Loggia The loggia as a go-between with the exterior

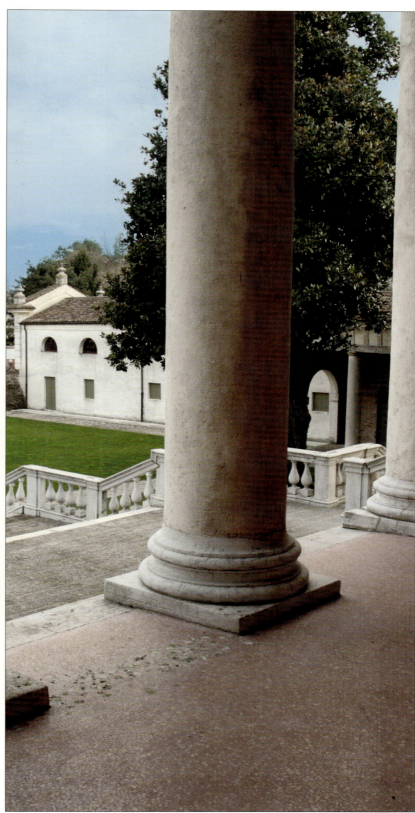

The loggias of Villa Emo Capodilista at Fanzolo
and Villa Badoer at Fratta Polesine.

The loggia as a go-between with the exterior   The Loggia   101

102　The Loggia　Walls accommodate and multiply space

The loggias of the Palladian Basilica (Vicenza).

Walls accommodate and multiply space   The Loggia

Villa Badoer at Fratta Polesine.

104   The Loggia   The main façade and consecration of the home

Villa Chiericati at Vancimuglio.

Villa Chiericati at Vancimuglio (side view).

The pierced wall of the loggia The Loggia 107

Villa Foscari alla Malcontenta.

Top: Portico opposite the Chapel in Villa Barbaro at Maser and the pierced wall in Villa Cornaro at Piombino Dese.
Bottom: Side arch of the portico in the Chapel in Maser and Villa Chiericati at Vancimuglio.

Controlling transparencies   The Loggia

Top: arches, intercolumniation and openings in Villa Almerico called "La Rotonda" in Vicenza; in Villa Barbaro at Maser and Villa Cornaro at Piombino Dese.

Loggias. The Palladian Basilica (Vicenza).

The ground-floor loggia. Palazzo Chiericati (Vicenza).

112 The Loggia   Architecture that breathes

3. Intersections. Spaces within Spaces

> "He no longer needs two-floor stratification in the façade of Il Redentore, they become a full four in the wisest of all intersections - the superimposed floors of the superb façade."[1]
> CESARE BRANDI

Palladio's works in general, but more in particular, his later works show how he was able to think and imagine architecture in ideal terms - like a set of transparent forms that live in the mind and can be combined, composed, merged, superimposed and intersected. This thought process is clearer when orders of different heights, parts that dialogue quite independently, co-exist in a design, spaces within spaces, spaces that penetrate each other. In some old architectural drawings this process is, so to speak, "evoked" before it takes place, like a hidden virtuality of the form to "co-grow," to be grafted and superimposed, much like events in a dream. Take for example the famous elevation of the small temple of Clitunno (London, RIBA, XI, 15r). Three orders of columns of two different heights are arranged on three different levels and seem to be waiting for a new balance achieved through transfer, movement, and superimposition. Another old drawing of the Diocletian baths emphasises the four orders of columns of different heights and a series of arches connecting these columns, grouping them like words which, placed all together in a preposition, acquire a very precise meaning. The fact the drawing is unfinished allows it to be read in "sections" that can be combined in a thousand different ways.

In his book on Palladio, *Learning from Palladio,* Branko Mitrovic credits Palladio with radical Platonism (perhaps it was unintentional, but it is nonetheless present in his compositional technique): this led him to see in his works a reflection or the incarnation of eternal and universal architectural concepts with their own individual reality, comparable to mathematical theories whose validity depends on how we use them. The artist's task is to discover, reveal and hint at them rather than reinvent them *ex novo*. The object of this aesthetic appreciation can either be recognition or the creation of a mental entity based on our perceptions. In actual fact, when we talk about an architecture and try and interpret it we don't think of a real image we can 'freeze' in a photograph; we have in our minds an image of the layout and everything our senses have registered from a distance or close up, inside or out, at the top or at the bottom. We create a mental image based either on the images we have or on the progressive discovery and recognition of a series of ideas that represent what Giedion defined the "Eternal Present."[1] According to Mitrovic, Palladio opted for the latter. One indication that this was his idea of architecture is his choice of orthogonal projections rather than perspective, and the fact that he never mentioned other architectural theories in the *Four Books*, theories repeatedly proposed by Vitruvius and accepted by nearly all theorists of architecture.[2] In fact, very rarely does Palladio use perspective in his drawings; in the treatise, perspective is used only to show the texture of walls, while the use of projections in plans, elevations and sections is as systematic as it is functional to the architect's analytical work. Some of the drawings in the treatise are in fact incomparable masterpieces in which superimposition and the way in which the three types of orthogonal projections merge gracefully suggest a concise process of understanding and knowledge of the object represented in the three dimensions of reality. For instance, the table showing the Corinthian trabeation (I, 17, p. 25). The capital is transparent, like a jellyfish and the forms, from the lower shaft to the abacus, are superimposed without reciprocally eliminating each other because the drawing is so simple: it shows the outlines without presuming to directly show plasticity (to be deciphered by the mind, not provided by the drawing). There are substantial differences between this drawing and a similar one in Vignola's treatise. Vignola uses the drawing to provide a realistic rather than an ideal description. By carefully using hatching, it anticipates the plastic and luminous effect of the mouldings. Quite rightly, Roberto Pane[3] notes that Palladio's graphic elegance is at its best in the table showing the spiral of the Ionic capital (I, 16, p. 20): a drawing in which the planes are superimposed and the technical information is so complete that it is as enjoyable as a painting or, better still, the explanation of a mathematical formula.

Further proof of Palladio's Platonism is the captious indication for the proportions of the orders of numbers very similar to those indicated by Vitruvius and even Barbaro for whom Palladio had

FIG. 42. DRAWING BY PALLADIO OF THE TEMPLE ON THE CLITUNNO (RIBA, XI, 15R).

OVERLEAF
FIGS. 43 AND 44. SCHEMATIC DRAWING OF THE TWO FAÇADES
OF SAN FRANCESCO DELLA VIGNA IN VENICE
(RUDOLF WITTKOWER, ARCHITECTURAL PRINCIPLES IN THE AGE OF HUMANISM,
LONDON 1962) AND PALLADIO'S DESIGN OF THE FAÇADE OF A CHURCH,
PERHAPS SAN FRANCESCO DELLA VIGNA (RIBA, XIV, 10).

done the drawings. In the Doric trabeation, for example, Vitruvius and Barbaro indicate the thickness of the moulding (called *tenia*) as being the diameter of the lower part of the column multiplied by 0.0714 that Palladio approximates to 0.75, passing from 1/14 to 3/40. With regards to the guttae of the trabeation, Palladio corrects Barbaro to 1/180 of the lower diameter of the column. The thickness of the abacus of the Ionic capital prescribed by Palladio differs from the thickness established by Renaissance tradition: the seven hundred and twentieth part of the diameter of the column measured at the base. Mitrovic writes: "The only conclusion we can draw is that this formula of the canon of the five orders in the *Four Books* belongs to an ideal system of orders different to anything that can currently be built or perceived once it has been built."[4]

Mitrovic is absolutely right when he says that Palladio had assimilated certain principles of Platonism. However, we should not forget that in Italian Renaissance culture, and Venetian culture in particular, Platonic and Aristotelian tradition are not always seen as alternatives, but leave enough room for mediation. This is clearly visible in Raphael's *School of Athens*, in which the two philosophers are walking together in the middle of the Bramantesque scene: one is looking upwards towards the heavens, the other downwards towards earth. If Raphael (who put Bramante on Aristotle's side and Michelangelo on Plato's side) had lived another fifty years he would probably have put Palladio in the middle. Plato's influence over Palladio is clearly visible in those parts of the treatise describing the construction of temples and churches: Palladio writes

> And therefore we also, that have no false gods, in order to observe the decorum concerning the form of temples, must choose the most perfect, and most excellent. And since the round one is such, because it is the only one amongst all the figures that is simple, uniform, equal, strong, and capacious, let us make our temples round. For which purpose this figure is particularly fit, because it being enclosed by one termination only, in which is to be found neither beginning nor end, nor are they to be distinguished one from the other; but having its parts familiar one to another, and all participating of the figure of the whole; in a word the extreme being found in all its parts, equally distant from the middle, it is exceeding proper to demonstrate the infinite essence, the uniformity, and the justice of God (IV, 2, p. 81-82).

I believe that this page, not without literary excellence, but above all packed with surprising clarity, means that Palladio had carefully read not only *Il Convito* but also the comments to the dialogue by Marsilio Ficino published in Italian in Florence in 1544 by the publisher Neri Dortelata. Ficino writes

> God who is the centre of everything, simple unity and pure Act, puts himself in all things. Not only because he is present in all things, but also because he has given an intrinsic part of himself to all the things he has made, a simple and important power, that is called the unity of all things: from which and to which, as if from a centre to his centre, all the other powers and parts of each part belong.[5]

Reading the comment by Marsilio Ficino, we would be right in thinking that Palladio concentrated on the part concerning the work of architects.

> If someone were to ask how similar the form of the body can be to the form and reason of the Soul and the Angel, I would tell that person to look at Architecture. The first thing an architect does is to conceive a design, a reason and an image in his mind: then he builds a house (as best he can) as his thoughts have indicated. So who would say that a house is not a body? And that it is very similar to the incorporeal idea of the artifice in whose image it was made? Certainly, it is similar in its incorporeal order rather than in its materials. Try and draw matter if you can: you can draw it with your mind. Now take matter away from the building and you will be left with order: no materials will remain: above all there will be order that comes from the artifice and the order that remains in the artifice. So, do this in the body of any man: and you will find the form of what is suitable with the approval of the soul, a simple being without matter.

Certainly, Palladio's design technique is based on an idea of order that coincides with the one proposed by Ficino: an order that introduces into the "body" of the house the incorporeal idea of the artifice that becomes the Soul, the inner nucleus that creates beauty.

In the façades of his churches (except for Santa Maria Nova in Vicenza), Palladio intersects two hierarchically distinct architec-

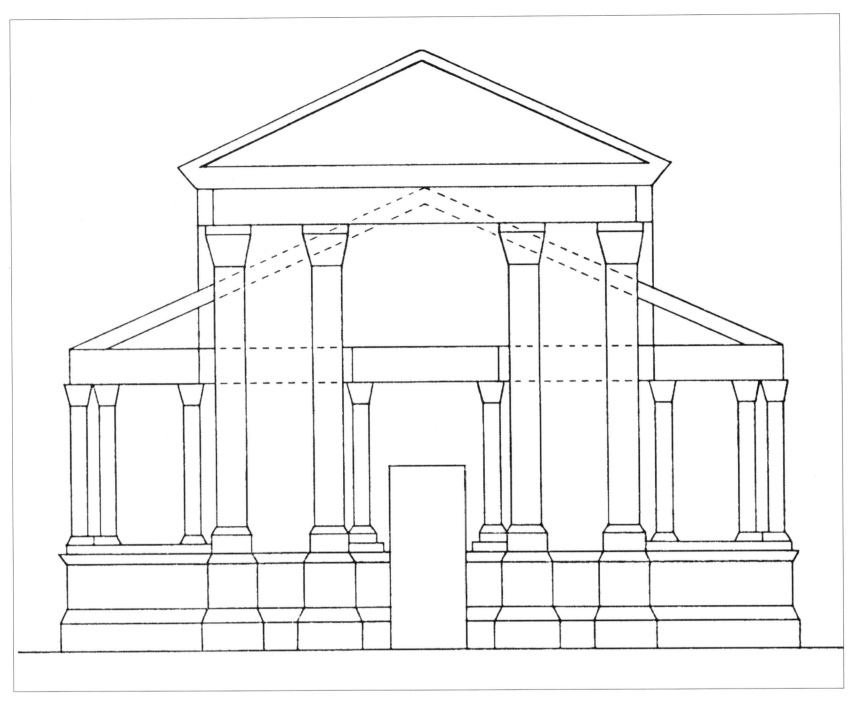

tural orders: a major order supporting the pediment, and two fragments of a minor order on the two sides facing the central nucleus. Wittkower in his book[6] has included a drawing of the façade of San Francesco della Vigna in which the tympanum created by the two inclined fragments of the side wings is completed so as to be superimposed on the lines of the central part. The drawing was considered a deliberate reference to the two realities present in a church: the divine and the human. Apart from its symbolic importance, an intersection in the façade of two temple aedicules had already been proposed by Francesco di Giorgio in his treatise, similar to Palladio's anthropomorphism later experimented by Bramante in the church of Roccaverano and by Baldassarre Peruzzi in Carpi. This intersection system made it possible to find a solution for the façades of basilicas, adopting a classical style without using the "impious" solution of the volutes proposed by Leon Battista Alberti in Santa Maria Novella – a solution that was to become very popular during the Baroque. A Palladian drawing (RIBA, XIV, 12), perhaps the façade of San Francesco della Vigna or San Giorgio (fig. 45), clearly reveals the problems inherent in placing the two aedicules side by side, even before using intersection.[7] The central part is still a simple tetrastyle while the lateral parts look like a temple *in autis* in which there is a third order belonging to an aedicule with a small monument inside. Another drawing, probably belonging to the same self-critical process, shows a sudden metamorphosis. The tetrastyle has become a triumphal arch which, thanks to the *cartelle* motif, recalls the arch in Ancona. The wings have maintained the traits they had in the drawing mentioned earlier, but the two orders (that of the smaller aedicule has disappeared) are raised on a base around the two centre columns, joined overhead by the very evident trabeation and attic. Instead, the way they unite the side wings to the outer columns of the tetrastyle is truly surprising. This is one of Palladio's typical *ars combinatoria* periods. The relationship between the parts is flexible yet depends on a precise analytical logic; it is used in the search for a balance that doesn't translate into a decrease in tension but

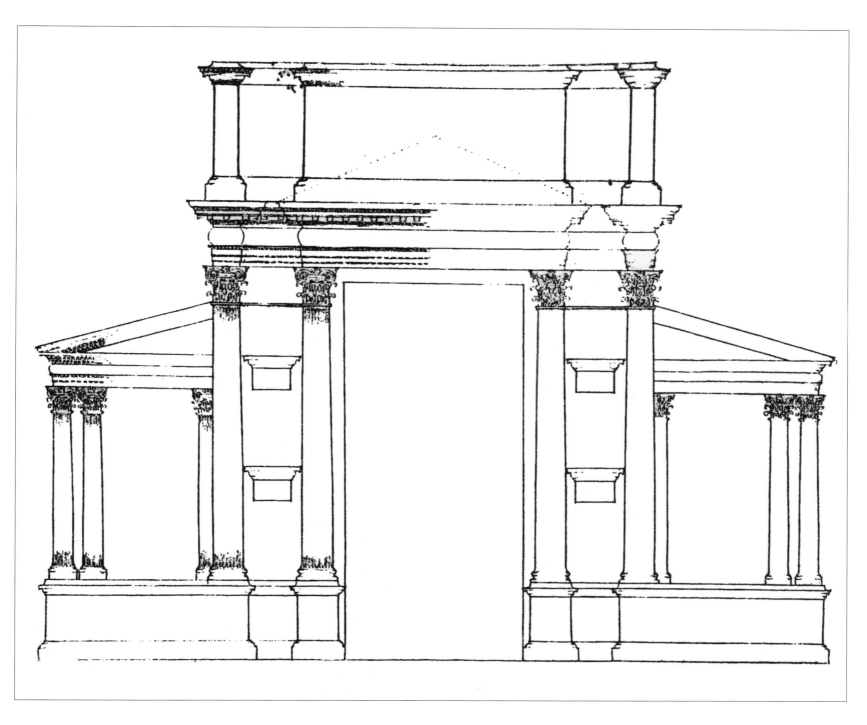

illustrates the many theories classical grammar provides to a learned connoisseur of its virtuality. In light of this research, the four very similar façades (San Pietro di Castello, San Francesco, San Giorgio and Il Redentore) have different *ars combinatoria* solutions. The fact that San Pietro and San Giorgio are not as good can be attributed to the posthumous work carried out by people who were less faithful to his drawings than those who built San Francesco and Il Redentore.

It's difficult to establish the role Palladio played in the building of San Pietro di Castello, because even if we accept the theory of an original model (as proposed by Pane and Puppi), Francesco Smeraldi certainly did modify the design described in the 1558 contract. But I prefer not to talk about it here given the crucial importance of autography ⁄ even if I don't agree with Wittkower who called it a pastiche that merged bits of San Giorgio, San Francesco and Il Redentore. The most obvious and convincing example of intersection can be found in San Francesco della Vigna, despite the reservations of many critics who don't seem to appreciate that Palladio was not aiming at the indisputable goal of static balance, but at a conscious dynamic balance that would convey the (never truly conclusive) importance of a "combined" design process. Like composing a symphony, in the façade of San Francesco the various elements play different, well-balanced roles. One indication of the overall design is visible in the side façade: here the two pilasters of the wings correspond, so to speak, to two layers of the façade ⁄ that of the order and that of the curtain wall.[8] A similar stratification is present in the central part where, in correspondence to the tympanum, there is a doubling of the framework that give breadth and depth to the frontal view. Combining the two systems was essentially achieved by executing a series of extremely refined ideas which, in my opinion, proves Palladio's involvement. The ideas are easily listed: 1) the first was to create a vertical gap between the central aedicule and the wings: this meant that the cornice of the wings was not to touch the central columns; 2) the second is the flattening of the cornice in the intervals between the two columns of the central

FIGS. 45 AND 46. DRAWING OF A FAÇADE OF A CHURCH WHICH COULD BE
SAN GIORGIO MAGGIORE IN VENICE (RIBA, XIV, 12, RIGHT).
PLANIMETRIC DETAIL OF THE SAME CHURCH SHOWING WHERE THE INTERIOR
AND EXTERIOR FAÇADES MEET (OTTAVIO BERTOTTI SCAMOZZI, *LE FABBRICHE E I DISEGNI
DI ANDREA PALLADIO RACCOLTI E ILLUSTRATI DA OTTAVIO BERTOTTI SCAMOZZI*,
VICENZA 1786, 2A ED., VOL IV, TAB. V).

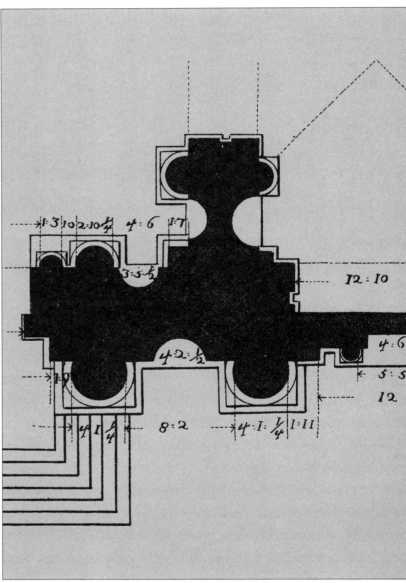

118　Intersections. Spaces within Spaces

OVERLEAF

FIG. 47. IL REDENTORE. VENICE (FRANCESCO ANTONIO MUTTONI, *ARCHITETTURA DI ANDREA PALLADIO... CON LE OSSERVAZIONI DELL'ARCHITETTO N.N.*, VENICE 1740-1748, VOL. I, TAB. 3).

FIG. 48. SAN GIORGIO MAGGIORE. VENICE (*IBID.*, VOL. I, TAB. 20).

aedicule, a trick I've already mentioned as being one of the most characteristic of his personal style: from the full overhang of the mouldings (each one was different) there is a shift towards contraction that turns plasticity and chiaroscuro into linearity, giving the intersection a trait I would call "mental" and avoiding its more drastic and violent effects; 3) the third involves raising the entire façade by putting it on a base similar to the one in the drawing RIBA, XIV, 10 (fig. 44), but arranged differently so as to create three frontal planes: that of the wings and portal (having in common the extension of the relative trabeations) and that of the curtain wall of the major order. Compared to the drawings I have mentioned, the pondered and subtle physical and "mental" parts of the building are all connected. The continuity of the mouldings of the attic base of the columns under the curtain wall belong to the first type[9] (a reference to the work by Antonio da Sangallo the Younger in the chapel of San Giacomo degli Spagnoli), as does the fascia under the panels that unite the wings to the central aedicule, panels which also run along the small channel/gap between the two parts. The rhythmic quality of the Corinthian cornice of the minor order (accentuated by the protruding parts of the modillions that at a distance unite the wings and the central door) belong to the second type, as does the repetition of the circular motif first in the Palladian window and then again above the entry doorway where it helps to make the proportions of the opening acceptable. These observations - which the reader might consider too anatomical and detailed - do, however, help to see beyond the seemingly quiet static of Palladio's design and appreciate the unsettling structuring force created by setting the parts against one another, listening to their reasons and, finally, emphasising the dialogue they establish.

Compared to the façade of San Francesco, the façade of San Giorgio rather than that of San Pietro di Castello, looks like a distracted viewer's sketch of a text spoken aloud by its author. Since we know that a model had been produced by Andrea in 1567,[10] we have to assume that forty years later the seventeenth-century builders were unable to understand the rules governing Palladio's grammar. Confirmation comes indirectly from Temanza who realised this and noted the discrepancies vis-à-vis the finished work. The fact is that continuity, correspondence and unification of the parts are replaced by simple 'matches' and an unpleasant violent interpenetration between the cornices and the shafts of the columns. *Concordia discors* is replaced by the monotony created by setting two overly similar trabeations on very different orders against one another. The intelligent arrangement of the rectangular cornices crowning the wall intervals is replaced by a series of dissimilar elements - the niches to the sides of the entrance and the aedicules with the funerary monuments on bases that are higher than the niches themselves. Nevertheless, seen from a distance San Giorgio does concretise Palladio's wonderfully intuitive idea of creating a sacred backdrop to the area around St. Mark's by designing a ring of churches that could play the role of "safeguard and protector of citizens" assigned in the treatise (IV, 1, p. 81) to the Christian religion.

The façade of Il Redentore is very different: perhaps construction began, like the rest of the building, before its designer died, but, in any case, it was completed before 1592. Here again we find two orders, two juxtaposed temple systems, slightly different in height, positioned so as to unite and avoid conflict and gaps. This time the two orders rise from a slightly protruding temple stylobate with a large staircase. The huge door is obliquely inserted in the central intercolumniation. Above the large tympanum there is an attic equal in width, so the façade, like a triumphal arch, ends in a straight line that acts as a base for three big statues that stand out against the blue sky: the statue of the redeemer in the middle and two angels with outstretched wings on either side. For Palladio, this solution is a step forward compared to San Francesco and San Giorgio. The different height of the two tympana at the impost corresponds exactly to the design of a series of individual chapels instead of naves. It allows Palladio to achieve absolute organicity between the interior and exterior, between the wall and the façade. From outside, above all when viewed at a distance, the building is easy to interpret. His decision to prefer a

Intersections. Spaces within Spaces

120 Intersections. Spaces within Spaces

Intersections. Spaces within Spaces 121

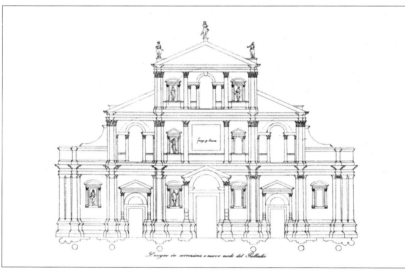
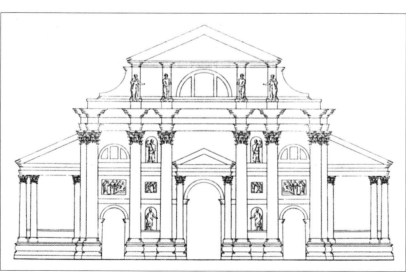

122 Intersections. Spaces within Spaces

FIGS. 49-52. FOUR SOLUTIONS FOR THE FAÇADE OF SAN PETRONIO IN BOLOGNA FROM THE ENGRAVINGS BY OTTAVIO BERTOTTI SCAMOZZI. BOTTOM, RIGHT: THE FINAL DRAWING BY PALLADIO SHOWING THE SOLUTION INSPIRED BY THE PANTHEON (WORCESTER COLLEGE LIBRARY, H.T. 68).

horizontal cornice to a second tympanum similar to that of the Pantheon (which Palladio very probably did initially envisage) meant he was able to prolong this thin cornice (combined with his favourite modillions) along the entire longitudinal length of the building, including the three apses and the choir. The same is true for the cornice of the wings which terminates only at the end of the series of side chapels. A third element is present in the façade, above the half tympana of the wings. This element completes and strengthens the compact nature of the plane of the façade and has both technical and aesthetic elements: the double buttress repeated eight times along the sides of the church to contain the thrust of the vault of the nave. When this element appears on the façade a half tympanum is grafted onto it creating the typical broken tympanum that Palladio so loved and employed in his first designs for villas (drawings RIBA, nos. XVII, 2; XVII, 15: figs. 61 and 56) as well as in such a superb manner in Villa Poiana (p. 163). The two small bell-towers and the perfect balance of the volumes of the cupola, the apse and the choir make it all the more plausible that Marcantonio Barbaro (who had been to Constantinople) did in fact tell his architect friend about the wonders of Haghia Sophia and the buildings recently built by Sinan.

Intersection was used in private buildings well before it became so important in church design. This is confirmed by several drawings of façades (which were never built) and, even more noticeably, by the façade of Palazzo Valmarana. In three drawings of the RIBA collection (XVII, 23, 26 and 19), the issue of a plastic link between the elements can be traced from when it was designed to when it was built. In the first (fig. 14) a weak link is created by the base of the order around the aedicules of the windows and each of the coupled pilasters around the small niches. The same elements are present in drawing n. 26 (fig. 15) but connected by the extension of the trabeation of the aedicules to the entire façade: the trabeation further compresses the niches, even establishing an upper limit. In the third drawing, the rusticated ground floor avoids mechanically repeating the same architectural elements on two floors and includes a tympanum to crown and differentiate the central part of the façade. During the early stages of his studies, turning the cornice of the windows into an aedicule with a tympanum (like the Pantheon) or a freely designed "Palladian window" allowed Palladio to achieve an organic whole (starting with a simple list of parts). He did this by intersecting two orders using archaeological examples: this paved the way for a more mature plan like the one in the drawing Zorzi identified as the home of Giuliano and Guido Piovene and Puppi considered to be Palazzo Da Monte and the architect's late masterpiece, Palazzo Valmarana. In the latter, Palladio draws on his extensive experience with the classical style to try and implement a small revolution. The architectural orders and the solutions proposed by Bramante and Raphael had breathed new life into research on buildings, but still, intercolumniation was very different to the one established by Vitruvius - much longer than the maximum three and a half modules. Even previous buildings built by Palladio had a wider intercolumniation in order to accommodate sufficiently wide windows. For Villa Valmarana and Palazzo Porto-Breganze, the adoption of a giant order left room for the windows without betraying Vitruvius, yet at the same time it allowed Andrea to experiment with new arrangements, changing proportions, joints and overhangs. The two buildings should be assessed together because they prove how important certain issues were for the architect: environmental conditions, flow of light and relationship with the sky. Palazzo Valmarana is located in a narrow street with a height/width ratio between the buildings of 1:3 and 1:4 and faces west. Palazzo Porto-Breganze faces north onto a large square. For the former, the architect chose a silvery chiaroscuro, small overhangs and imperceptible vibrations: he implemented an architectural *stiacciato*, perhaps to imitate Donatello in Padua. For the latter, he chose a rounded shape, pronounced overhangs and an oblique composition so that the galleries (their supports resting on a mysterious architrave) appear compressed by the shafts. The space between the bases and the very recessed win-

FIGS. 53 AND 54. TWO PARTICULARLY ELEGANT GRAPHIC TABLES OF THE *FOUR BOOKS*. THE CORINTHIAN CAPITAL (I, 16) AND THE COMPOSITE TRABEATION (I, 18).

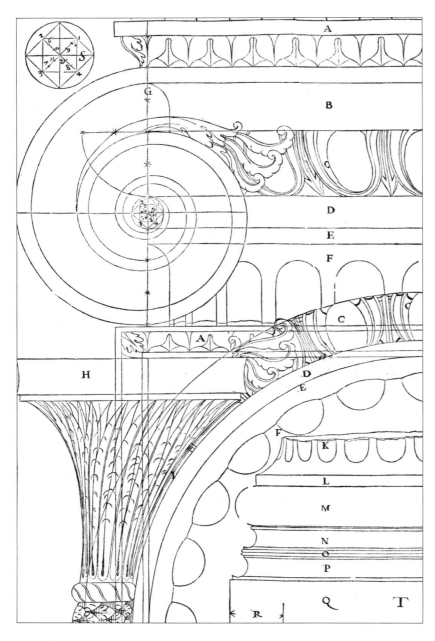

dows become an ambiguous space immersed in the shadows. Designed to be seen from different viewpoints, from a distance and close-up, the building has both plastic and pictorial aspects influenced as it was by the lasting impressions left on Palladio during his first trip to the Forum of Nerva. In Palazzo Valmarana, while repeating and flaunting his pact of loyalty to Vitruvius (who apart from forbidding intercolumniation greater than 2.5 times the lower diameter of the columns, in the Basilica in Fano had proposed an intersection with two orders), Palladio proves he is also a free-thinker. He replaces the neat arrangement of pilasters at the ends with "lame" intervals in which the minor order develops in the overhangs and the cornice of the window acquires a tympanum. *In extremis*, to provide support for the crowning cornice, he uses two slender figures of soldiers in bas-relief who seem to have adventurously descended from the cornice itself. In fact, the statues are not included in the engraving in the treatise and were unfortunately never built. Oxymoron, irony, deconstruction, destruction of the image? Or quite simply a compromise between the splendour of the building and the rather dull countryside? Certainly an end that opens rather than closes, an oneiric detail, today we would call it surreal, like Wim Wenders' Berlin Angel in *Der Himmel ueber Berlin*. However it tells us that Palladio's imagination was not influenced by classicist orthodoxy or mannerist licence.

The intersection technique suggests a step-by-step telescopic depth that shifts from the *moment of ideation* to the moment of interpretation and carries us, as if in a dream, into the secret materiality of the mind. This led Fiocco to talk about "spaces that grow within spaces"[11] as a specific trait of Palladio's architecture. If you look at Il Redentore from the entrance, it looks like a large apsidal room with a break that suggests a transept. Taking a few steps forward, you can see the area of the pendentives and the drum of the cupola; but you have to get almost to the steps of the presbytery to see the two side apses and realise that further along there is a central organism, three-quarters of which is almost freely developed. The link between the church area and the

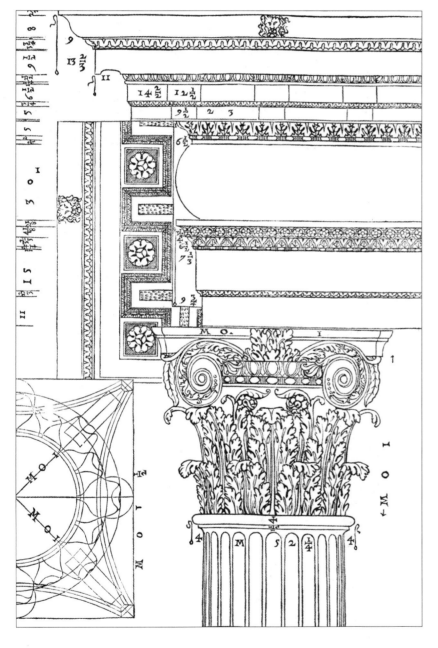

domed space is one of the high points of Palladio's syntactic teachings. In fact, the arch we see at the back of the church, replicated in the transparent apse, rests on two pilasters, but receives visual force for the two columns next to it, creating an extraordinary plastic and luminous effect (figs. 73 and p. 137). This same coupling (pilaster/column) is also present in the central organism where the columns are intended to highlight the diagonal pylons supporting the pendentives of the cupola. Closer examination of the complexity of the cornice in this particular point reveals the degree of refinement Palladio had achieved after years of research and experience in the field of classical language and how this language had become for him a *language of the soul*, a source of absolute and timeless truth to be joyfully discovered again and again through toil and labour. The recurrent theme of the half-circle and the arch as an archway, niche and nymphaeum is another indication of Palladio's creative bond with Roman architecture. From the entrance onwards, visual polyphony is created by the arches of the cadenced girder, the niches between the columns and the niches of the chapels arranged on orthogonal planes. This polyphony emphasises space and forces one to see the same form in progressively bigger shapes - from the smallest niches to the biggest arches. Under the cupola, the three apses intensify the design of the half-circle, uniting niche and arch. Ultimately, the idea of the arch is again present in the drum of the circular cupola where the openings are positioned in such a way so as not to hurt the eyes of viewers and make the latter imagine a circle of celestial signs - executed with all the talent of a man of the theatre.

I should point out that one key tool in this intersection technique applied to space is a conscious strategy of natural lighting achieved not only through the position of the windows, but by shaping the walls to find those "gaps," those soft spots that dematerialise surfaces and emphasize continuity through a sort of chiaroscuro vibration. Here too, the church of Il Redentore is a triumphal achievement with effects that recall "Leonardo's nuances." First of all, the column is set against the niche. On the

Intersections. Spaces within Spaces

Fig. 55. Façade and courtyard. Palazzo Valmarana (Vicenza).
Preparatory drawing for the xylograph of the *Four Books* (RIBA, XVII, 4).

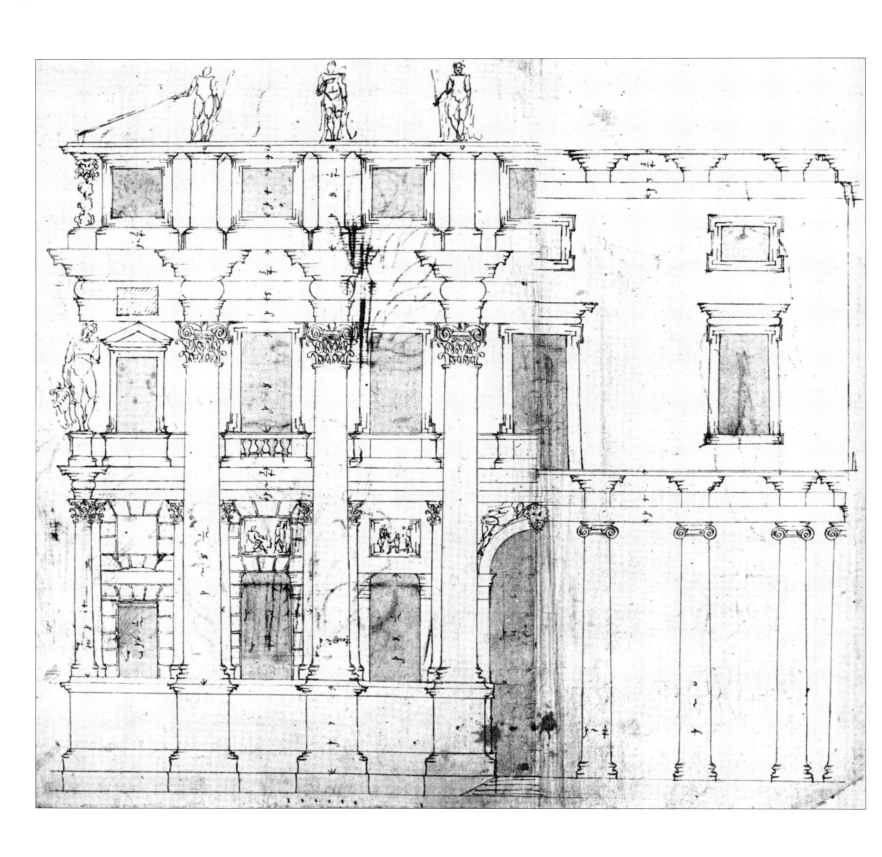

126   Intersections. Spaces within Spaces

one hand, building materials congregate in the convexity of the shafts where light converges and escapes; on the other, excavated material that captures light, condenses it and lets it softly fade. These dual effects reach incomparable heights in the transparent apse where the apsidal conch recaptures the design of the niche above the four columns that stand out against a background that is sometimes dark, sometimes light, depending on the time of day. None of Palladio's other works, but I would be so bold as to say no other similar architecture, gives this feeling of space, of the diastole and systole of the sunrise and sunset against the horizon, but also the passing of clouds or simply the change that takes place in images when they enter and remain in our memory, acquiring new nuances when we move in space (pgs. 198-199).

"Spaces within spaces" is also an appropriate definition for San Giorgio where Palladio develops the ideas he originally planned for the reconstruction of San Pietro. The basic plan is a domed central structure with two additional spans at the entrance that lengthen the building longitudinally. In the background, there is a very distinct quadrangular space with round columns not against the wall: this is the presbytery, separated from the choir by a transenna on two orders. Here too there are combinations and intersections of independent parts: the two traditional orders of the nave, the simplified order that frames the transenna; the nave and the presbytery; the central aedicule behind the altar with a third order; the distant but gracefully composed image of the choir. Palladio's main concern seems to be to give visibility to the possibility of expanding sideways into the luminous space of the naves and to concentrate on the altar and transenna. The pillars between the three naves are complex parts, made up of half-columns facing the main nave and a pair of pilasters supporting the dividing arches. These pilasters separated by a half-column of the same height, in turn support arches and vaults of the minor naves lit by thermal windows. The cupola springs from the point where the nave and transept meet and ends in two apses. Palladio's use of the orders reveals his expertise and his incredibly flexible style - continually introducing novelties that "fit the bill." Note the withdrawal of the overhangs in the cornice of the minor order (contrary to what happens in the façade built posthumously) which penetrates the shaft of the column with measured grace; note the gap that divides the rear transenna from the order letting the cornice of the lower order of the transenna touch the nearby pilaster without entering it. These expedients come from Roman architecture - for example the autographed relief of the Arch of Jupiter Ammon in Verona (RIBA, XII, 22v). However, to be seen and understood, a person needed independent judgement and an anti-academic instinct, something the architect maintained throughout his life.

Palladio made one of his most acute observations on intersection after suffering a humiliating defeat when consulted about the completion of the church of San Petronio in Bologna. When asked for his opinion in 1572, he said he was against continuing the façade based on the *todesco* design of the base (already finished). But in the end Andrea approved a mediocre project by Terribilia in order to save at least part of the construction. When other consultants voiced their concerns, he drafted two compromise designs (fig. 50) packed with Palladian windows, tympanums broken at the base, aedicules and statues - words from his own personal vocabulary - but he did it with such cynicism and indifference that it cannot but make a reader think of all his misfortunes during that period and his probably need for compensation. In a gesture of creative pride, without being asked and convinced that no-one would listen to him, he proposed two solutions in an ambiguous drawing; the two solutions reflected his research on the façades of basilicas, in particular for Il Redentore. His dissolutive nature emerges in the solution studied on the right side of the page (fig. 52): the façade of Palazzo Valmarana, however, shows that he promptly quashed that particular temptation. The four columns around the entrance aedicule are moved forward, making the cornice more complex; the columns are crowned with statues that repropose the model of the triumphal arch together with that of the honorary column. In the solution studied on the left side of the page, the characteristics of San

Francesco, San Giorgio and Il Redentore reappear in a contradictory and dramatic image, packed with an amazing potential for development. The half tympana of the wings, in keeping with the style adopted for the façade of Il Redentore, are almost as high as the central tympanum, while at the top a horizontal cornice crowns the volume flanked by another two half-tympana. The design anticipates this "role game": this advancement and retreat, division and coupling of architectural words, pronounced with different timbres, makes one regret that Palladio's adventure/defeat ended in the most conventional of designs, taken from the Pantheon, and illustrated in the Oxford drawing found by Harris[12] (fig. 51).

[1] SIGFRIED GIEDION, *L'Eterno presente. La nascita dell'architettura*, Milan 1965.
[2] Cfr. PAOLO PORTOGHESI, *Natura e architettura*, Milan 1999.
[3] BRANKO MITROVIC, *Learning from Palladio*, New York 2004.
[4] ROBERTO PANE, *Andrea Palladio*, Turin 1961.
[5] MARSILIO FICINO, *Sopra lo Amore*, Lanciano 1934, pgs. 29, 65 and 71.
[6] RUDOLF WITTKOWER, *Architectural Principles in the Age of Humanism*, London 1962.
[7] Lionello Puppi certainly refers to San Giorgio due to the similarities of the monuments inside the aedicules (LIONELLO PUPPI, *Palladio*, Milan 1973, p. 367).
[8] Cfr. RENATO CEVESE, *L'opera del Palladio*, in *Palladio*. exhibition catalogue, Milan 1980, pgs. 86-87.
[9] Cfr. PAOLO PORTOGHESI, *Roma del Rinascimento*, Milan 1971, p. 84, fig. 365.
[10] PUPPI, *Palladio* cit., p. 210.
[11] GIUSEPPE FIOCCO, *L'Esposizione dei disegni di A. Palladio*, in "Arte Veneta", 1949, p. 184.
[12] JOHN HARRIS, *Three Unrecorded Palladio Designs from Inigo Jones' Collection*, in "The Burlington Magazine", 1971, pgs. 31-37. The drawing is housed in Worcester College. Another similar drawing was published in GIANGIORGIO ZORZI, *Le chiese e i ponti di Palladio*, Venice 1966.

Tympana and cornices. San Francesco della Vigna (Venice).

Intersections. Spaces within Spaces

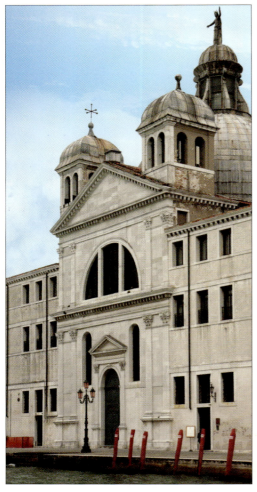

From top to bottom, left to right:
Façades of the Zitelle (Venice),
San Francesco della Vigna (Venice),
San Giorgio Maggiore (Venice),
Santa Maria Nova (Vicenza),
the side entrance of the Cathedral in Vicenza
and the façade of Santa Maria di Castello (Venice).

Intersections. Spaces within Spaces   The façade as a projection of the interior

IL REDENTORE (VENICE).

Left: Cupola and ceiling.
San Giorgio Maggiore;
Right: Cupola and ceiling.
Il Redentore (Venice).

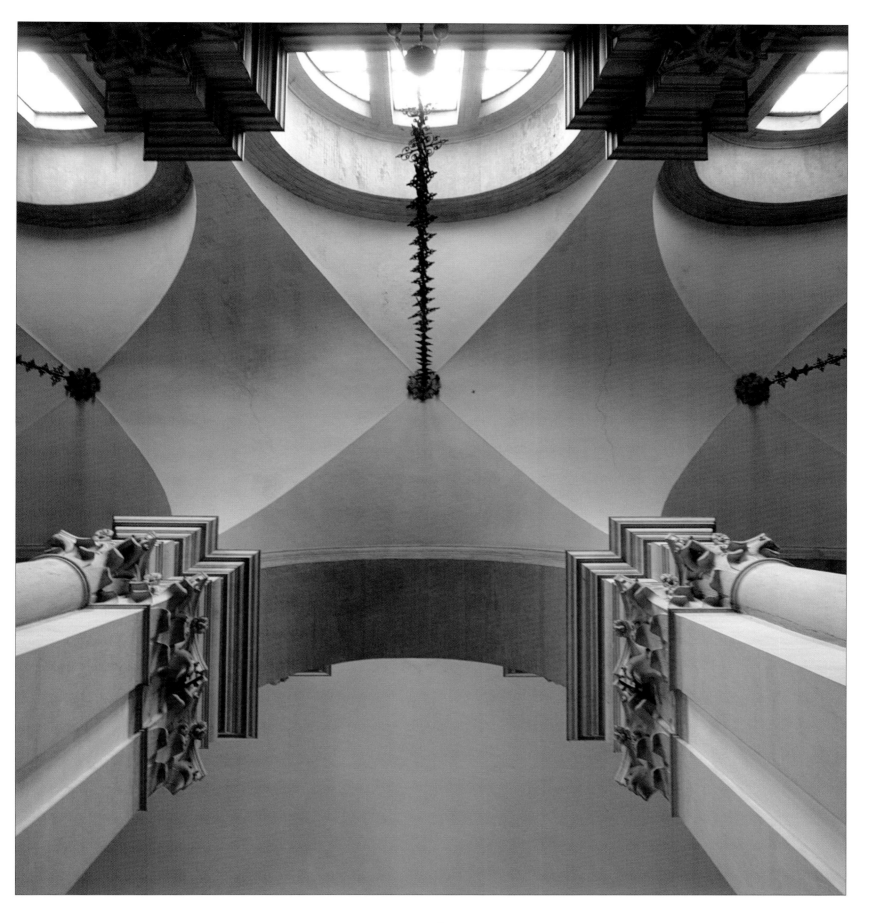

Cross-vaults of the minor naves.
San Giorgio Maggiore (Venice).

Spaces within spaces   Intersections. Spaces within Spaces

INTERNAL FAÇADES.
SAN GIORGIO MAGGIORE
AND IL REDENTORE (VENICE):
THE CENTRAL PARTS RECEDES
AND ENLARGES THE OPENING.

Intersections. Spaces within Spaces The internal façade as a "break"

In the church of Il Redentore in Venice,
a central plan breaks and ends the longitudinal nave.

136   Intersections. Spaces within Spaces   Centrality as catharsis

Centrality as catharsis   Intersections. Spaces within Spaces   137

Three pictures of the hall of Palazzo Thiene (Vicenza); centre, right and bottom: two details of Villa Serego at Santa Sofia di Pedemonte and Palazzo Schio (Vicenza).

138   Intersections. Spaces within Spaces   Joints and intersections in the rustic order

From left to right, top to bottom:
details of Villa Pisani at Bagnolo,
Villa Serego at Santa Sofia di Pedemonte, Villa Pisani,
Palazzo Antonini (Udine), Palazzo Thiene,
Villa Pisani, the Town Hall (Cividale),
Palazzo Poiana and Palazzo Civena (Vicenza).

Joints and intersections in the rustic order   Intersections. Spaces within Spaces

Intersecting orders. Palladian Basilica (Vicenza).

140 Intersections. Spaces within Spaces   Interpenetration of the orders

Palazzo Barbaran(o) and Casa Cogollo (details).
Right: Palazzo Valmarana in Vicenza (details).

Interpenetration of the orders   Intersections. Spaces within Spaces   141

A COMPOSITION WITH JUXTAPOSED FLOORS
BREAKS PERSPECTIVAL CONTINUITY.
THE STAGE OF THE TEATRO OLIMPICO (VICENZA).

From perspective to stage sets Intersections. Spaces within Spaces   143

The violent intersection of the façade of San Giorgio in Venice and the subtle, discreet façade of Il Redentore in Venice.

144 Intersections. Spaces within Spaces   Conflict and organicity

4. Bareness and Horror Vacui

"All these solutions: the naked wall, sharp corners, frameless windows, are an indication of modesty and poverty in contrast to columns which are always associated with a sort of nobility, a certain idea of grandeur, even when they're not load-bearing columns. It's the two together that is surprising and, if I'm not mistaken, exceptional. This is clearly Palladio's initial intention."
ANDRÉ CHASTEL

"It's the bareness of the wall that makes the thrusts extreme and it's the bareness of the wall that removes all the grace of the architecture. The less visible the architecture, the more beautiful the work; if it weren't visible at all, then the work would be perfect."
MARC-ANTOINE LAUGIER

Not only was Palladio unwilling to invent decoration, he constantly distanced himself from the stereotyped image of honest moderation and carried out an exercise which swung between nudism and *horror vacui*. So for some of his buildings Chastel created a category he called *bareness*[1] and Ackerman, *cubism*,[2] while for other buildings some people talk about a decorative explosion interpreted in an expressionist manner as a way to destroy form. *Aurea simplicitas* is one of the objectives Palladio always set himself, convinced that this did not mean forsaking decoration altogether. On the contrary, he considered it should only be used functionally: a word often misinterpreted, but which means the ability to communicate symbols, meanings and values through decoration.

Contrary to what many critics say, the initial design of Villa Godi at Lonedo already reveals precise choices and the intention of the architect to use the volume as a crucial, expressive tool, defining openings and complexities. The central motif of the loggia assigns the role of the wings to other volumes and is designed very sparingly, using flat fascia instead of cornices; these fascia are like a thin red line running through many of his other works and are illustrated in Chapter One. In the idealised drawing of the villa, later included in the *Four Books*, Palladio, now sixty, describes anachronistically what he would have done thirty-eight years later, or rather, what he would have liked the client to allow him (the stonemason - aspiring architect) to do when he was twenty-four. The spontaneous simplicity of Villa Godi is visible in some of Palladio's drawings executed when he was young and living in London (RIBA, XVII, 1r and 27). In Villa Poiana at Poiana Maggiore, he already achieves an extremely elegant celebration of simplicity through a process of "simplification," a process that was to become popular again during the Enlightenment, in works by Boullée, Soane and Gilly, and in twentieth-century architecture by Perret, Muzio, and Piacentini as well as in Terragni's early works. The villa is one of his masterpieces designed after his trips to Rome and his hands-on knowledge of Roman monuments, the works of Bramante and his pupils. The trabeation broken under the tympanum, already illustrated in the drawings in London (figs. 56-61), was inspired by the thermal baths and aedicule of Trajan's Market, while the crown of circular oculi comes from Bramante's nymphaeum in Genazzano and the cupola in Capranica along the Via Prenestina. Instead, the design of the windows is unique: a cornice *alla cappuccina* surmounted by a small shelf supported by a series of interlinked prismatic brackets fastened to the back wall by a thin moulding. A bare, pure form achieved by "taking away," by disassembling an aedicule and reassembling it after having removed all elements not crucial to its grammatical enunciation. And since two of the windows of the façade towards the garden belong to the loggia, their pure shapes are left untouched by the outline of the frame and the overall design acquires an incomparable metaphysical rigour. A series of platonic ideas come down to earth from Hyperuranus, this bare (but not cubist) Palladian window surrounded by openings that emphasise its force, a game of fascia and prismatic and cylindrical blocks. It is a gift Palladio gives to lovers of *architecture as language*, who around these gypsum forms of fake stone, crossed by thin, illusory fugues of mortar, can enjoy the force of the absolute or imagine "casings" of any form or colour, order, capitals or decorations or, even without touching the forms, imagine different materials, crystalline transparencies, marbles and metallic reflections. Isn't the real reason for Palladio's universality, this 'pleasure to imagine' that architecture so often gives us?

Another supreme moment of simplification is the corner of the base in Villa Poiana in which the various fascia of differing heights, without features and figurations, mime the embrace Palladio writes about in the *Four Books:* "The discharged part, or set-off, which is on the outside, may be covered with a fascia and a cornice; which, surrounding all the building, will be both an ornament, and a kind of bond to the whole. And because the angles partake of the two sides, in order to keep them upright, and united together, they ought to be made very strong and solid with long hard stones, holding them as it were with arms" (I, 11, p. 11).

Figs. 56-59. Four drawings by a young Palladio. A façade and a plan considered by Lewis to be Villa Valmarana di Vigardolo (RIBA, XVII, 15R); a plan of Villa Pisani at Bagnolo (RIBA, XVII, 18V); a sketch, probably of Villa Valmarana (RIBA, XVI, 4V) and a sketched plan of Villa Pisani (RIBA, XVII, 2V).

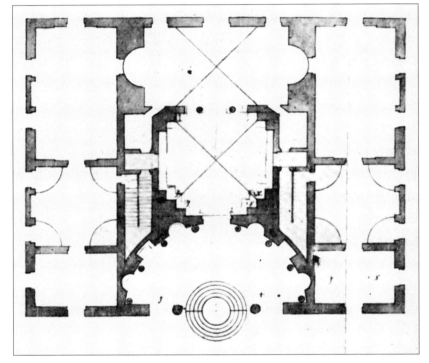

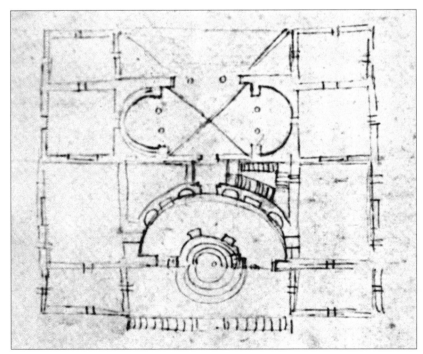

146　Bareness and Horror Vacui

Another example of Palladio's "bareness" can be seen in his later works: Villa Pisani at Montagnana and Villa Cornaro at Piombino Dese with their frameless windows, and Villa Zeno which, perhaps due to the fact it has been abandoned seems to be the poorest and most laconic of the Palladian villas. The lack of any decorations suits its melancholy air; it is almost a declaration of how simplicity is a defence against the ravages of time. Even in his urban architecture Palladio provided his clients with a terse and eloquent atmosphere, two sides of the same coin. In the Convent of Charity, for example, if the courtyard courageously achieves the perfection and expressive power admired by Goethe, in the façade along the canal (now *rio terà* of Sant'Agnese) the windows have only a squared-off stone frame set back a few centimetres from the wall surface. The solemnity of the building and its relationship with the sumptuous interior (underlined by the terracotta cornices superimposed on three floors), coexist with the rhythm of the openings floating in the middle of the walls.

The absolute balance between bareness and decoration characterises one of Palladio's major works, the first he built in Venice: the Convent of the Lateran Canons near the Church of Charity. His declared goal was to rebuild, as far as possible, the old house described by Vitruvius. Unfortunately, in 1630 a fire destroyed what was the most attractive part of the building, the famous Corinthian hall to which Temanza probably refers in his biting quatrain: "It isn't a bad thing if Palladio goes whoring / if indeed he wants to / because he does so to encourage them to build / an ancient atrium in the centre of Carampane." A fifteenth-century style courtyard still exists in the area known as Carampane: it might have been part of the famous brothel referred to in the poem. Undoubtedly, the vestibule of the church of Charity with its giant coupled columns and compluvium must have fired the imagination and malicious irony of the Venetians who disapproved of such an obvious homage to Rome. This same trait is present in the unfinished Bramantesque cloister that recalls the architecture of the Vatican with its famous frescoed loggias painted by Raphael.

The Lateran Canons were instead pleased with this reference to Rome and allowed the architect to build in Venice what in Vicenza he had only been able to dream about for the courtyard of Palazzo Iseppo da Porto: a space full of shadows, lit from above, in which columns were to play a key role as a matrix of space. The tables of the Convent with "greater detail" (some of the best in the treatise) show how he used *aurea simplicitas* in the frameless windows and how only the capitals, trabeation and ever-present statues had negligible decorative details. In the design of the courtyard, the haphazard texture of the bricks is used to draw attention to the surfaces, as if to imitate plaster worn and weathered by time and the elements - so typical of old monuments. In actual fact, the carefully constructed surfaces of the cloister are covered in red brick intentionally produced and laid with layers of lime so thin they make the Imperial *opus testaceum* pale in comparison. Only the bases, capitals and keystones of the lintels are in stone. Goethe really liked these surfaces which he defined as being built in terracotta rather than brick. But the masterpiece of daring and talent is what Goethe called "the most beautiful spiral staircase in the world"[3] to one side of the building next to the (now covered) canal. Free from any and all academic scruples, Palladio lit this room by placing oversized windows on the side of the façade towards the old church. Inside, he created a laconically monastic space by inserting monobloc stone steps into the ovoid envelope of the walls, leaving an empty space of almost two metres in the middle: the intended effect was to draw people's attention to its users. Goethe wrote: "one never tires of going up and down the staircase." In fact, from the top it's possible to see bits of the Grand Canal and a series of niches placed haphazardly, suggesting pauses and moments of silence as well as references to the gentle gradient of its helicoidal movement.

Palladio uses decoration sparingly, at least until he designed the Basilica where the mascarons (inspired by the Roman monuments in Verona) emphasise the keystone of the arches and the statues of the coping. For the first time in Palazzo Iseppo da

FIGS. 60 AND 61. TWO DRAWINGS OF VILLA VALMARANA DI VIGARDOLO (RIBA, XVII, 1 AND XVII, 2).

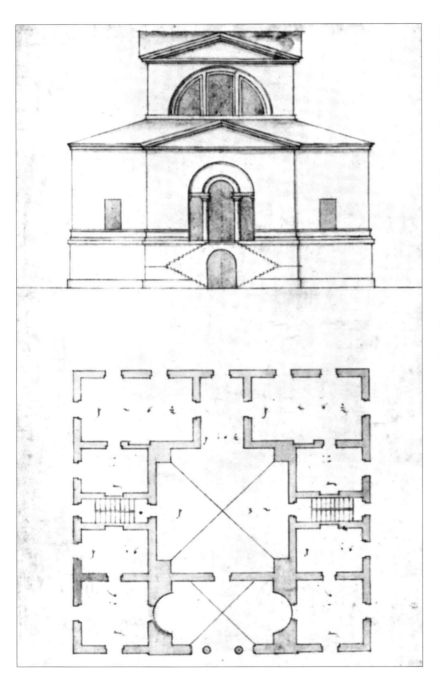

Porto, there are reclining figures on the tympana of the windows as well as garlands that hang down the sides between the windows and the columns. These designs were repeated in Palazzo Chiericati, Palazzo Barbaran(o) da Porto and, in a different way, even in the Loggia del Capitanio. As far as the human figures are concerned, the decorations and statues were used to create continuity along the ascending lines of the order, up to the skyline. Their purpose was to provide some sort of symbol to the manor house, while the festoons and garlands were used to recall the festivities and temporary installations built during important celebrations. Starting with Villa Barbaro, in 1560 these decorations become more commonplace and a new relationship between sculpture and architecture began to be part of Palladio's work. The villa commissioned by Daniele and his brother Marcantonio (who Palladio credits in his treatise for having invented an oval staircase) began with an iconological design. This design was visually and artistically recreated by Douglas Lewis,[4] while Marcello Fagiolo[5] reproduced the plan. Apart from the theme of reconciliation (the two-winged imperial eagle crowned by a papal tiara and the head of the Egyptian ox, symbol of Peace), Lewis indicates *universal harmony* as an interpretative key: this concept was expressed using pagan gods which lead the visitor in from the entrance and accompany him in his itinerary inside the building where a symbolic figure stands in the middle of the main room: Peace dressed as Venice and Aristodama ("Woman of Bounty"), an obvious reference to the double pagan and Christian interpretative key, loyal to the humanistic concept of continuity. The complex figurative iconology appears to have been inspired by the *Description of Greece* by Pausanias who tells us how he went as a supplicant to the sanctuary of Trophonius at Lebadeia and subjected himself to the ritual of mysteries.

The fact that in the *Four Books* (II, 14, p. 49-50) Palladio did not cite Paolo Veronese, author of the pictorial decorations, has inspired a romanticised tale of a dispute between the architect and his clients or that the latter abused the former, a tale that

Bareness and Horror Vacui

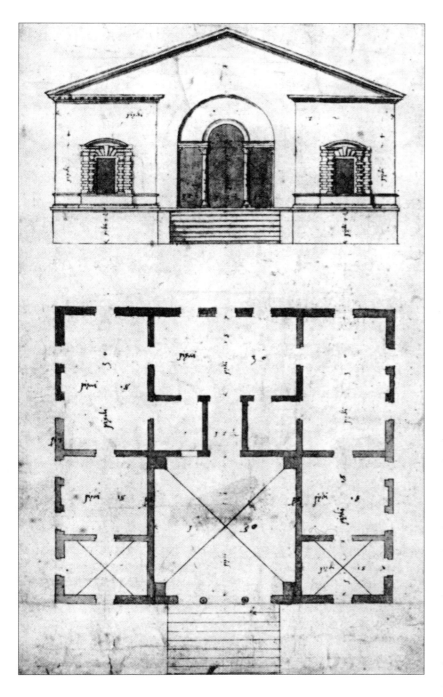

leaves the listener rather confused and which I personally do not believe. There seems to be multiple reasons for this disagreement: the "broken tympanum" of the façade, the reduction (from four to two) of references relative to Palladio's collaboration in the second edition of Vitruvius commented by Daniele Barbaro, the layout of the pictorial decoration and several details, as well as the unsuccessful intersection between the main building and the *barchesse*. Regarding the tympanum, this is not an anti-Palladian solution. On the contrary, it is one of Palladio's most characteristic designs. In fact, it's not the tympanum that is broken in Maser, but the trabeation underneath. The same thing occurs in Villa Poiana and in several of his youthful designs (figs. 56-61) as well as in the frescoes by Zelotti in Villa Emo, cited in the treatise. It's worth noting that when designing the doors and windows for Villa Barbaro, Palladio adopts the "ornate style" used in the pictorial decoration of Villa Godi at Lonedo which, based on the drawing in fig. 37, we know to have been designed by Palladio himself. Regarding the war over the references, it is highly unlikely that Daniele (who helped Palladio in every way to become successful in Venetian society) would show his displease in such a petty way - a reaction more in keeping with a modern art historian than a Renaissance diplomat. Regarding the unsuccessful grafting of the *barchesse*, the pre-existent parts of the main building provide a much better explanation than the alleged dispute between the architect and his client. We still have to explain the silence about Veronese, who even Palladio clearly mentions and defends as a painter when referring to the frescoes in Palazzo Iseppo da Porto (II, 3, p. 40). So why not mention the pictorial cycle in Maser, undoubtedly one of the most important in sixteenth-century Venice? The omission certainly begs an answer, but this negative one doesn't seem the most appropriate. It should be said that decorators were not always cited in the treatise, and although Palladio's attitude towards them is not prescriptive, he was tolerant and respectful of personal independence. I don't think we can say that all the decorators mentioned in the treatise (Giallo Fiorentino, Battista Franco, Bernardino

Bareness and Horror Vacui

150 Bareness and Horror Vacui

FIG. 62. SIDE VIEW OF THE LOGGIA DEL CAPITANIO IN AN ENGRAVING BY OTTAVIO BERTOTTI SCAMOZZI, *LE FABBRICHE E I DISEGNI DI ANDREA PALLADIO RACCOLTI E ILLUSTRATI DA OTTAVIO BERTOTTI SCAMOZZI*, VICENZA 1786, 2ª ED., VOL. I, TAB. XV.

India, Anselmo Canera, Battista Maganza, Giovanni Indemio, Gualtiero Padovano and Battista del Moro) successfully helped to portray the very strict numeric harmonies studied by the architect. So the omission might be completely accidental or due to a temporal delay. Focusing more on substance, Veronese's frescos enhance rather than deform Palladio's spatial sequence. Furthermore, if they introduce elements foreign to his style (for instance, twisted columns or balustrades), they do it more discreetly than the frescoes by Zelotti in Villa Godi for which Palladio himself designed architectural views (as shown in fig. 37). Perhaps Palladio did not fully appreciate the affinity between Veronese's style and his own ⁄ sometimes closeness creates distance ⁄ but he certainly had no reason to use this ambiguous and much too hypocritical formula of silence to rebuke the artist who in the refectory of the Convent of San Giorgio and in Villa Barbaro allowed him to tackle two of the best pictorial images of the spiritual climate that had nurtured both artists (despite their age difference) during those wonderful mid⁄sixteenth⁄century years.

The presumed slight towards the gullible Palladio by the Barbaro brothers is highly unlikely, given that they considered him their equal. In my opinion, there is another explanation for the differences in Villa Barbaro (which in any case anticipate the decorative opulence of the Loggia del Capitanio and the Teatro Olimpico): the client/architect relationship that Filarete describes as being similar to a relationship between a mother and a father as parents. The more a client has his own intellectual approach, the more the architect is tempted to create a genuine "portrait" of his client in his design. To all intents and purposes Villa Barbaro is a double portrait, like the one Raphael did for his Venetian friends Andrea Navagero and Agostino Beazzano. We know Palladio went to Rome in 1554 with Daniele and it's very possible that when he was there he met Pirro Ligorio who had begun to build his Garden of the Esperidi in Tivoli. An extremely important meeting, if you think that Palladio was one of the greatest connoisseurs of classical architecture and Pirro was a very talented antique dealer, as well as being the most imaginative and assertive interpreters of old figurative tradition. Villa D'Este (praised by Daniele in his introduction to his own *Vitruvius*) played an important role in inspiring the use of water in Maser, in particular the creation of the pool and nymphaeum. Its architectural structure is too stern and subtle to be attributed only to Vittoria who superimposed his plastic exuberance on a sombre and extremely elegant framework of fascia and borders culminating in a strong projection of the cornice supported by simple prismatic modillions. The nymphaeum provides access to the grotto with the spring: this also seems to be in keeping with the description provided by Pausanias.

> The fountain forms a small lake, which serves for the fish⁄pond. From this place the water runs into the kitchen; after having *watered the gardens that are on the right and left* of the road, which leads gradually to the fabrick, it forms two fish⁄pond, with their watering place upon the high road; from whence it waters the kitchen garden, which is very large, and full of the most excellent fruits, and of different kinds of pulse (II, 14, p. 49).

As mentioned earlier, building on Palazzo Valmarana began in 1566; it is the best example of interpretation of the site. The narrow road suggests the use of flattened relief and the rejection of a specific tectonic effect. However, the rhythmic vibration of the surfaces (achieved using decoration and the design of the order) did not produce dramatic effects and contains no visible heresies, except for the ironic presence of the two Roman soldiers descended from the cornice to single⁄handedly support its terrible load. Only in the Loggia del Capitanio does Palladio become "irritating": let's be clear, he becomes irritating for neo⁄classicists like Milizia, as well as for anti⁄classicists like Zevi who, under the entry for Palladio in his *Encyclopaedia of Art*, writes of an

> [...] imposing syntactic absurdity that mixes crude Michelangelo⁄style decorations and echoes of the arches of Septimius Severus and Orange. The refined barrel vaults of the porticoes in Palazzo Chiericati and La Rotonda are abnormally enlarged and digress into the entire side wall where the fascia of the piano nobile, with a Palladian window, looses all contact with the lower half. On the main façade (the enormous swollen

FIGS. 63 AND 64. THE STAGE OF THE ROMAN THEATRE IN A XYLOGRAPH DESIGNED BY PALLADIO FOR THE BOOK ON VITRUVIUS COMMENTED BY DANIELE BARBARO (1567) AND THE STAGE OF THE TEATRO OLIMPICO IN AN ENGRAVING BY OTTAVIO BERTOTTI SCAMOZZI (*LE FABBRICHE E I DISEGNI DI ANDREA PALLADIO RACCOLTI E ILLUSTRATI DA OTTAVIO BERTOTTI SCAMOZZI*, VICENZA 1786, 2ᴬ ED., VOL. I, TAB. I.).

half columns oppress the pilasters behind), the very shallow relief of the imposts of the arches emerges only to expose this deliberate imbalance. What is most amazing - much more than the fragile cornices contrasting the massive brackets of the balconies or the controversial breaks in the architraves - is the fact that two orders of different height (the order of the giant columns of the façade and that of the sides) neither dialogue with or intersect each other: they remain juxtaposed and incommunicado on orthogonal fronts. A senile and anticlassical fury explodes in this unfinished and badly restored building that uses architectural frames (writes Pane, 1961) 'as if they were leftover pieces forcefully inserted in a new and different cadence' now devoid of any compositional structure. It would be appropriate to add that 'a Michelangelesque style was used only for the paintings' in other words, ruined, wrecked and without any function whatsoever. In no other work, not even in the spectral fragment of Palazzo Porto-Breganze did Palladio achieve the same paradoxical degree of informality.

These arguments, very similar to those used by neoclassical critics, have not convinced modern critics who are tired of using ambiguous and flexible words like mannerism and anticlassicism: the latter absolve Palladio for heresies based on an attitude increasingly free from linguistic certainties and ready to experiment with new syntactic links. What isn't plausible is that Palladio changed his design of the side façade after the victory at Lepanto. The inclusion of a triumphal motif later on allows us to grant extenuating circumstances to Palladio for the lack of a link between the order (on which the Palladian window rests) and the orders of the main façade. In my opinion, the loggia designed by Palladio clearly shows how experienced he had become when it came to classical orders; it also proves he had an untiring penchant for experimentation. The accuracy of the intersection can be taken for granted, not only for the orders, but for all the individual elements present in many old buildings and used, as far as the architrave is concerned, in the Bollani altar in San Giorgio Maggiore. However, the use of the column instead of the pilaster strip is an important experiment that differs from the works by Michelangelo, for instance, Palazzo dei Conservatori and the apses in St. Peter's: it shows he tried to forge his own new path ahead. For the half columns to acquire the necessary dynamic force, the wall should not be a continuation of the half columns, neither should the latter be too close together. This is where Palladio uses decoration to neutralise the mass effect of the wall, to reduce it to a vibrant surface that doesn't join, but on the contrary, divides. Consequently, the huge windows, resting on protruding triglyphs, float on a neutral background. The fact that they are raised means they can exercise an upwards thrust that breaks the architrave: this proves that the compositional elements dialectically contrast one another and interact until they achieve reciprocal penetration. An important drawing by Palladio, the one for the completion of the building in Brescia housed in the Tosio-Martinengo gallery, clearly reveals a trend (prior to the intersection technique) in which compositional elements, aedicules, tympana and columns are joined through tangency. It also shows that decorations were used to fill the interstitial empty spaces and make the surfaces vibrate without effacing them.

On the side towards Via del Monte, we can see the hidden structure. The real second order is not the one with the slender frames supporting the just as slender archivolts, but the one which in the main façade facing the square appears only through the protrusion of the balconies that divide the dripstone of a composite cornice dotted with modillions. In fact, on this side too, the columns support a similar yet wider gallery. The Palladian window above the central arch stands out against a chiaroscuro backdrop thanks to a tiny decoration of festoons and victory trophies; at both ends, the two soldiers of Palazzo Valmarana again make their surreal appearance. Anticlassicism, mannerism, neo-late-ancient style? The all too broad categories coined by critics can be used either to absolve or condemn or to assign points as if this were an exam: at times, this influences even perception and hinders interpretation and the decoding of forms. We cannot deny that Palladio continued to use his method (i.e., a style based on antiquity considered as a virtuous world to be explored) to learn, to learn to grow, and even to contradict himself. The man who designed the Loggia del Capitanio is the same man who thirty years earlier hesitated to combine pilasters, windows and trabeations: but

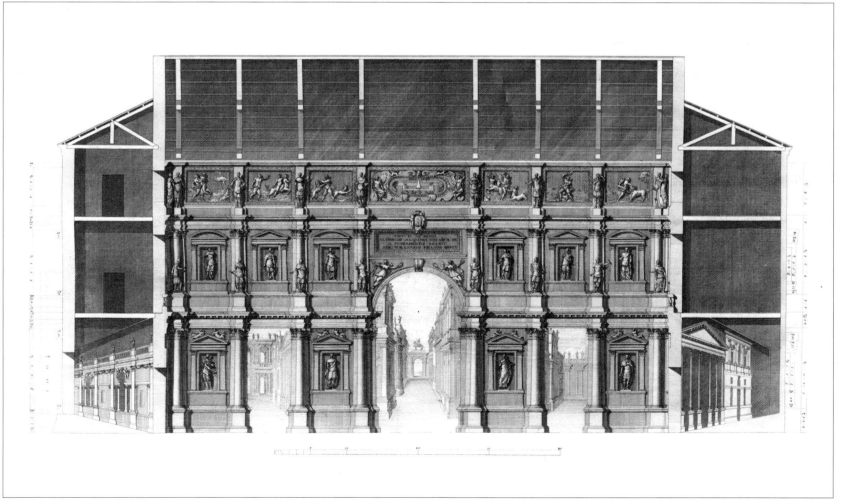

Bareness and Horror Vacui 153

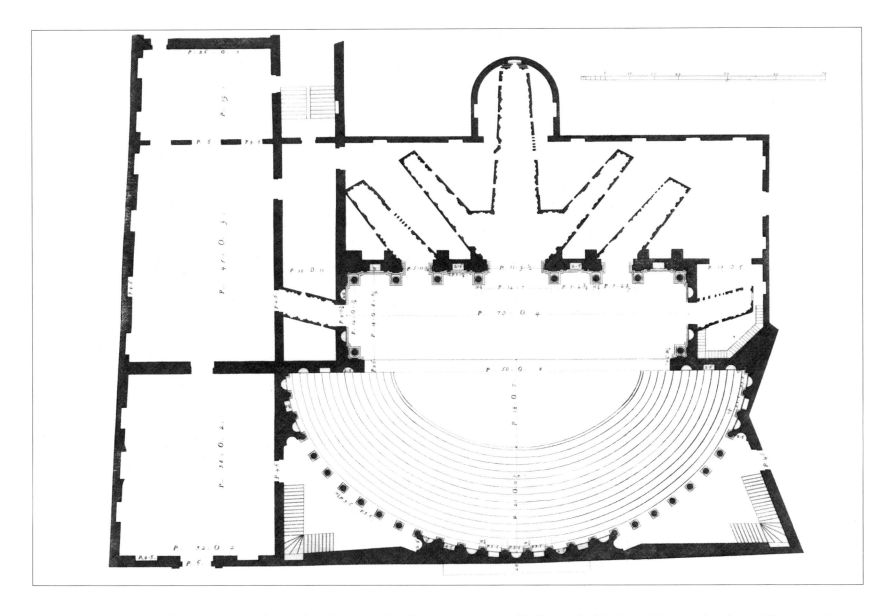

now he had completely mastered style, its flexibility and infinite assets. His acquired maturity led him to use it *ad organum plenum*, to the limits of virtuosity - certain to pave the way for those who came after him. And this is exactly what happened: almost a century later, Bernini and Borromini, each in their own way, used his discoveries to find their own truths, while maintaining the teachings of the ancients, so that, they too, *leaned on the shoulders of giants*. To draw the most daring of all his designs (the façade of the first project for the Louvre) Bernini succeeded in creating an unusual synthesis between the Basilica in Vicenza and the Loggia del Capitanio. Borromini instead accurately evoked the order of the loggia in the first courtyard of the house of the Filippini family and was to use the Palladian metaphor of embrace for the unsuccessful project of St. Paul's, unfortunately never built.

One of the classical decorative motifs that appears more frequently and incisively in Palladio's later works is the garland of flowers and fruit; it recalls impermanence and, therefore, an atmosphere of festivity. Not present in any of the works Palladio designed up to Villa Barbaro, it is present in the project for Palazzo Thiene, including in the engravings of the treatise. In Palazzo Iseppo da Porto, Palazzo Chiericati and Villa Montano Barbaran(o) pendant garlands appear to the sides of the windows. Palladio probably loved this garland motif because it was originally used to decorate the human body and because its double curve expresses the influence of weight on the form of a flexible group of vegetal elements. The garland reappears in the doors of the Basilica in Vicenza (built for the same client who commissioned La Rotonda), in Palazzo Porto-Breganze and in a famous drawings (which once belonged to Giorgio Vasari) for a funerary monument.[6] Two years before he died, Palladio defended this decorative element in a letter to Giovan di Pepolli regarding the designs for the façade of San Petronio in Bologna, in open contrast with his colleagues:

> About the festoons which they say are so flawed and detract from the seriousness of the work, I say that there are not so many that reasonably more could not be added: but I don't know where they get this German idea that festoons, greenery and fruits detract from the seriousness of the work, never did the ancient Egyptians, Greeks and Romans use so many ornaments in their works as they did in sacred temples.

In the temple-shaped pavilion built in the lagoon for the visit of Henry III of Orleans in 1574, all the capitals are joined by garlands hanging free in space. The same thing is repeated - with an unforgettable note of festive originality - in the portico of the small temple in Maser where inside the house the motif is repeated thirty-six times in the frieze of the impost of the cupola, an

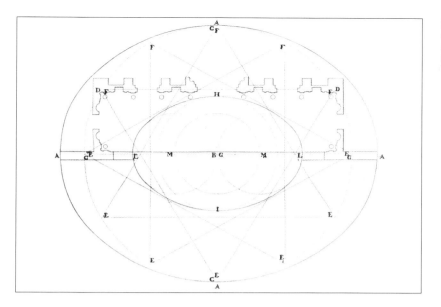

FIGS. 65 AND 66. PLAN OF THE TEATRO OLIMPICO AND THE GEOMETRIC DIAGRAM OF A PALLADIAN CONSTRUCTION BASED ON VITRUVIAN RULES (OTTAVIO BERTOTTI SCAMOZZI, *LE FABBRICHE E I DISEGNI DI ANDREA PALLADIO RACCOLTI E ILLUSTRATI DA OTTAVIO BERTOTTI SCAMOZZI*, VICENZA 1786, 2ᴬ ED., VOL. I, TAB. II AND ILL. ON P. 29).

obvious indication that the Maestro had no doubts about the "good reasons" expressed in that controversy.

The intensity of the decorations, the fullness of the forms as a metaphor of the fullness of being and therefore of theatrics, is certainly one of the characteristics of the Teatro Olimpico even if Palladio's last work is significant primarily because it represents, almost absurdly so, his goal to revive all aspects of antiquity, above and beyond its exemplary historical importance. With regard to buildings, villas and temples, his typological approach is based on his philological knowledge of ancient works used to develop unusual and creative solutions. With regard to the theatre, he proposes a real restoration completely different from contemporary trends adopted in Renaissance theatre. By developing an earlier tradition, from sacred plays to the Globe Theatre, Renaissance theatre had already laid the groundwork for the dynamic and successful development of the "Italian theatre," sacrificing a fixed stage in favour of a clear separation between the rigid architecture of the hall and the illusionary and changing architecture of the stage.

The retrospective and "academic" nature of Palladio's choice matured within the circle of enlightened members of the *Accademia Olimpica*. It was quite a heroic choice because its goal was to imbue an architectural work with a "fashionable trend," i.e., to use temporary constructions to conjure up the image of the ancient theatre; it was therefore an attempt to restore taste. This has given Vicenza the privilege of maintaining a *unique* building; its amazing appeal has continued to seduce the great names of modern theatre who over the centuries have accepted, often very willingly, the anachronistic challenge of introducing traces of modernity into this amazing architecture.

The genesis of the theatre is, of course, "literary" because it is based on the combination of the rules in Vitruvius' treatise, Alberti's considerations in *De Re Aedificatoria*, Serlio's reconstructions and the theatrical events Palladio either studied live or about which he was at least indirectly informed - the theatre in Verona, the so-called Berga theatre in Vicenza, the theatre on Mount Zaro in Pola, the Roman theatres that still survived. However, we shouldn't forget that Palladio had already contributed to the "fashionable trend" of building temporary constructions. In 1561-1562, in Palazzo della Ragione (which he himself had turned into a Basilica) he built a theatre for the plays *Amor Costante* by Alessandro Piccolomini and *Sofonisba* by Giangiorgio Trissino. Paolo Chiappini, then the secretary of the *Accademia Olimpica*, has left us a short description of this wooden theatre:

> Through the door on the right you can see houses with an excellent view, through the one on the left, a countryside with lots of trees, while other houses are visible through other doors [...] and through these doors people exited, and since they exited from the best view, all the doors had two of the said columns per side [...] with gilt capitals, bas-reliefs and pedestals. Between the columns there was a niche with free-standing, life-size, fake bronze statues; above the niche was a small chiaroscuro painting and [...] a festoon hanging between one column and another. This order was in the upper part, between the columns, that supported [...] the frieze and architrave, which were composite [...] below was the large door [...] above, above was a big fake gilt chiaroscuro painting with beautiful figures [...] Above the circle of the arch of the main door there were two painted Victories in the above-mentioned colours and style and in the middle of the arch hung the gilt crest of the *Accademia* i.e. the Olympic Circles [...] The perspective plane was fake in a floor with squares, very pale and with fascia that decreased towards the centre of the perspective and drew the attention of the onlookers, and all this small space was open to the eye, etc.[7]

Certainly thanks to the stage set built in Vicenza, a few years later - in 1565 - Palladio was asked by the *Compagnia della Calza* to design another temporary theatre for a biblical drama written by Count De Monte: *L'Antigono*. We don't know much about this second work, but we do know it was very taxing and trying for Palladio. In fact in a letter to his friend Vincenzo Arnaldi he wrote: "I have done penance for my many past and future sins." Apart from these works which preceded his design for the *Olimpico*, another tassel in Palladio's preparation was his theoretical interpretation of Vitruvius' ancient theatre for Daniele Barbaro who used it in his monumental translation of Vitruvius' works (1556). It includes a comment on the fifth book of *De*

Fig. 67. Drawing attributed to Marcantonio Palladio for the Teatro Olimpico in Vicenza (RIBA, XIII, 5).

156   Bareness and Horror Vacui

FIG. 68. DETAIL OF THE DRAWING ON THE PREVIOUS PAGE.

158 Bareness and Horror Vacui

Architectura and an extremely polished appendix of "mobile images": these were small engravings glued onto the pages of the book with a piece of string so that they could be rotated around a point. The editor Francesco Marcolini suggested these engravings be cut out on a thick piece of paper and accurately follow the outline of the building; they were used to demonstrate how it was possible to mechanically join two theatres together in a single amphitheatre (something Vitruvius believed Curio had already done in the past).

The plan of the theatre in Vitruvius' edition is a possible reconstruction of the Roman Theatre in Vicenza which had a decidedly baroque, tri-apsidal, non-mobile stage. For the Olimpico, Palladio preferred a rectilinear proscenium (because of the space available) or something similar to the one designed for Barbaro. Given that the former prison cells granted by the Municipality were very small, in his design of the orchestra pit Palladio turned Vitruvius' circle into an ellipse. The differences between the theory and the actual construction lie mainly in the decorations which were not only ornate but also plentiful, above all the disproportionate number of statues of academy members. Apart from these statues which were disturbing in themselves, every panel, every little piece of space not used for the frames of the orders was packed with decorations and bas-reliefs. Reclining figures were positioned above the central archivolt and on the tympana of the aedicules of the first order; the labours of Hercules were illustrated in the six panels of the attic with the crest (a circus) of the Academy in the middle; symbolic bas-reliefs adorned the panels in the wings of the proscenium. It really looks as if a sudden *horror vacui* had taken hold of Palladio who had accustomed us to a certain laconicism and poise. Is this senile regression or the deliberate creation of an atmosphere that was "theatrical" and therefore festive, unreal and oneiric? Or is it another arbitrary interpretation of a more serious project changed by its executors and challenged by the ambitions of certain academics to be "remembered by posterity" and who "paid" to have their sculptured images fill every nook and cranny of the theatre?

Perhaps all these things are true, but first of all we must admit that the work is *entirely* in keeping with Palladio's design, because the stage sets visible through the openings of the proscenium were meant to be there and correspond to what can be seen in the engraving in the Vitruvian edition. It is of little consequence whether it was indeed Scamozzi (who had always had an inferiority complex vis-à-vis Palladio and had spread the rumours that Palazzo Thiene was designed by Giulio Romano) or, as Zorzi writes, his son Silla who actually built it, because in any case all they did was implement a clearly expressed decision in something considered ephemeral.

It is strange, but as we will see logical, that so many negative circumstances (which we have listed here) did nothing to subtract from the theatre's profound and long-lasting attraction, from that sort of charm or spell that it weaves over those who enter and are honest with themselves. It's true that the theatre was an archaeological exercise, an attempt to revive something that had been dead for centuries, rather than a way to understand the lesson it teaches or absorb whatever novelty it communicates. Of course, ancient plays are staged in theatres, so it's a place where things are revived, but a theatre belongs to the civilization that wanted it in the first place, the civilisation it somehow represents. Its role is to compare two ages: the present and the past. Palladio was a past master at achieving this using the methods we have tried to identify - intersections, harmonies, changes in use and concrete execution. In this his last work there is no subtraction, distance or estrangement, but identification and escape into the past. Despite its lack of colour, there is nothing gloomy about the theatre. The glint of gold and bronze (fake, but for this much more genuine) in the ephemeral theatre of the basilica gives the theatre a festive air. When visiting it alone, you get the impression the party has just ended, you can hear its echoes in its muted acoustics. When instead you see a play, you get the same impression you would listening to a Stradivarius: our ears hear a sound from another age. It is a theatre where the living and the dead, the statues of the academics, the actors, musicians and spectators are all present.

Perhaps thanks to all those statues. Remember? In the *Four Books* (IV, 8, p. 89) Palladio wrote about the Forum of Nerva: "Nor should any body wonder, that I have put such a number of statues in these edifices, because one reads that there were in Rome so many, that they seemed there a fecond people". Since the design of the Olimpico is a "choral" initiative it does not have the gloomy appearance of a private, solipsistic image, perhaps because it is a theatre, the temple of fiction and enactment of truth, a place to meet and observe, a place which, thanks to the imaginary separation between the stage and the public Palladio turns into something magical and oneiric with all those statues and ornate decorations. We don't know whether he actually wanted those statues or whether he put up with them. His own statue is not there: we will never know if out of modesty or because, in the words of Maganza, "I know that the poor man Andrea earned a lot but he spent it all." The magic of a square theatre, of a theatre within a theatre, is there (long before Bernini or Pirandello discovered it) ready to be seen by anyone entering the theatre where old ladies sitting in corners gesticulate like ballet-dancers and the stern architecture invites involvement and participation. As in the Gewandhaus in Leipzig where Bach used to play, the Latin inscription, *res severa, verum gaudium* would not be out of place.

[1] ANDRÉ CHASTEL, *Le nu de Palladio*, in "Bollettino del Centro Internazionale di Studi di Architettura Andrea Palladio", XXII, 1980, p. 33.
[2] JAMES H. ACKERMAN, *Palladio*, Turin 1972, p. 32.
[3] JOHANN WOLFGANG GOETHE, *Travels in Italy*, London 1846.
[4] DOUGLAS LEWIS, *Il significato della decorazione plastica e pittorica a Maser*, in "Bollettino del Centro Internazionale di Studi di Architettura Andrea Palladio", XXII, 1980, p. 203.
[5] MARCELLO FAGIOLO, *Il contributo all'interpretazione dell'ermetismo in Palladio*, in "Bollettino del Centro Internazionale di Studi di Architettura Andrea Palladio", XIV, 1972, p. 357.
[6] Cfr. LIONELLO PUPPI and DONATA BATTILOTTI, *Andrea Palladio*, Milan 2006, fig. 476, p. 348.
[7] GIANGIORGIO ZORZI, *Le ville e i teatri di Andrea Palladio*, Vicenza 1969, p. 276.

THE PIGEON HOLES IN THE TURRETS
OF VILLA EMO CAPODILISTA AT FANZOLO.

Bareness and Horror Vacui

Villa Poiana at Poiana Maggiore (façade).

The simple style of the base in Villa Poiana at Poiana Maggiore and, opposite, in Villa Zeno at Cessalto and in the rear façade of Villa Barbaro at Maser.

164 Bareness and Horror Vacui   Aurea simplicitas

Aurea simplicitas Bareness and Horror Vacui 165

Palladian window. Villa Godi at Lonedo.

166 Bareness and Horror Vacui   Sharp corners, fascia and simplified cornice

Top: Palladian windows and doors in the Convent of Charity (Venice) and in the side façade of Villa Foscari alla Malcontenta; Bottom: Palladian windows and doors in Villa Pisani at Bagnolo and in the rear façade of Villa Foscari alla Malcontenta.

Sharp corners, fascia and simplified cornice Bareness and Horror Vacui

Simple openings in the interior and exterior walls
of Villa Poiana at Poiana Maggiore
and, below right, in Villa Foscari alla Malcontenta.

Bareness and Horror Vacui   Proud modesty

Villa Foscari alla Malcontenta (detail).

Proud modesty   Bareness and Horror Vacui

The Exhedra. Villa Barbaro at Maser.

170 Bareness and Horror Vacui   Decorations and festivities

Façade and exhedra (details), Villa Barbaro.
Window (detail), Palazzo Iseppo da Porto (Vicenza).
One of his favourite fretwork panels. Palazzo Civena (Vicenza).

Decorations and festivities   Bareness and Horror Vacui   171

Loggia del Capitanio (façade), Vicenza.
Below: Palazzo Barbaran(o)
and Palazzo Porto-Breganze (details), Vicenza.

172 Bareness and Horror Vacui   Horror vacui

The Teatro Olimpico (detail), Vicenza.

Horror vacui Bareness and Horror Vacui

Festoon in the Barbaro Chapel at Maser, in the façade of Villa Barbaro and in the Loggia del Capitanio in Vicenza.

174   Bareness and Horror Vacui   Crystallised festivity

Crystallised festivity   Bareness and Horror Vacui   175

THE TWO FIGURES RESTING ON THE SLOPING PITCHES
OF THE PEDIMENT IS A RECURRENT THEME IN PALLADIO'S LATE WORKS,
FOR EXAMPLE IN THE TEATRO OLIMPICO IN VICENZA.

176 Bareness and Horror Vacui Architecture and figures

5. Numbers, Music, the Absolute

"Divine is the force of numbers when compared rationally, nor can we say there is anything more important in the creation of this universe we call world than the suitability of weight, number and measurements with which time, space, movements, virtues, speech, artifice, nature, knowledge and everything divine and human is made, grows and becomes perfect."
DANIELE BARBARO

"In my youth Palladio was one of my best friends, a great secret inspirer, a person who does not inspire with words but with other means, for example music."
GUIDO PIOVENE

Palladio's biographers concur that it was Giangiorgio Trissino who introduced Palladio to the classics and persuaded him to change his own name from Andrea di Pietro della Gondola to Andrea Palladio. Lionel March[1] has recently discovered a curious detail about this change of name which probably took place during an investiture at the Trissino Academy. Using the equivalence codes between numbers and letters written by Agrippa von Nettesheim in her *De occulta Philosophia* published in 1533, the name Andreas Paladius (written in Latin, as it is on the frieze of the small temple at Maser) corresponds to the numeric values of 32 and 34. Multiplying the two numbers gives a figure of 1088 which, again using Agrippa's codes, corresponds to the word Vitruvius. So Palladio did not apparently base his pen-name on that of the angel in Trissino's tragedy, but on a cryptic reference which was to seal his fate as a reincarnation of Vitruvius. Even if March's finding might raise some eyebrows, it's true that both Palladio and his learned friends Giangiorgio Trissino and Daniele Barbaro were involved in a number cult and were also interested in traditional Pythagorean mathematics and its use during the Renaissance. When Palladio talks about architecture, he almost always speaks of proportions. In a letter to Count Giovan di Pepolli he writes: "architecture is nothing but the proportions of the limbs of a body, so well is one symmetrical and correspondent to another, and another with another, that together they harmoniously create majesty and decorum." Or in the same letter he goes on to say, "that a body with limbs which together have harmonious proportions will lead to the beauty that the ancient Greeks used to call Eurhythmy which simply means that no more well-balanced body could ever be wished for."

The letter would seem to recognise an explicit anthropomorphism in Palladio's architecture, something generally denied by the critics. However, Palladio considers harmony between the parts and the whole as a sign of creation: the human body is only one of the many possible outcomes and numeric ratios constitute its secret structure.

The fact that a number cult can lead to the creation of a link between architecture and music is almost inevitable. Rudolf Wittkower studied Palladian architecture in his book published in 1949 to try and find these deliberate links.[2] An explicit statement by Palladio also pointed in this direction. In a letter he wrote after being asked for an opinion by the supervisors responsible for the construction of the new basilica in Brescia,[3] he said

> [...] for the beauty and shape of the building to delight all those who enter, like the correct balance of voices is harmony to our ears, so are the right measurements harmony to our eyes, and we are truly content without knowing why, except for those who study to understand the nature of things.

It was normal for Palladio who considered himself one of "those who study to understand the nature of things" to try and achieve (following in the footsteps of Leon Battista Alberti) "harmony to our eyes," even using the analogy known as the "balance of voices." Nevertheless, many scholars have recently tried, with a greater or lesser degree of respect towards the great art historian, to refute Wittkower's conclusions when he states that Palladio loved musical proportions.

The subject is clearly explained in chapter 21 of Book One of the *Four Books*: "the most beautiful and proportionate of manners of rooms, and which succeed best, are seven, because they are either made round (tho' but seldom) or square, or their length will be the diagonal line of the square, or of a square and a third, or of one square and a half, or of one square and two thirds, or of two squares." The advocated proportions are 1:1; the root of 2:1; 3:4; 2:3; 3:5; 1:2, in other words, in musical terms (except for the root of 2), unison, fourth, fifth, major sixth and the octave. In the next chapter, Palladio gives his solution to the problem of proportionality, the relationship between the three measurements concerning the length and width of a room and its height.

The first manuscript draft of the chapter, entitled *of the height of the rooms* (I, 23, p. 28-29), had a theoretical premise that did not appear in the printed version. Here, after having deftly defined

Fig. 69. Ptolemy's Diatonic tetrachord
(*Le Istituzioni armoniche del rev. Gioseffo Zarlino*, Venice 1562, p. 122).

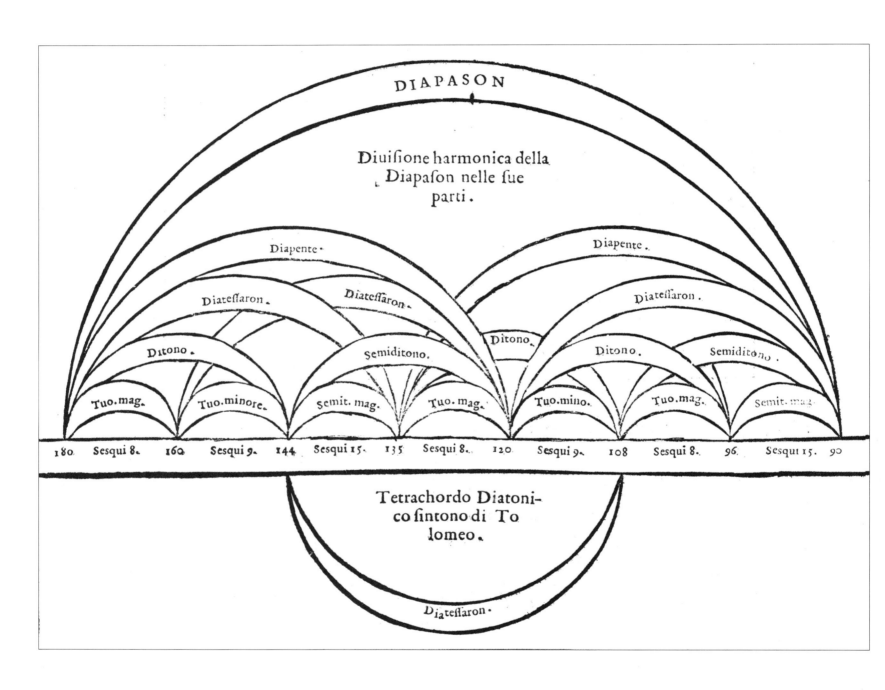

178 Numbers, Music, the Absolute

the concept of proportion, distinguishing between geometric, arithmetic and harmonic proportion, Palladio illustrates his favourite measurements for these operations. Instead in the final version, he omits any and all theoretical difficulties in the obvious intent (being a foreman himself) to allow even unskilled labourers to understand the concept.

Of the six methods of geometric construction, the first three refer to square rooms. For these Palladio proposes that the height (in the case of vaulted rooms) be increased by a third. For rooms with flat ceilings, he proposes the height be the same as the sides. In the case of upper floors, the height should be reduced by a sixth. The third method involves rooms with different widths and heights: he proposes that the height be half the sum of the two, i.e., an arithmetic average. The numeric example is that of a 12 x 6 rectangle with a height of 8. The fourth method, with the same conditions, involves a geometric solution: the height of the rooms becomes the height of an equilateral triangle inscribed in a semi-circumference whose diameter is equal to the sum of the two sides: this is a geometric average and the numeric example is a 16 x 4 rectangle which will give a height of 8. In the fifth method, Palladio proposes to start with two proportional rectangle triangles The catheti of the first are made up of half the sum of the sides and the measurement of the width, while the catheti of the second are the length and established measurement of the height: this is what mathematicians today call a pondered average. As a numeric example, Palladio suggests a sequence of numbers and how to use them. With regards to proportionality, the manuscript edition is more extensive and explicitly defines the objective of the third method as an "arithmetic means," the fourth as a "geometric means" and the fifth as a "harmonic means."

Opposition to Wittkower's theory regarding the reasons for Palladio's choice of proportions is based on a broader approach to the problem by including both more buildings in the equation and taking into consideration the comments by Bertotti-Scamozzi as well as others expressed more recently. The first attempt to make a comprehensive comparison of the proportions illustrated in the drawings of the treatise was carried out by Eugenio Battisti who in 1973 provided and commented on a list of 96 proportions.[4] He found out that five of them were used repeatedly (more than 15 times), thirty were used only once and the others at most four times. Without confuting Wittkower's conclusions, Eugenio Battisti, as an expert musicologist, stressed that Palladio tended to prefer non-Pythagorean scales based on semitones and quarter tones. This would link Palladio's visual harmonies to certain aspects of contemporary music, from Orlando di Lasso to Gesualdo da Venosa. In 1982, Deborah Howard and Malcolm Longair[5] carried out an in-depth study with tables relating to the treatise and surveys it was based on. Fifty-five percent of the time Palladio used his preferred options. Later on, in the 2002 re-edition of Silvio Belli's treatise,[6] Lionel March proposed the interesting theory that Palladio - who knew Belli - might have calculated his preferred proportions based on indications in Belli's treatise[7] in which there are four arithmetic, geometric, harmonic and counter-harmonic ratios which coincide with those indicated by Palladio. Last but not least, Branko Mitrovic in his book, *Learning from Palladio*,[8] openly refutes Wittkower's theory, even if he found what could be considered proof of its validity. In fact, he declares that four of the five preferred ratios are certainly based on music and only one (with a root of 3) presents problems insofar as its relationship with musical theory was proven only when Gioseffo Zarlino's *Istituzioni Armoniche* was published in 1558. He then goes on to reject the idea that Palladio could have discovered this before Zarlino when in fact everything points to the fact that Palladio and Zarlino might have met and discussed this issue before the publication of the *Four Books*.

It is absolutely improper to imply that Wittkower advanced his theory because it was in line with the times and that by doing so he justified contemporary architecture for having discarded the use of orders and turned architectural style into a mere matter of volumes and proportions. In actual fact, Wittkower explicitly

Figs. 70 and 71. Two tables from the *Four Books* showing the Corinthian entrance hall (II, 6, p. 124) and the "Room with Four Columns" (II, 8, p. 133).

states in his book that the myth of proportions belonged to an age gone by and is irreconcilable with modern times dominated as it is by science. He ends his book with a quote from Julien Gaudet (1901): *Les proportions, c'est l'infini*.

If the meticulous research by Branko Mitrovic did not actually confute Wittkower's theory, it did contribute to clarifying the fact that Palladio did not only use his preferred proportions, but also many others (as Mitrovic himself admits) as well as irrational ratios which were also part of his repertoire - a fact demonstrated by Paul Hofer[9]: the entrance hall of Villa Godi has a ratio between the sides of 1:6185, a number incredibly similar to the golden section which is a periodic number where the first five numbers are 1,6180.

Having said all this, let's examine Palladio's interiors with an open mind. Using his preferred ratios, did Palladio achieve his goal of rationally controlling form? And is the human eye able or not to recognise and therefore appreciate these ratios? Debate over perception clarifies that it depends on practice, personal sensibilities and the period in time. In the sixteenth century, a trained eye was able to appreciate what we, perhaps, no longer can.

However, when you enter a building designed by Palladio, you often feel drawn towards musical qualities such as rhythm, thematic repetition and the feeling of harmony caused by the dual presence of the same proportions in contrasting elements that are part of a complex image. Once inside, you often realise that the feelings you have are part of a deliberate design, carefully arranged as if they were chapters in a book. Palladio reveals his poetics in the concept of unity in multiplicity and in "correspondence" between the parts.

> Beauty will result from the form and correspondence of the whole, with respect to the several parts, of the parts with regard to each other, and of these again to the whole; that the structure may appear an entire and complete body, wherein each member agrees with the other, and all are necessary to compose what you intend to form (I, 1, p. 1).

Palladio applies this concept of composition not only to the physical, material and tangible parts of the building, but also to space,

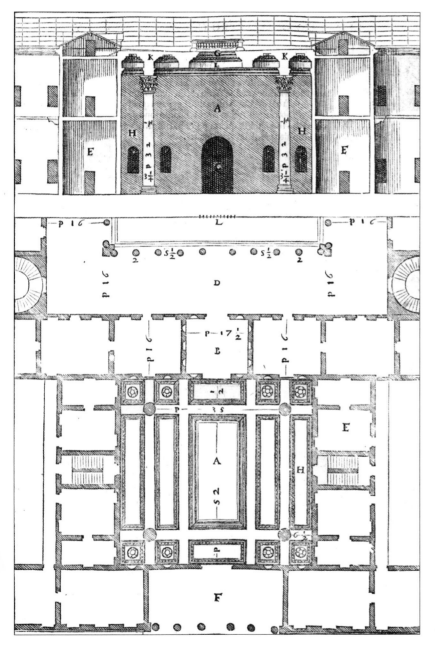

to the immaterial parts registered by the mind. He elaborates what our senses perceive and to do this he needs numbers, because in a certain sense numbers are its secret structure, the skeleton of space. We cannot deny that his faith in numbers is more religious than esoteric in nature because Palladio considers numbers have a "soave harmony" that they are proof of the supreme perfection of God:

> And indeed, if we consider this beautiful machine of the world, with how many wonderful ornaments it is filled, and how the heavens, by their continual revolutions, change the seasons according as nature requires, and their motion preserves itself by the sweetest harmony of temperature; we cannot doubt, but that the little temple we make, ought to resemble this very great one, which, by his immense goodness, was perfectly completed with one word of his; or imagine that we are not obliged to make in them all the ornaments we possibly can, and build them in such a manner, and with such proportions, that all the parts together may convey a sweet harmony to the eyes of the beholders, and that each of them separately may serve agreeably to the use for which it shall be appointed (IV, Preface, p. 79).

Certainly the regularity of the forms and the way they are arranged in his rooms as well as the relationship between a series of rooms that follow on from one another and initially look like *enfilades*, communicate a sense of the absolute, of peacefulness and balance. Since we normally focus on understanding the characteristics behind the overall project, we are surprised when we turn and look upwards to see and compare these measurements, these carefully studied ratios, that we see and recognise them again and again. Just look at the square ceiling of the hall in Villa Barbaro, the circular ceilings in La Rotonda and Palazzo Thiene, the cruciform ceiling of Villa Pisani and Villa Malcontenta, the octagonal ceilings of Palazzo Chiericati and Palazzo Thiene: each one reveals Palladio's efforts to create an absolute unity which, in the eyes of the beholder, can produce an even greater unity of analogies and assonance, of subtle correspondences that we compare in a mental process very similar to that of fade-outs in films. In Villa Malcontenta, where the frescoes superimpose on the perception of pure geometric forms the illusion of a design that suggests a dif-

Numbers, Music, the Absolute 181

FIG. 72. FAÇADE OF PALAZZO VALMARANA IN AN ENGRAVING IN THE BOOK BY CHARLES-ÉTIENNE BRISEUX, *TRAITÉ DU BEAU ESSENTIEL DANS LES ARTS*, PARIS 1752. THE BOOK DESCRIBES THE PALLADIAN FAÇADES AS MODELS OF HARMONY BECAUSE THEY OBEY THE RULES GOVERNING MUSICAL HARMONY. SEE THE QUOTATION FROM THE TEXT REFERRING TO THE TABLE ON PAGE 184.

182 Numbers, Music, the Absolute

ferent spatiality, we feel even greater pleasure thanks to the dual perception of an internal tension between the two images which is not opposition, but intersection, albeit achieved here by using two different styles.

Palladio's ambition to create absolute spatial configuration is also visible in his design of the tetrastyle hall and the room with four columns. It is a well-known fact that, after the problems presented by Vitruvius' treatise and the lack of precise archaeological proof, Renaissance culture was unable to reliably recreate the design of a Roman building, something that was to be achieved only after so many ruins had been brought to light during excavations in Pompeii. Palladio was no exception and, from a purely archaeological point of view, his reconstruction of a private home in ancient Rome looks out of scale and unreliable. Nevertheless, Vitruvius' idea of a tetrastyle hall, graphically illustrated by Palladio for the second edition of Vitruvius by Barbaro (1567) and later improved upon in the *Four Books* (II, 8) (figs. 70 and 71), is confirmed by a series of high-quality rooms. He understood the structural advantages of placing the four columns near the corners because this reduces the space between the beams and allows them to be narrower. Palladio, however, believed it was more important to gauge space against the structure of order, introduce columns and impose an obligatory division on the ceiling because this would imprison space and limit the arbitrary nature of formal choices. Two examples of the organic nature and elegance achieved using this method are Villa Cornaro at Piombino Dese and Palazzo Antonini in Udine. In Villa Cornaro the first floor room opens onto the columned loggia in the centre of the building. The interpretation of the architectural order is cunning and subtle; the architrave of the trabeation runs along the four sides and unites the columns two by two where they are closest together; the rest of the trabeation runs like the architrave along the walls and plastically characterises the four cross beams of the coffered ceiling. Without the support of the architrave the cross beams would have weakened the structure which, on the contrary, since it has no useless parts, fulfils its role of support and union to perfection. The fact that Palladio did not use pilasters shows how foreign academic impositions were to him; the pilasters would have softened the contrast between the circle of walls and that sort of canopy structure emphasising the centrality of the room. In Udine, where the room is on the ground floor and is more a hall than a room, he introduces a variant into this system: the architrave uniting the columns two by two continues until it intersects the wall and rests on a small capital which acts as a corbel, avoiding fifteenth-century archaisms. Palladio really preferred a four-column room. He proposed it again in Villa Thiene at Quinto Vicentino, in Palazzo Dalla Torre in Verona, in his design for a site in Venice, in Palazzo Capra, in the Convent of Charity in Venice and in Villa Mocenigo at Marocco. The same design is repeated in vaulted rooms, for example, the hall of Palazzo Iseppo da Porto, Villa Pisani at Montagnana and Palazzo Barbaran(o) where, however, the plastic ornamentation of the vaults overshadows the subtle game of proportions. The lack of accurate measurements and the fact that the measurements of the façades are not included in the treatise makes it difficult to express a general comment on the proportions of the elevations in Palladio's architecture. However, we should examine the way in which the façades of Palladio's buildings were analysed, particularly in the eighteenth century, when he was becoming an internationally renowned figure. Several buildings designed by Palladio are illustrated and commented in the splendid edition of the *Traité du Beau Essential dans les Arts* by Charles-Étienne Briseux, published in Paris in 1752, with its copper engravings and rich rococo friezes. In particular, Palazzo Valmarana (fig. 72), used as a perfect example of how rules can indirectly control and ensure "essential beauty." The description exploits musical terms long before Rudolf Wittkower wrote his much criticised book nearly three centuries later:

> The width of the façade is in a ratio of 3:2 compared to its height, which in music is a fifth. The height, divided into six parts, including the pedestal, its base and attic, each have one part. The other four are for the huge columns and their trabeations, so that the pedestal and the attic have

a 1:4 ratio compared to the rest, a ratio of double octave. The ground floor is half the height of the building. The pedestal and base have a 1:2 ratio compared to the minor order above, which is a ratio of an octave. The trabeations and underlying part have the same ratio, 1:2. The height of the ground floor, the building and its width have an arithmetic proportion of 1:2:3 which produces an octave and its fifth. The overall height of the building, that of the ground floor above the pedestal, the height of the latter and that of the minor order, the height of the first floor and that of the attic have a 2:2 proportion and a 1:2 proportion, i.e. the ratio of an octave. The height of the ground floor and that of the first floor including the trabeations, the height of the ground floor above the pedestal and the height of the first floor under the architrave are 2:2 or 2:3, which is a fifth.

The three parts of this trabeation have a 3, 4, 5 proportion, which give a fourth and major third. The trabeation has a 1:5 ratio with the height of the column, a double third. The attic has the same ratio with the major order and the pedestal is proportionate to the rest of the height of the building.

Anyone who has seen the buildings designed by Palladio agrees that they are immediately captivating. This instant pleasure comes undoubtedly from the right ratios between the main parts of the building established by Palladio using the rules of harmony. These are rules that create the beauty of the works of this famous architect. How will the members of Perrault's faction react to such convincing experimental solutions? Will they, as always, say it is purely the effect of talent and taste?

[1] LIONEL MARCH, *Architectonics of Humanism*, London 1998.
[2] RUDOLF WITTKOWER, *Architectural Principles of the Age of Humanism*, London 1962.
[3] ANDREA PALLADIO, *Scritti sull'architettura (1554-1579)*, edited by Lionello Puppi, Venice 1998, p. 78.
[4] EUGENIO BATTISTI, *Un tentativo di analisi strutturale del Palladio tramite le teorie musicali del Cinquecento e l'impiego di figure retoriche*, in "Bollettino del Centro Internazionale di Studi di Architettura Andrea Palladio", XV, 1973, p. 211.
[5] DEBORAH HOWARD and MALCOLM LONGAIR, *Harmonic Proportion and Palladio's Quattro Libri*, in "Journal of Architectural Historians", 41, 1982, pgs. 116-43.
[6] LIONEL MARCH, *Forward to On Ratio and Proportion. The Common Properties of Quantity*, Florence 2002.
[7] SILVIO BELLI, *Della Proporzione, et Proporzionalità, Communi Passioni del Quanto, Libri Tre*, Venice 1573.
[8] BRANKO MITROVIC, *Learning from Palladio*, New York 2004.
[9] PAUL HOFER, *Palladios Erstling: die Villa Godi Valmarana in Lonedo*, Basel 1969.

The main hall. Villa Almerico called "La Rotonda" in Vicenza.

Numbers, Music, the Absolute

Ceiling, Palazzo Chiericati (Vicenza).
The Main Hall, Villa Pisani at Bagnolo.

186 Numbers, Music, the Absolute   Preferred proportions

The Room of the Four Columns.
Villa Cornaro at Piombino Dese.

Top: ceilings in Palazzo Thiene (Vicenza) and Villa Barbaro at Maser;
Bottom: two ceilings, Palazzo Thiene (Vicenza).

188 Numbers, Music, the Absolute   Preferred proportions

The Room of the Four Columns.
Villa Cornaro at Piombino Dese.
The Main Hall. Villa Pisani at Bagnolo.

Preferred proportions   Numbers, Music, the Absolute

The Main Hall.
Villa Foscari alla Malcontenta.

190 Numbers, Music, the Absolute The heavens on the ceiling

The heavens on the ceiling Numbers, Music, the Absolute 191

Ceiling of the Hall, Villa Poiana at Poiana Maggiore.
Beamed ceiling. Villa Valmarana at Vigardolo
Octagonal ceiling. Palazzo Chiericati (Vicenza).

192 Numbers, Music, the Absolute   Favourite forms and proportions

Round windows in the hall of Villa Poiana at Poiana Maggiore.
Room in Palazzo Chiericati (Vicenza).
Cross-vault frescoed by Bernardino India. Villa Poiana.

Favourite forms and proportions   Numbers, Music, the Absolute

Vaulted ceiling in an irregular space.
Hall of Palazzo Barbaran(o) (Vicenza).

194   Numbers, Music, the Absolute   Flexibility and geometric absoluteness

View from the four loggias.
Villa Almerico called "La Rotonda" in Vicenza.

196 Numbers, Music, the Absolute   Opening onto the countryside

Opening onto the countryside   Numbers, Music, the Absolute   197

The transparent apse. Il Redentore (Venice).

198   Numbers, Music, the Absolute   Circles and semicircles in concert

Circles and semicircles in concert   Numbers, Music, the Absolute

Symbiosis between real and illusory space
Perfect harmony between the frescoes by Paolo Veronese
and the Palladian structure in the Hall of Olympus. Villa Barbaro at Maser.

6. The Joys of the Worksite

> "... and because that bridges thus made, are strong, beautiful, and commodious; strong because all their parts mutually support each other; beautiful, because the texture of the timbres is very agreeable and commodious, being even and in the same line with the remaining part of the street."
> ANDREA PALLADIO (III, 7)

Palladio was very pleasant and learned in his conversation, which pleased the gentlemen and persons with whom he talked as much as it did his workmen; he kept them happy and treated them cordially so that they worked happily and willingly. He liked to teach generously all the terms of Art, so that all the bricklayers, stonecutters or carpenters understood everything about the measurements, terms and objects of Architecture.

This excerpt from the first biography of Palladio by Paolo Gualdo, written in 1617 by a person who probably knew him personally (when Palladio died Gualdo was 27), paints an intense and lively picture of a Palladian worksite: a small group of people governed by the strategic and organisational skills of a man who appreciated military art (in particular, Julius Caesar) and had an innate penchant for teaching - something that shines through the pages of the *Four Books*. A somewhat similar portrait of Borromini has been handed down to us by one of his clients Brother Giovanni di san Bonaventura who followed the maestro around every day when he worked on the construction site of San Carlino: "... Francesco himself handed the *cuciara* to the bricklayer, straightened the *cucirino* for the stucco worker, gave the saw to the carpenter, the chisel to the chiseller, the tile to the tile-layer, and the file to the iron-beater." The difference between the two architects is so obvious, above all if you think they were both once humble stone-cutters and both became great architects. Borromini taught his workmen how to forge matter and use form to breathe life into it. Palladio focused on teaching people about terms and measurements, in other words, he taught language like a linguist, convinced that each object should be "called" by its proper name, that it should be different from any other, measured, shaped and coherent with all the other parts.

To work with pleasure - this is where the basic traits of his Venetian personality emerge: the feeling of friendship that breaks down class barriers; the use of a dialect that enhances the excitement and speedy reactions that spontaneously surface during dialogue and therefore involve the objects that are being mentioned. Palladio was a great technician who also considered the economics of his profession. He saw it as an "alchemic" profession that can transform even the most humble material when the latter is bestowed with the dignity and character of a carefully designed shape.

In a letter addressed to the administrator of the Basilica in Brescia written in 1567, Palladio sings the praises of brick structures, emphasising their resistance to fire which made them more suitable than stone:

> Regarding the material to be used for columns and cornices, in my opinion, in your church Your Excellency should build the columns of the main nave and small naves in stone as far up as hands can reach and then in baked brick, except for the part above the cornice because what is made of baked brick will be covered in plaster that will accompany and unite one and the other, so the entire building will be strong and beautiful. I can say this because I've seen old buildings, few of which are without adornments and all covered in plaster and even though they are over 1500 years old, the plaster is still beautiful as if it had been laid yesterday, and it can be seen in all the ancient temples of Rome and Naples and many other places [...]. Building columns, vaults and other parts in baked brick, even this is not new, on the contrary, it was a technique widely used by the ancients and lasts longer than stone. Old buildings in baked brick remain more intact than those in stone and the reason is easy to see: stone can be attacked by fire and split, something that doesn't happen to baked brick.

Palladio ends by mentioning the worksite where he was working that year: "and now in Venice even San Giorgio Maggiore is being built in brick, a construction I am building and which I hope will bring me honour, because buildings are appreciated for their shape and not what they are made of."

All his life, Palladio never swerved from this technical and ethical principle. Thanks to its aesthetic characteristics and representational nature, important buildings were to be made of stone, for example the Basilica in Vicenza and the façades of Venetian churches. However it could be replaced by fake stone above all in private homes. This could be achieved by covering the brick with a thin layer of marble plaster, *marmorino*. During his visits to Rome Palladio had seen new buildings made of stone (the temple by Bramante or Porta Santo Spirito) or covered in stone (Palazzo dei Massimi), but he had also seen stone use sparingly in the courtyard of the Belvedere and other buildings, in other

FIGS. 73 AND 74. TWO DRAWINGS BY PALLADIO TESTIFYING TO HIS INTEREST IN THE CONSTRUCTION TECHNIQUES USED IN ROMAN ARCHITECTURE. A DRAWING OF THE BALBI CRYPT WITH NOTES INDICATING THE PARTS MADE IN STONE AND THOSE IN BRICK (RIBA XI, 2R), AND A DRAWING OF THE TERRACING ABOVE THE ROMAN THEATRE IN VERONA (RIBA, XII, 22R).

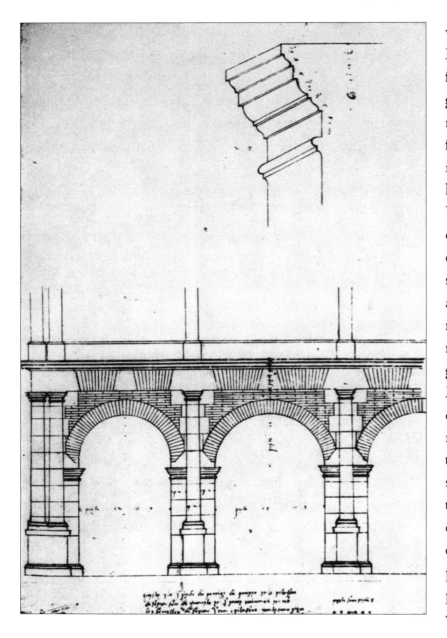

words in more detailed parts such as the base, cornice or capital. His clientele in Vicenza (whose "business" penchant was carefully studied by Giovanni Zaupa[1]) would never have accepted ‚ given their pre‚capitalistic sensibilities ‚ a purely symbolic investment like that of live stone. Palladio's fortunes were probably also furthered by the fact he could produce just as good and long‚lasting a result with less cost to the client (maintenance was evidently still underestimated).

What I would like to emphasise here, however, was not that he chose *marmorino* to replace stone (used only as far as one's hands could reach and therefore where it was possible to actually feel the stone), but rather that Palladio could creatively deal with and accept economic production and constructive simplicity. Recent restoration on Villa Malcontenta and the Teatro Olimpico has revealed the finishing technique used by Palladio. In 1965, this gave Renato Cevese food for thought: he saw that in Villa Malcontenta there was a gap in the plaster covering part of the columns of the portico just above the stone base. He guessed that its thickness was not part of Palladio's design which envisaged that the surfaces of the terracotta bricks with which it was made should have remained visible, creating a chromatic contrast with the white surfaces of the walls. "If the shafts had been built to be covered in *marmorino*" ‚ he wrote ‚ "it would have been useless to execute such a diligent and orderly facing which almost completely hides the mortar used to hold the bricks together, made perfectly curved on purpose."[2] The restoration ‚ probably supervised by the current owner, Countess Foscari, wife of Tonci, an excellent historian and architect ‚ has done a reasonably good job in restoring the original white/red colour, giving the splendid villa an amazing visual quality which was previously lacking. Even if we cannot be mathematically certain that the restoration fully corresponds to what Palladio had in mind, we have to admit that the different textures (next to one another in a logic of superimposition suited to the architectural orders) reinforce the volumetric perception and give the building back its independence compared to its surroundings. It replaces the "romantic"

202 The Joys of the Worksite

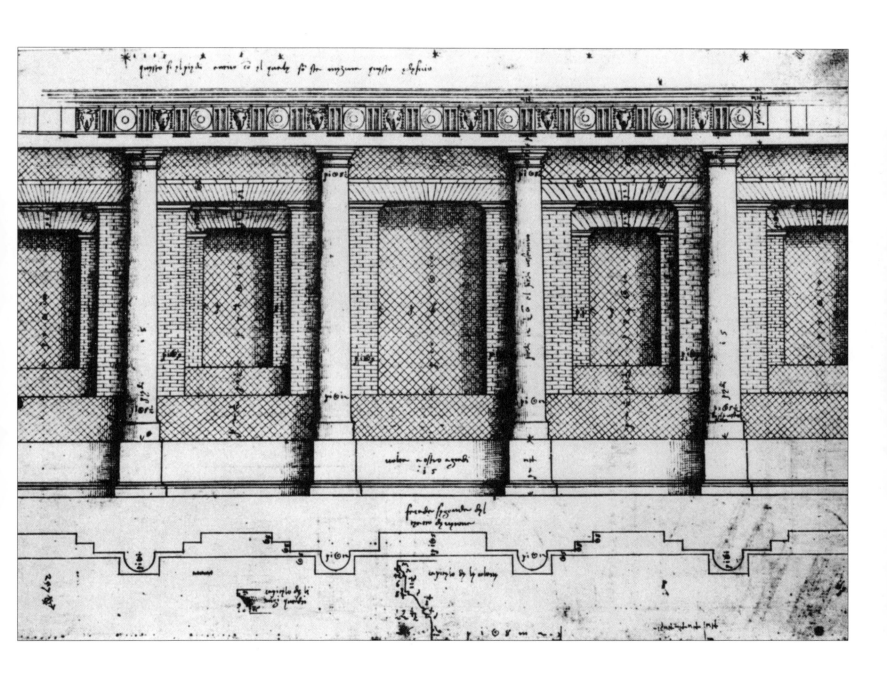

FIG. 75. THE TABLE OF THE *FOUR BOOKS* SHOWING THE COURTYARD OF PALAZZO ISEPPO DA PORTO IN VICENZA WITH THE TERRACOTTA SIDE ARCHES CONNECTING THE FRIEZES OF THE COLUMNS SO THAT THE ARCHITRAVES CAN BE PLACED PERPENDICULAR TO THE PLANE OF THE FAÇADE (II, 3, P. 106).

image (in the worst sense of the word) of a building that fades into and is camouflaged by the environment, with a "classical" image of absolute balance that neither contrasts nor is absorbed by its natural surroundings. The same problem of dual colour was and will be a problem in future restorations of the Loggia del Capitanio, even though in this case, the differences in height of the stone bases (excluding the plaster) suggests that the beautiful, perfectly smooth terracotta columns could be whitewashed with a thin glue to reduce the contrast. However, in some cases Palladio actually wanted to use this contrast to emphasise his building technique. One example would be the courtyard of Palazzo Iseppo da Porto which in the beautiful xylograph in the *Four Books* has a trabeation without an architrave and an elegantly designed frieze of stone ashlars joined by small brick arches - a solution probably inspired by the excellent illustration by Giuliano da Sangallo of the portico of the Balbi crypt highlighting the complexity of the walls (fig. 73).

Palladio's technical skills are confirmed by the frequency with which he was involved with difficult building problems. They also shine through in the brilliant illustrations in his treatise, the precision of the building details and clear explanations. So clear that he has been credited with inventing certain types of trusses and floors, called "Palladian floors" which are nothing but a sort of *opus incertum* made with pieces of stone slabs. On the contrary, Palladio did indeed invent the wooden structures of certain bridges illustrated in the treatise; these bridges were as cheap to build as they were compositionally elegant. The problem that had set his imagination on fire, or what Pier Luigi Nervi called the architect's static intuition, was to eliminate intermediate pylons in the river to avoid them being hit by free-floating tree trunks that then had to be carried on carts. His solutions shows he knew of, or had invented, the principle of reticular structure, arranging planks of wood in such a way as to create different types of rigid rectangular or triangular frames to that the thrust shifted from one element to the other, linking them in a chain like the ashlars of an arch. Palladio writes (III, 7 p. 65): "and because that bridges thus made, are strong, beautiful, and commodious; strong because all their parts mutually support each other; beautiful, because the texture of the timbres is very agreeable and commodious" (figs. 76-79).

Palladio as a "worksite expert" shines in particular in his design of rooms in villas and houses, rooms that are not part of the aulic series of halls and exclusive apartments, but which constitute a crucial corollary. These are mainly ground floors or even cellars and storerooms defined by Louis Kahn as "service spaces." Palladio concentrated intensely on these rooms: he did not introduce any decorative or superfluous elements, but focused on purity of forms, on the simple concatenation of the vaults that support the floors above but also confer abstract solemnity to these normally neglected parts. For example, the cellar of Palazzo Thiene (p. 212) where it's possible to see the way the bricks are arranged, as a curtain wall, in blocks, in a herringbone pattern, based on a construction concept constantly influenced not by aesthetics but by the self-respect of the architect and bricklayer. In other places, the surfaces of the plastered vaults look as if they are sculpted by shafts of light, divided by graceful patterns of lines that correspond to the joints or intersections between the vaults and lunettes. In La Rotonda, under the round room, there is an annular vault supporting the floor of the first floor which rests on the side walls as well as on a large hollow column, a sort of canopy that is connected to the ring by four pairs of lunettes which touch at the vertex, two by two, in an extremely complex surface pattern (pgs. 216-217). In the hollow centre of the huge column, the grille can be seen from below, with the faun's head acting as a filter for the rainwater entering through the hole at the top of the cupola. It also let in cooler air from the rooms underneath. It was Palladio who told us that in the sixteenth century in the Veneto region fresh air was introduced naturally. Today we would call it a bio-climatic system (pgs. 210-211).

> The ancients used to warm their rooms in this manner. They made their chimneys in the middle [...] and when they were not willing to have chimneys, they then made in the thickness of the walls some tubes or

The Joys of the Worksite 205

FIGS. 76-79. THE RIALTO BRIDGE AND THREE EXAMPLES OF SINGLE SPAN ARCHES ILLUSTRATED IN THE *FOUR BOOKS* (III, 9, P. 211; III, 9, PP. 207, 208 AND 209).

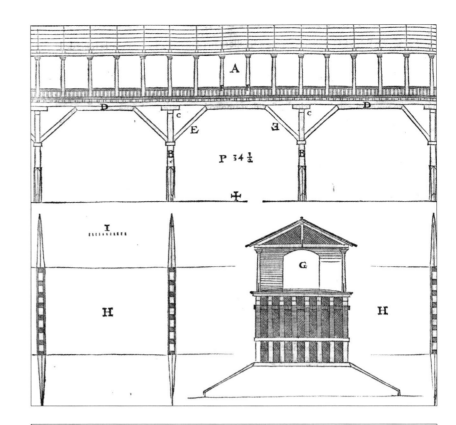

pipes, through which they conveyed the heat of the fire that was under those rooms, and which came out of certain vents or holes that were made at the top of those pipes. Almost in the same manner, the Trenti, *Vicentine* gentlemen at *Costoza*, their villa cooled the rooms in the summer, because there are in the mountains of the said villa some very large caves, which the inhabitants of those places call *Couali*, that formerly were quarries (which I believe Vitruvius means, when, in the second book, wherein he treats of stones, he says, that in the *Marca Trivigiana* a sort of stone was dug up, which was cut with a saw like wood) in which some very cool winds were generated, and which those gentlemen conveyed to their houses through certain subterraneous vaults, by them called ventiducts, and with pipes like the abovesaid, they convey that cool wind through all the rooms, by stropping and unstopping them at pleasure, to receive more or less of that cool air according to the seasons. And although this very great convenience makes this place wonderful, what makes it still more worthy of our admiration, is the prison of the winds, which is a subterraneous room built by the most excellent Signor Francesco Trento, [...] to beautify which, and make it worthy of the name, he has neither spared cost or care (I, 27, p. 33).

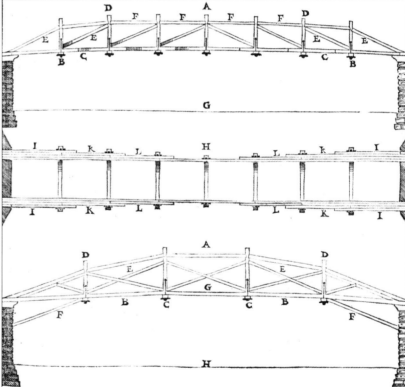

We know that this tale is true because it appears in the description of Villa Trento, called *Eolia* in Longare di Costozza. The fact Palladio wrote at length about this issue shows that he was particularly interested in those "tricks of the trade" that could increase a house's liveability. It also allows us to suppose that the pattern of holes in the central room of La Rotonda might actually act as coolers.

Another indication that Palladio was a expert workman, particularly familiar with the technologies used in the Veneto region, comes from a passage in the *Four Books*: "The piles are to be driven so close to one another, as not to leave space for others to come in between. Care must also be taken to drive them rather with blows frequently repeated, than such as are violent; that so the earth may bind the better to fasten them" (I, 8, p. 7). "It's clear, writes Giancarlo Turrini,[3] that he understood the importance on the one hand of frequent "blows" to pack the earth by reducing volume and, on the other, the need for vibration to achieve consolidation."

Palladio's technical skills are particularly evident when he designs staircases which in Renaissance architecture had been assigned a rather marginal role. Leon Battista Alberti talks about

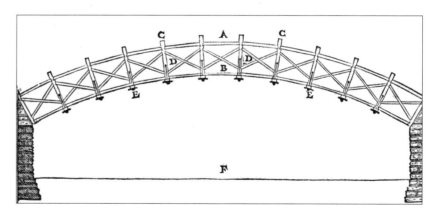

206   The Joys of the Worksite

FIG. 80. THE STAIRCASE IN CHAMBORD CASTLE.
AN IMAGINARY INTERPRETATION BY PALLADIO IN THE *FOUR BOOKS* (I, 18, P. 89).

stairs in *De Re Aedificatoria* as an element that makes designing building difficult: "*Qui volent scalis non impediri*, and adds, *scalas ipsas non impediat*," "if you don't want stairs to obstruct, don't obstruct stairs." Leonardo and Bramante were not interested in creatively designing stairs, but in the sixteenth century stairs were still normally built to one side, like a purely functional element. It was above all Palladio and Vignola who tackled the problem and came up with innovative solutions, paving the way for the scenic designs of the Baroque era. In the *Four Books*, there are echoes of the studies carried out in Europe in the part dedicated to the staircase in Chambord (fig. 80):

> Another beautiful sort of winding stairs was made [...] by order of the magnanimous King Francis, in a place by him erected in a wood [...] there are four staircases, which have four entrances, that is, one each, and ascend the one over the other in such a manner, that being made in the middle of the fabrick, they can serve four apartments, without that the inhabitants of the one go down the staircase of the other, and being open in the middle, all see one another going up and down, without giving one another the least inconvenience (I, 28, p. 35).

The narrative vision of people who can see but not come into contact with one another reveals the psychological focus behind Palladio's choices, a focus which led him to write about oval staircases with an empty space in the middle with a certain amount of personal satisfaction (for instance, the one in the Convent of Charity judged by Goethe to be "the most beautiful spiral staircase in the world") (p. 220). Palladio writes (I, 28, p. 35): "They succeed very well that are void in the middle, because they can have the light from above, and those that are at the top of the stairs, see all those that come up, or begin to ascend, and are likewise seen by them". The need for symmetry persuaded Palladio to place the staircase in the narrower part of the geometric plan repeatedly present in the villas illustrated by Wittkower (fig. 1), but there are also examples of a more scenic position, for instance in Palazzo Dalla Torre in Verona where the oval staircase is in axis compared to the entrance, or in Villa Trissino at Meledo (fig. 82) or Villa Ragona where the plans in the treatise

The Joys of the Worksite 207

suggest that the parallel ramps go in opposite directions. Instead in Villa Barbaro, the parallel ramps go in the same direction, leaving a hole in the middle: a design that was to become typical of the Baroque double staircase. Chastel supports Palladio's decision not to follow contemporary trends and repeat a Bramantesque staircase ("a double reversed movement"), built at the end of the Vatican courtyard of the Belvedere. However, I believe it's a pity that the stairs and concave portico in the drawings normally associated with Villa Pisani at Bagnolo were never built: they are one of the most original and courageous spatial inventions in the dialectic relationship between interior and exterior (figs. 38, 39, 57, 59).

[1] GIOVANNI ZAUPA, *Andrea Palladio e la sua committenza*, Rome 1990.
[2] RENATO CEVESE, *Appunti palladiani*, in "Bollettino del Centro Internazionale di Studi di Architettura Andrea Palladio", VII, 1965, p. 305.
[3] GIANCARLO TURRINI, *Aspetti costruttivi e strutturali nell'opera di Andrea Palladio*, in *Andrea Palladio. Nuovi contributi*, Milan 1988, p. 127-135.

Window-sill. Villa Poiana at Poiana Maggiore.

The Joys of the Worksite 209

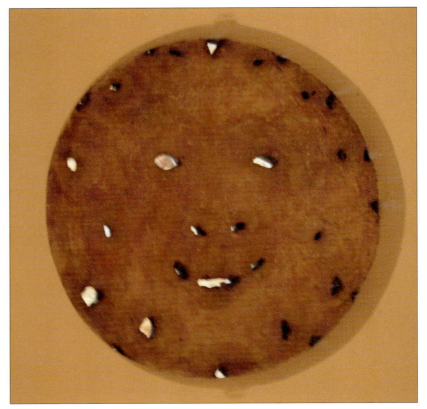

The wooden ceiling of the loggia, Villa Foscari alla Malcontenta. The underside of the mask of a faun in the middle of the main room in Villa Almerico called "La Rotonda" in Vicenza. The mask allowed rainwater to run away and fresh air to enter the floor underneath; Below, the wooden architrave in Villa Badoer at Fratta Polesine and Villa Pisani at Montagnana.

210 The Joys of the Worksite From the heroic to the everyday

The mask of a faun in the middle of the floor of the main room in Villa Almerico called "La Rotonda" in Vicenza. The mask allowed rainwater to run away and fresh air to enter the floor underneath; Below, the kitchen sink in Villa Godi at Lonedo.

From the heroic to the everyday   The Joys of the Worksite

Left, cellars in Villa Pisani at Bagnolo and Palazzo Thiene (Vicenza); right, cellars in Palazzo Thiene and the Loggia del Capitanio (Vicenza).

212   The Joys of the Worksite   Bricks and stone

Palazzo Thiene (Vicenza) and Villa Thiene at Quinto Vicentino (details); Below, a stone base inserted in a brick wall (Villa Thiene) and the Doric trabeation in the Convent of Charity (Venice) in terracotta brickwork.

Bricks and stone   The Joys of the Worksite

Ground-floor rooms.
Villa Foscari alla Malcontenta.

214   The Joys of the Worksite   The majesty and humility of vaults

The majesty and humility of vaults   The Joys of the Worksite   215

The annular room under the main hall in Villa Almerico called "La Rotonda" in Vicenza. The extrados of the circular vault in a room in Palazzo Chiericati (Vicenza).

216 The Joys of the Worksite   The geometric theorem of the vaults

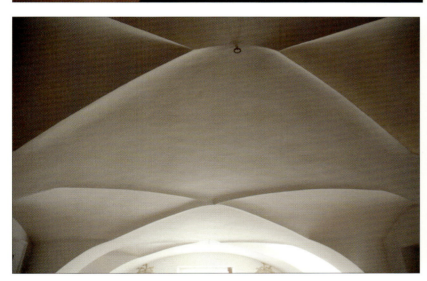

Ground floor of Villa Almerico (Vicenza) and Villa Poiana at Poiana Maggiore (details). centre: corridor of the Teatro Olimpico (Vicenza).

The geometric theorem of the vaults   The Joys of the Worksite   217

Two vaulted rooms.
Ground floor, Villa Godi at Lonedo.

218 The Joys of the Worksite   Space sculpted by light

TOP AND RIGHT: BASEMENT IN VILLA CORNARO AT PIOMBINO DESE AND GROUND FLOOR ROOMS IN VILLA FOSCARI ALLA MALCONTENTA.

Space sculpted by light   The Joys of the Worksite   219

The staircase in the Convent of Charity (Venice).

Springing point of a vault (detail).
Villa Almerico called "La Rotonda" in Vicenza.

Aurea simplicitas   The Joys of the Worksite

Top: stairs in Palazzo Chiericati (Vicenza) and, bottom, in Villa Foscari alla Malcontenta.

222 The Joys of the Worksite   The vertical passage technique

THE STAIRS IN VILLA PISANI AT BAGNOLO.

The vertical passage technique The Joys of the Worksite 223

A BRICK VAULT IN THE CELLAR OF PALAZZO THIENE (VICENZA)
WITH ONE OF PALLADIO'S FAVOURITE PIERCED GRILLES IN THE CENTRE.
THESE GRILLES ARE OFTEN FOUND IN THE VILLAS AND BUILDINGS BUILT BY PALLADIO.

The Joys of the Worksite   "So that they worked happily and willingly"

7. The Palladian Landscape

"The roads [...] ought to be beautiful and delightful to travellers [...] being in them able to see at a great distance, and besides to discover a good deal of the country, whereby great part of the fatigue is alleviated, and our minds (having always a new prospect before our eyes) find great satisfaction and delight."
ANDREA PALLADIO, III, 1

When talking about his childhood Guido Piovene[1] wrote:

> The city and the countryside echoed each other and almost forced me to pass from one to the other to achieve the perfect mix. But I felt as if the quality of space changed. It was always the same ideal space, either weaker or stronger, a constant in and out between the countryside and the city or city and the countryside, and I never really crossed a border because there wasn't one, not even an imaginary one in my mind. This model inspired me with an ideal or at least a human model, a model inspired by Venetian civilisation and by its way of designing cities: a man who, in the same breathe, is both a city dweller and a country gentleman, social and solitary and, I'd like to add (especially when I think of villas - although the link is less obvious), realistic and lyrical, practical and contemplative.

This physical and human landscape so passionately imagined by the Venetian writer owes much to Palladio - to his graceful agricultural designs. He was the one who provided a group of clients fired by the common goal of transforming their own relationship with the land into a plan that could turn this goal into architectural and landscape excellence.

Historical circumstances had paved the way for a particular model of rural settlement which combined agricultural labour and residential villas. Faced with the difficulties pursuant to the wars in the early sixteenth century and the inevitable reduction in trade with the East, the Venetian aristocracy had concentrated on the economic advantages to be reaped by reclaiming the marshes around the lagoon and promoting an agriculture based on new production criteria. Contrasting opinions about this reclamation are provided by two contemporaries, Girolamo Priuli and Alvise Cornaro. Priuli writes:

> Since the Venetian nobles and citizens had become rich, they wanted to enjoy this success and life's pleasures, amusements and other delights in the countryside, giving up maritime navigation and travels which were more troublesome and tiring, but from which come all wellbeing. And however dangerous was the mainland for the entire city, something we all know and are aware of, the inebriated nobles, citizens and populace started to buy land and houses on the mainland paying double their worth, spending 25 ducats for a piece of land that didn't yield even 3% a year: they built houses and palaces on this land [...] and [...] the revenue they obtained was spent in meals, amusements and enjoyments, but it was never enough and capital had to be added [...]. So what happened was that some were so enamoured of these pleasures, amusements, soft delicacies of the mainland - which were of no use whatsoever - that they abandoned the seas, sailing and travels.[2]

There was however a positive image in contrast to this catastrophic one, written by Alvise Cornaro who Palladio cites and praises in the preface of the first of the *Four Books* and who certainly played an important role in his education and training. Cornaro wrote to his friend Sperone Speroni:

> I have bought that without which I was born. Even if my parents were very rich, I bought it thanks to the best and most worthy means - in other words holy agriculture - and not thanks to weapons and toil and other people's misfortunes: nor by sailing the seas, source of endless dangers.[3]

The contrast between the sea from which "comes all wellbeing" and the sea "source of endless dangers" reveals the psychological difference that existed between the two generations and the distance between those who moralistically regretted the past and those who accepted change in order to develop new sensibilities, a new way of considering the mainland and its seductive visual landscapes. Showing his newfound sensibility towards this novelty, Cornaro writes:

> But above all I enjoy travelling, departing and coming back to places and towns I consider beautiful when I pass through them. Some on the planes, some on the hills, near rivers or springs, full of beautiful houses and gardens: nor are these delights and amusements any less sweet or dear because I cannot see properly or hear what is easily said to me or because some other of my senses is not perfect, they are all (thank God) perfect, especially taste; since I enjoy the simple food I eat much more, anywhere I might be, more than the delicacies I used to eat during my disorderly life.[4]

Cornaro offsets Priuli's haughty considerations by offering his own practical experience, expressing an ideology of life in the countryside that echoes Alberti's ethics which the latter based on Roman writers like Varro, Horace and Cicero, but Cornaro makes more hedonistic and rational.

In recent years, specialist studies have been carried out to find out

Fig. 81. A building on the shores of a canal (Civic Museum, Vicenza). The fact it is located in the Veneto region is confirmed by the presence of a jetty as well as by the central motif: a version of the group types with a Main Hall that crosses the entire lot, to which the Palladian window and triforium of the upper floor are well suited. An excellent example of Palladio's graphic skills and his penchant for a balanced and transparent chiaroscuro.

226   The Palladian Landscape

more about the clients who commissioned Palladio to build their villas and homes. The results of these studies, based on documentary sources involving not only the history of architecture, but also general history and economics, are very important. A theory has developed regarding the families who helped Palladio in his professional career: the Godi, Valmarana, Thiene, Angarano, Arnaldi, Gualdo, Piovene, Civena, Saraceno, Chiericati, Gazzotti, Capra, Trissino and Repeta families. It suggests that this group shared a widespread interest in political power, had novel religious ideas and economically-driven ideological motives. Recently Giovanni Zaupa[5] identified other less well-known individuals (his neighbour Alberto Monza, Giacomo Pagello, Rizzardo and Francesco Alidosio, Antonio Terzo, etc.). Zaupa discovered the latter were all in close contact with one another (including with the Florentine family of the Pomponazzi). This explains the support Palladio received from this group of noble artists and financiers as a man who could use architecture to express their common vision of change. It's debatable whether this goal and the existence of the group coincided with what has been called an "international republic of money" that used the protestant reform to assist the growth of nascent capitalism. In my opinion, it is a far cry from Palladio's idealistic mentality whose attitude towards money is well known thanks to his friend Maganza and his famous distich (cfr. p. 160).

> But perhaps he will not reap much less utility and consolation from the country house; where the remaining part of the time will be passed in feeling and adorning his own possessions, and by industry, and the art of agriculture, improving his estate; where also by the exercise of which in a villa is commonly taken, on foot and on horseback, the body will more easily preserve its strength and health; and finally, where the mind, fatigued by the agitations of the city, will be greatly restored and comforted, and be able quietly to attend the studies of letters, and contemplation (II, 12, p. 46).

It's true that Palladio talks about "increasing happiness" by exercising "holy Agriculture," but in the context of many other activities - observing, decorating, walking and contemplating.

It's reasonable to assume that Palladio was more interested in observing and contemplating, because this was his particular task - to help his clients see, decorate and contemplate. These three actions are the key to his landscape architecture which doesn't focus on how the architect places his architectures in the landscape (sometimes in a very sensitive manner, sometimes indifferently), but on his ability to make his architectures reveal or contribute to building a *landscape*, a landscape as an aesthetic element to be experienced and contemplated. It is this seeing and observing that he *builds* in a dual creative relationship: what can be seen through the architectural structure (the loggias, windows, raised platforms) that frame the views over the landscape and the image of the architectures in their own habitat, for examples, fences, volumes, centres of light, welcoming spaces, big houses or small towns with places to work or meditate. I believe that there's much to be said for Ugo Soragni's objections in 1980[6] to the idea that Palladian villas were an expression of a capitalistic plan: he identified differences between Palladian typologies and the real needs of a farm as illustrated by contemporary treatises on agriculture. He believed that the group of clients wanted to protect and exert direct control over their properties as well as force the peasants to respect the feudal agreements and thereby contrast the demands of the Venetian state. The fact the villas were left unfinished and that the successful reclamation of land by the Pisani family in Bagnolo led to the relocation of the buildings needed for rice growing (placing them further away from the towns) testifies to the utopian and anything but progressive nature of the agricultural policies of the nobles in Vicenza, united in their opposition to the power of Venice, rather than in their sponsorship of a European attitude. It's not surprising that the no less utopian nature of Palladian villas remained imprisoned in the pages of a treatise or was broken down into disjointed fragments.

As I've already mentioned, the main difficulty in trying to understand Palladio's philosophy is to tackle what might appear to be a contradiction but which, instead, is a sign of the architect's great powers of synthesis. In other words, the dual presence in his

Fig. 82. Villa Trissino at Meledo in the xylograph of the *Four Books*: "The situation is very beautiful, because it is on a hill, which is washed by an agreeable little river, in the middle of a very spacious plain, and near to a well frequented road. Upon the summit of the hill, there is to be a round hall, encompassed with the rooms, but so high, that it may receive its light from above them" (II, 15, p. 162).

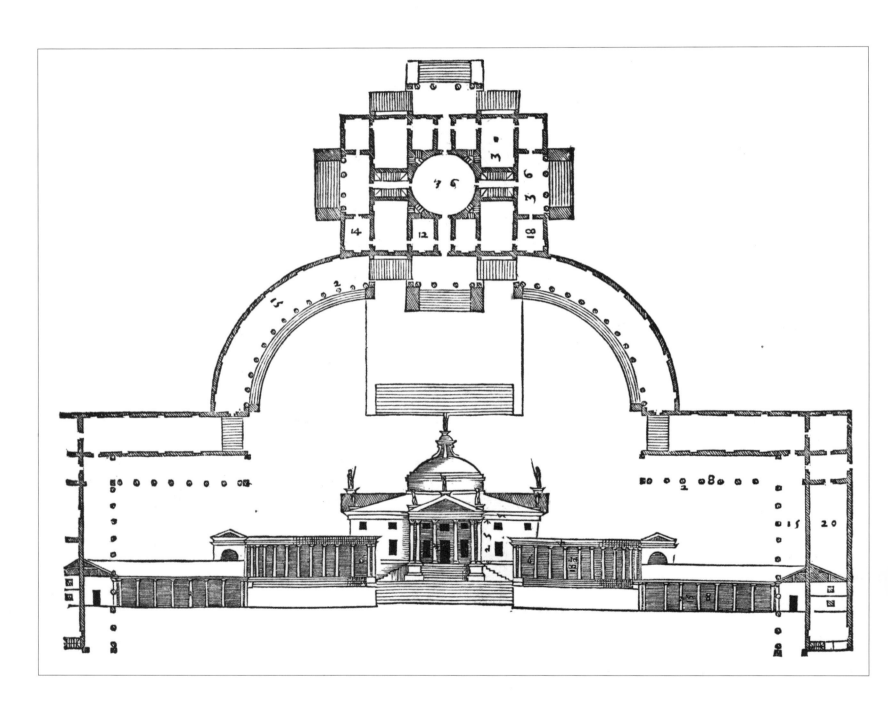

228 The Palladian Landscape

architectures of a strong rationalist element and a sensual approach that imbues the architecture with a sense of real presence, material solidity and a persuasive, pervasive ability to excite the senses and celebrate the fullness of being. In Palladio's aesthetics, this unsettling duplicity and *naturalness* is a sine qua non condition for innovation.

> The invention of the caulicoli is very beautiful, that are under the rose, which bind one another together, and seem to spring out of the leaves. Hence, as well by this, as by many other examples scattered throughout this book, it is evident that an architect is not restrained from departing sometimes from the common custom, provided such a variation be graceful and natural (IV, 24, p. 104).

Finally, in the addendum to the first book published in all the editions after the first one, Palladio states that the floor underneath has to be a fifth of the one above and if three floors are built the lowest should be a sixth less than the intermediate one and adds:

> With this proportion, by experience, a symmetry greatly pleasing to the eye is created, very similar to what one sees in canes where the taller they are the less the nodes, since taller things show greater weakness, therefore it is necessary for them to be shorter.[7]

Given that naturalism has been exploited and abused in the history of visual arts, we cannot use it to explain Palladio's statements about his model of a relationship with nature. According to Palladio, the architect has to represent not its forms, but its principles and laws, as well as what reason and the senses draw from the immensity and richness of nature. On the one hand, there was an attempt to press this approach by theorising a compliance that would involve adaptation to the environment (which seldom happens) and, on the other, an attempt to theorise a dreary, rationalist approach disconnected from the perceptive and sensual nature of natural images. What's missing here is that the architect's goal was to exploit laws and archetypes to create a responsive volume made of transfigured and vibrant materials that offer themselves up to the light to be imbued with life and human warmth. So, even though what we can assume from Palladio's writings does not necessarily coincide with the way he develops his poetics, it's worth recomposing the fragments that allow us to get a better understanding of the aesthetic ideas he expresses in words. The explicit statement of Palladio's concept of nature starts solemnly:

> I say, therefore, that architecture, as well as all other arts, being an imitatrix of nature, can suffer nothing, that either alienates or deviates from that which is agreeable to nature; from whence we see, that the ancient architects, who made their edifices of wood, when they began to make them of stone, instituted that the columns should be thicker at the top than at the bottom, taking example from the trees, all of which are thinner at the top than in the trunk, or near the root (I, 20, p. 25).

His conviction is based on a premise, the imitation of a nature that belonged to the popular beliefs of his age and sinks its roots in the genesis of architecture expressed by Vitruvius; but Palladio wants to give these statements a didactic flavour and clarifies that it involves imitating the laws of nature and not forms. The example that follows illustrates this approach: "And because it is very probable, that those things are depressed upon which form great weight is put, bases were placed under the columns, which, with their bastoni and cavetti, seem to be crushed with the burden laid upon them" (I, 20, p. 26). Since the deformation of objects under pressure from a thrust is a law of nature, then if the form of the base suggests the effect of that weight this naturalness gives it an aesthetic importance. Or "... the manner of building cannot but be blamed, which departs from that which the nature of things teaches... framing as it were another nature, and deviating from the true, good and beautiful method of building"(I, 20, p. 26). Regarding his gothic designs for San Petronio, argumentatively Palladio further clarifies his thoughts about nature:

> With regards to the objections of those brilliant architects, I will briefly answer, although I'm not obliged to reply to objections made indirectly and by people I do not know and who do not sign their names, and I

The Palladian Landscape

know for certain that if I had been present, they would not have been so bold, because I have done nothing in my drawings, partly drawing on the ancients, partly on modern examples ⁄ therefore done by good architects ⁄ that I cannot forcefully defend. And with regard to the problem of putting together Corinthian and composite order, because they are not suited, I answer that the Corinthian and the composite have nothing to do with the rustic and the Doric, although the ancients did it, putting them quite rightly on top, a polite and lightweight style above a solid and simple style, imitating nature in this, mother and teacher of all good things, where trees and branches are full of flowers and leaves and their feet of hard bark.[8]

This natural metaphor reappears when he talks of the pattern of bricks used to reinforce a stone wall. Palladio compares them to "ligaments" (I, IX, p. 9) which hold the other parts together, or again, when speaking about the layout of rooms, he recommends symmetry so that "the whole building has a certain convenience to make it beautiful and graceful," or when he repeatedly talks about the wings of the *barchesse* that "come out of the fabrick [...] to join the master's house with that of the villa"(II, 15, p. 52), or in the case of Villa Trissino "like arms tend to the circumference" and that for this form "seem to receive those that come near the house" (II, 17, p. 55).

Speaking about bridges, the naturalistic proposal is just as eloquent and inspiring. It echoes that penchant for dialogue highlighted by Diedo in his biography: "The pilasters that are made for the breadth of the river, ought to be in number even; as well because we see that nature has produced all those things of this number, which being more than one, are to support any weight, as the legs of men, and all other animals can justify" (III, 10, p. 68). On the topic of anthropomorphism, Palladio is certainly more reticent than Francesco di Giorgio or Alberti. Even though he doesn't cite its magnificent and iconological aspects, he does take for granted its normative and metaphorical value speaking often of buildings as "bodies" whose limbs are "one with the other and the other with the one symmetrical and correspondent" so that they "create majesty and decorum."

In keeping with what nearly always happens to an artist who is also a theorist, Palladian critics have tried to compare the ideas illustrated in his treatise and, more in general, in his writings, with the works that were actually built or designed: theory versus practice. They often concentrate on the inevitable contradictions, also because the *Four Books* represent a very specific period in his life, his more mature period, while his works span a much longer timescale from youth to old age and reflect substantial changes in his sensitivities. From this point of view, the treatise represents the systematic account of a philosophy to which each work is somehow adapted in order to privilege its theoretical value and provide the reader with a single, coherent method. This adaptation of practice to theory and ideas to examples can also be found in the works of Francesco Borromini who, as noted by Joseph Connors,[9] while preparing a series of engravings of his works, did not hesitate to change certain elements of his own constructed works to improve and perfect the theory behind them or at least adapt them to what he felt at that time.

Apart from the ambivalent meaning of the word naturalism coined for visual arts and unsuited to the world of architecture, there is no doubt that Palladio's sensibility for nature and the landscape and his ability to imagine it architecturally induced him to respect and honour nature in his designs. These traits emerge clearly in his written words. The gentleness towards nature that they seem to express (which Vitruvius spoke about in the preface to Book II) should not be confused with a search for smooth continuity. La Rotonda says it all. Palladio considers the landscape as a theatre and the building as a sort of actor.

> The site is as pleasant and as delightful as can be found; because it is on a small hill (this inspired Jefferson to design Monticello in Virginia), of very easy access, and is watered on one side by the *Bacchiglione*, a navigable river; and on the other it is encompassed with most pleasant risings, which look like a very great theatre, and are all cultivated, and abound with the most excellent fruits, and most exquisite vines: and therefore, as it enjoys from every part most beautiful views, some of which are limited, some more extended, and others that terminate with the horizon; there are loggias made in all four fronts (II, 3, p. 114).

FIG. 83. CANALETTO, "CAPRICE VIEW WITH PALLADIO'S DESIGN FOR THE RIALTO BRIDGE" (WINDSOR CASTLE, ROYAL COLLECTION).

The Palladian Landscape 231

Fig. 84. Axonometry projection of Palladio's second project for the Rialto bridge (Roberto Pane, *Andrea Palladio*, Turin 1963, p. 309).

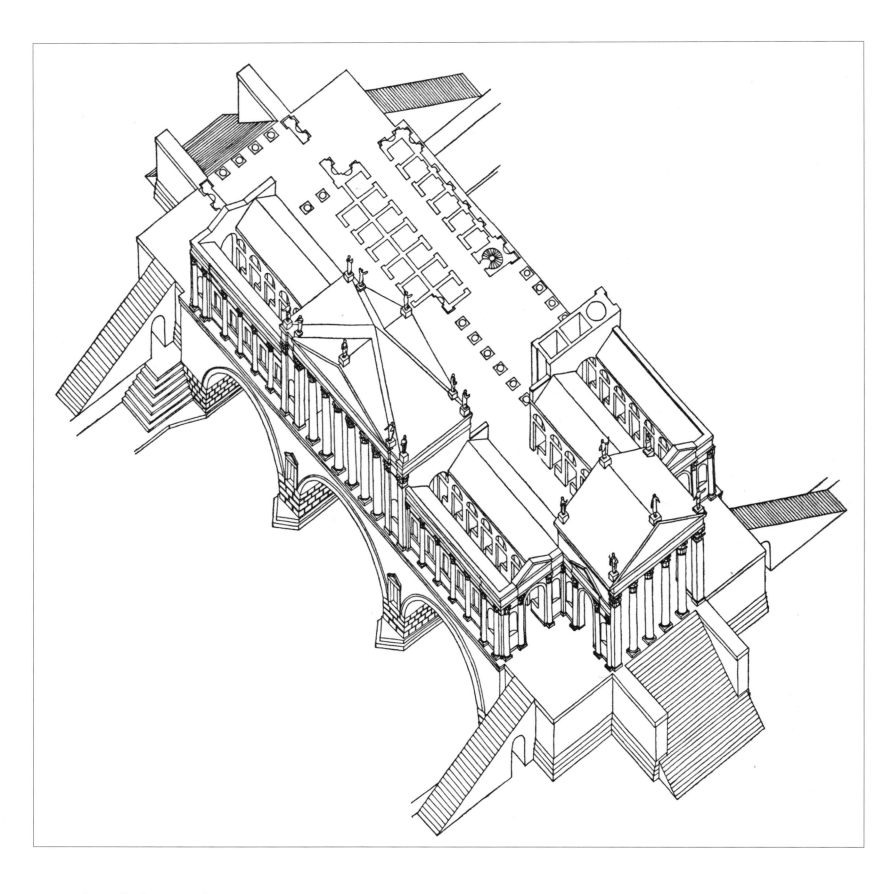

232   The Palladian Landscape

This simple, serious description is extremely literary: when speaking about the horizon it somehow echoes Leopardi's sonnet *Infinity*. It's true that Palladio does not talk about his feelings, but when he describes a place (comparing the distant horizon with the near horizon of fruit trees and vines), he does infer it. We should remember that in Europe there is another architectural masterpiece, the Philharmonic Hall by Hans Scharoun that the author himself describes as having been inspired by the sight of the vines along the sloping banks of the Rhine. This masterpiece is a theatre to listen to music and in Berlin the vineyards were turned into balconies and the vines into devoted spectators. When open to metaphor, architecture performs this miracle: a landscape becomes a theatre by exploiting "holy agriculture" and plays a unifying role. A building in the middle of a metaphorical "theatre" nestling among gentle hills becomes an orchestra that plays a tune, turning the endless variety of the natural scenery into a cosmic order. Some critics have complained about the non-correspondence between the physical characteristics of the landscape and the cruciform shape of La Rotonda. They note that if three of the staircases are connected in some way or another with the land, the third ends on a gradient that jeopardises function, forcing anyone descending the stairs to turn into a narrow space. Apart from the attractive balcony jutting out into the void at the end of the stairs, we should remember that Palladio interprets landscape by comparing it to the cosmic order; he doesn't deny that there is a difference between absolute unity and the absolute multiplicity of nature, on the contrary he emphasises it because he can use it to indicate the solution *ab initio* in the creative act.

Very few buildings in the world have generated as many dissenting views as La Rotonda. Some believe that its strict unitary concept represents the supremacy of pure human rationality, intentionally opposed to the variety and infinite multiplicity of the landscape. Instead, others think that it is an abstract interpretation of a real landscape poetically described by its author. Still others consider that, thanks to its graceful assembly of spaces, it is a building that is self-explanatory, whose only visible intent is to communicate its structure. Again, others see it as a complex symbolic machine that its client, the learned priest Almerico, asked Palladio to design to portray his own personality and his own beliefs. For Marcello Fagiolo, it is the manifest image of a universal religious nature, an exploration of the overall principles that influence religion all over the world and, therefore, can be considered like a mandala (figs. 87 and 88) or a sign of the Kabala. For Lionel March, if La Rotonda is turned into numbers that correspond to the most important measurements established by its creator (15, 26, 72), it could represent, from an esoteric point of view, the Gods surrounded by angels. For others, La Rotonda is just a "myth" to be destroyed, an allegedly typological invention inspired by two Islamic-style buildings in Palermo built by the Normans, the *Cuba* and the *Zisa*, mentioned in Leandro Alberti's book, *Descrizione di tutta Italia*, published in Venice in 1561.[10] Still others believe that if it is considered as it was originally intended as an "aulic villa on a little hill" it would not have warranted so much attention and that, only after it was turned by Scamozzi into "a simple manor house in the middle of a farm" did it become "something more compared to its foolish fame won in over four centuries, a "dubious and exploitable icon".[11]

In a providential digression in his book *Storia generale dell'Arte*, Giulio Carlo Argan found a precious interpretative key for Palladian villas which is worth citing here:

> Palladio presents the problem very clearly: it involves inserting a solid form, a geometric and volumetric construction, into a natural yet always different space, and finding a satisfactory relationship, indeed a perfect balance, between these two realities. Natural, infinite space should become tangible in the final shape of the building; it has to overcome the limits of its own finiteness by establishing, in unison, a relationship with infinite natural space.

It's easy to say that anyone who stands in front of this building, trying to find a kernel of truth, ends up by considering it a mirror that reflects their own thinking, expectations, doubts and certainties. The building has allowed many critics and writers to paint

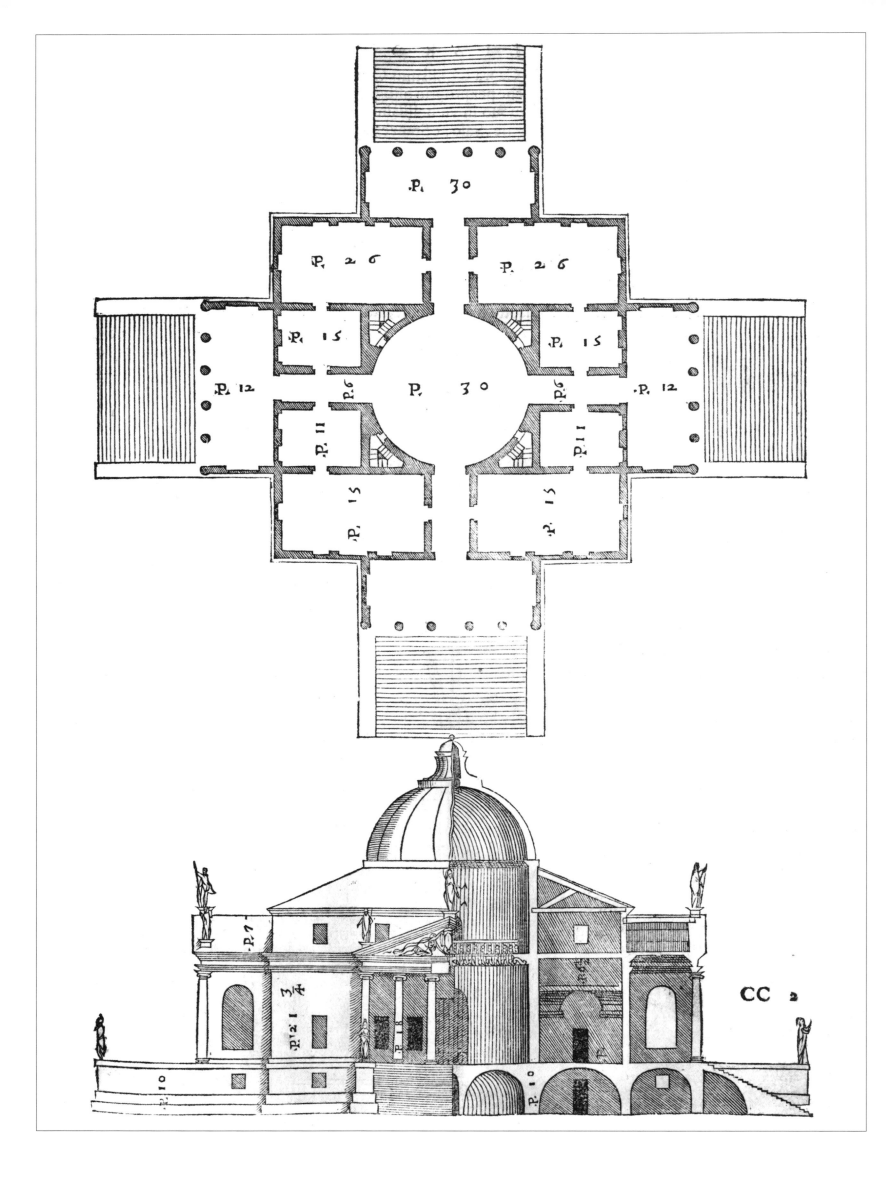

FIG. 85. VILLA ALMERICO CALLED "LA ROTONDA" IN THE XYLOGRAPH OF THE *FOUR BOOKS* (II, 3, P. 115).

their own self-portrait when commenting on the building. However, isn't it this ambiguity, this intriguing aspect that forces people to "confess," a common trait of many masterpieces in which their provocative enigmatic greatness is emphasised and stressed? And isn't the enigma, the unanswered question, the secret meaning of this work created by an enthusiastic scholar of types, something that proudly stands beyond and above every possible type? Palladio does not consider it a villa. In the *Four Books* he includes it among the buildings at the end of the second book, but as Hofmannsthal rightly points out: "What crowns the hill in Vicenza is no longer a temple, no longer a house, it is more than either. An immortal dream, a miraculously designed symbol towards which the distant hills seem to be drawn, the impetus of turbulent waters which finally reaches it and flow around it and rest softly on the four staircases, redeemed by a symbol."[12]

Let's examine how Palladian architecture created the landscape Piovene described in the pages we cited earlier. I believe three traits are the most meaningful: the feelings and mood inspired by his most important works and their relationship with the sky, something that has made people talk about an "architecture that breathes"; the horizontal nature and stratification of the buildings; and the way the walls connect with the land or, better still, the way in which the architect makes his buildings rise up out of the ground. The first still requires a contribution from twentieth-century literature. Comisso[13] wrote: "I survive on landscapes, I recognise the origins of my blood in the landscape. It penetrates my eyes and gives me strength." When talking about Palladio:

> Vicenza with its hills, clear flowing rivers, fertile plains and pale skies, is populated with people who live and enjoy looking at things and Palladio built for the delight of the eyes of its citizens [...] He felt that these mainly light, perhaps Celtic eyes, were asking for harmony and cunning patterns and gave them arches, loggias, columns, porticoes, robbing space from the air [...]

In a much more incisive and profound manner, Guido Piovene credits Palladio's works with an air of radiance:

> I found the buildings to be always different, as if, seemingly imprisoned in rigid classical modules, they had a strange power to contract and expand, to change with the weather. Indeed, they themselves created a mood, as others have already mentioned, they tended to overflow, to invade external space. They had a radiant quality to them [...] I found myself faced with a paradox; an architect who created maximum aperture using closed forms.[14]

At this point perhaps we could use the concept of "openness" the way Rilke used it in the *Duino Elegies* and was commented on by Heidegger in *Off the Beaten Track*, like being in the world, like animals without conflict. "Animals and flowers are what they are without realising it; they possess that indescribably open freedom which for us is present (just for a moment) only during the early stages of love, when people see in another, in their loved one, their own immensity, as well as in elevation towards God."[15] Many factors contribute to creating this atmosphere, this inhaling and exhaling in Palladio's works: some are linked to the classical style and are therefore quite common; others are more personal and secret - the chiaroscuro of the loggias, the pattern of the holes on the walls, the superimposition and intricacies of different rhythms within the confines of classical orders, the series of dentils, of trusses, the contraction and expansion of the cornices, the projecting trabeations on the columns and the way they withdraw into the walls, the swollen convex friezes and the contractions of the scotias in the attic bases, the quality of the building materials, the whitewashed marble which often revealed the underlying brickwork, the lead of the domes and lanterns (pgs. 248 and 249) different to all the rest because covered in slabs and shaped using simplified mouldings to provide an impenetrable defensive shield of lead against the wind and the weather. One of the most personal elements of the diastole and systoles of Palladian architecture, similar to a musical instrument in an symphony orchestra, is the contraction and expansion of the cornices depending on their position and therefore the role given to them by the architect. This contraction and expansion is clearly visible in Villa Cornaro, in La Rotonda and in the façades of

The Palladian Landscape 235

FIG. 86. VILLA FOSCARI ALLA MALCONTENTA IN THE XYLOGRAPH OF THE *FOUR BOOKS* (II, 14, P. 150). NOTE THE WALL CROWNED WITH BATTLEMENTS USED IN THE DESIGN AROUND THE *HORTUS CONCLUSUS*, DOUBLED IN DEFERECE TO BILATERAL SYMMETRY.

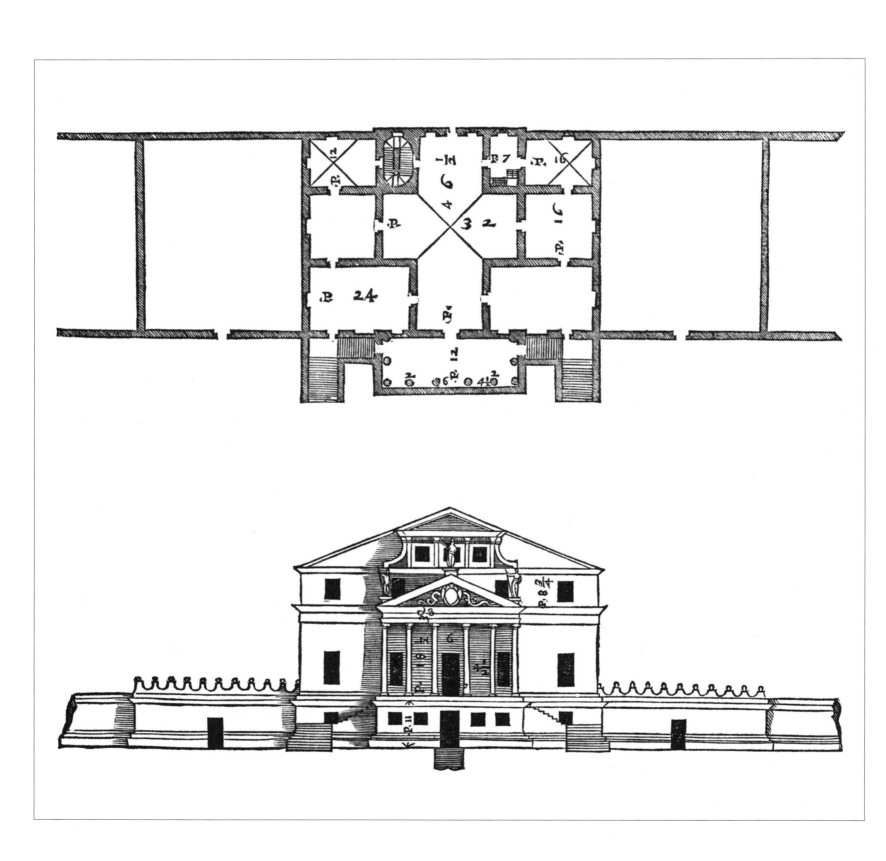

236 The Palladian Landscape

Fig. 87-88. Two versions of Villa Almerico as a *mandala* (André Corboz, *Per una analisi psicologica delle ville palladiane*, in "Bollettino del Centro Internazionale di Studi Andrea Palladio", XV, 1973, p. 259 and fig. 169).

Fig. 89-90. The xylographs in the *Four Books* of Villa Repeta at Campiglia (II, 15, p. 163) and Villa Pisani at Bagnolo (II, 14, p. 146).

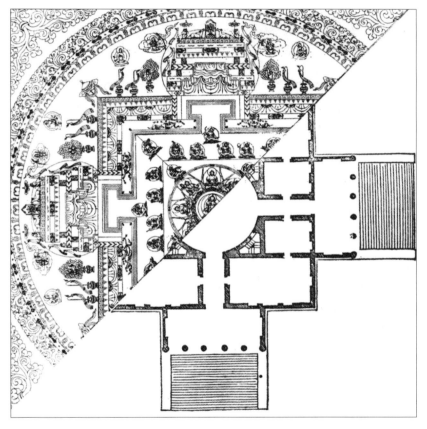
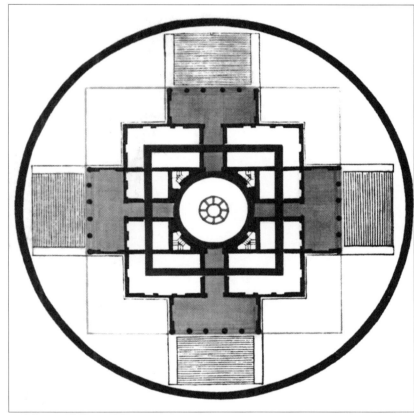
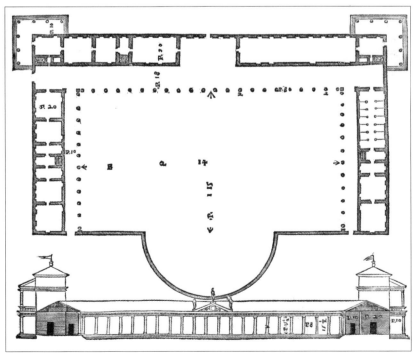
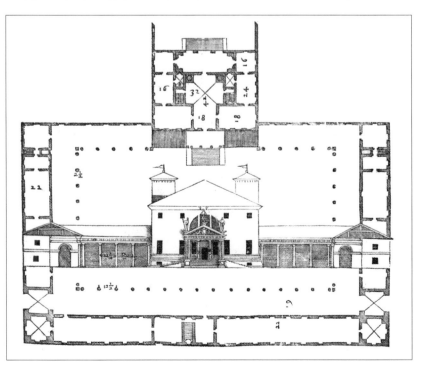

The Palladian Landscape 237

Fig. 91. The plan of an ideal city in Vitruvius commented by Daniele Barbaro (Vitruvius Pollio, Marcus, *De architectura libri decem, cum commentariis Danielis Barbari, electi Patriarchae Aquileiensis, multis aedificiorum, horologiorum, et machinarum descriptionibus, et figuris*, Venice 1567).

Fig. 92. Engraving by Juan Caramuel (*Architectura Civil Recta y Obliqua*, Vigevano 1678, articulo III, lamina XIV) with the plan of the city of Hochelaga in Canada copied by Giovan Battista Ramusio (*Navigazione et viaggi*, vol. III, Venice 1556) that André Corboz believed to be inductively designed by Palladio.

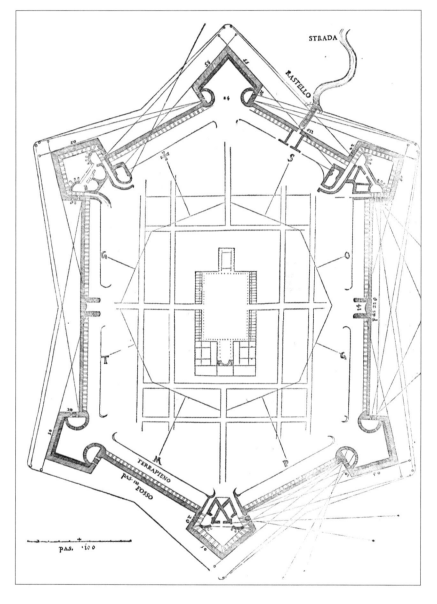
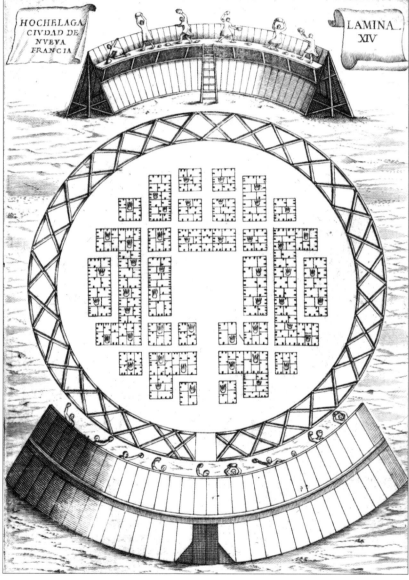

238 The Palladian Landscape

San Francesco della Vigna and Il Redentore. Finally, a reference to one of Palladio's linguistic anomalies: the pilaster strip tapered like a column, extremely rare in old buildings and instead convincingly adopted to fight the rigidness of the lines and introduce into matter an assonance with biological forms.

The way a building is connected to the ground is always part of any study of Palladio's work. He uses the podium, the base, the pedestal, the stairs and ramps to mediate between floors. While the podium in Palazzo Chiericati is useful to make the building slip towards the open space of the Island, the staircase in Villa Badoer connects the building with its concave wings by creating an intermediate level that spreads out sideways. In Villa Poiana, the convex semicircular staircase superbly mirrors the arch of the Palladian window, suggesting a process of transposition and reversal of the semicircular design; in Villa Emo Capodilista at Fanzolo, the ramp gives the temple portico a feeling of accessibility which softens its monumental appearance, while in Villa Caldogno, the triadic form of the ramp provides dynamism and material vibrations to the loggia.

One of the constants in Palladio's works is the way they dialogue with the sky. This is achieved mainly by his use of cusps which interrupt the upper profile of the buildings, eliminating that sense of closure. His first statues, a consolidated custom in the sixteenth century, appear in the drawings for the courtyard of Palazzo Thiene and in those of the façade and courtyard of Palazzo Iseppo da Porto (figs. 7 and 75). However in the xylograph of the treatise all the villas (except for Villa Godi, Villa Ragona and Villa Serego at Santa Sofia) have statues. Statues are everywhere, in the buildings, façades or courtyards. The only exception is Palazzo Chiericati and in the building designed for a site in Venice illustrated in the *Four Books* (II, 17, p. 54). The small flags instead appear on the turrets of the dove-houses in Villa Pisani, Villa Saraceno, Villa Repeta, Villa Thiene at Cicogna and Villa Serego (figs. 90, 89 and 2), as well as in the reconstruction of the villa of the ancients, thereby excluding the possibility that they were inspired by the sea. This dialogue with the sky certainly played an important role in the configuration of the lanterns of Palladio's domes, the characteristics of which we have mentioned elsewhere. Inspiration came from the Rafaelesque cupola of Sant'Eligio degli Orefici (the presence of the same type of lantern in a relief in the mausoleum to Romulus along the Via Appia should be attributed to a theoretical reconstruction). The idea was developed on many occasions: in San Giorgio, in the cupola of the Basilica in Vicenza, Il Redentore and the Zitelle: it has its own character thanks to the base which "radiates" compared to the statues crowning the buildings (pgs. 248 and 249). Skylines must have fascinated Palladio, as did the ends of rather low walls for which he invented these 'tops' by combining concave segments and by putting stone balls on the top of this sort of battlements. This finishing is visible in the outer wall of Villa Badoer and the side doors of San Giorgio Maggiore; it could be an addition by those who came after him, but the treatise shows that it played an important role on the tops of the walls of the mysterious enclosure around Villa Foscari alla Malcontenta (fig. 86). So undoubtedly this mythical detail that appears to be irreconcilable with classicism and was inspired by the endless different types of Venetian battlements was invented by Palladio himself, by the dreamy levity of some of his unexpected ideas.

The Palladian city is there before our every eyes, Vicenza, his city of choice. By building the monuments that grace its city streets and squares, he created a pervasive, dominant image that influences its atmosphere, its welcoming yet austere character, its spirit and soul.

Recalling Alberti's metaphor, Palladio speaks of the house as if it were a small city and the city as if it were a big house: an intimacy that expands and dilates into an urban context which closes in on itself, contracts and becomes intimate. Sometimes Palladio escapes from the real, realistic and solidly rooted city and imagines something more regular and organic, the ideal city imagined as a defensive system, much like the one illustrated in Barbaro's *Vitruvius* (fig. 91), or the ideal reconstruction of the mythical Hochelaga (fig. 92), drawn successfully by André

Corboz[16] for Giovann Battista Ramusio: technical exercises and graphic elegance that have little to do with the natural genesis of the city so well described in the *Four Books* when he talks of the need and the pleasure of being "with friends."
In the preface of Book One, he writes:

> It being very probable, that man lived formerly by himself; but afterwards, feeling he required the affection of other men, to obtain those things that might make him happy, (if any happiness is to be found here below), he naturally sought out and loved the company of other men; so districts were made of many houses, and many districts then created cities and public spaces and buildings.

Desire and love, these are the reasons why cities exist: this is the legacy, the power, the provocation that still fires Palladian architecture, the message left in the walls, columns, spaces, words created by the hands of this architect, Palladio - hands that went from cutting stone and shaping space to developing ideas and during that time exploited all the possibilities provided by this marvellous part of our mortal body.

---

[1] GUIDO PIOVENE, *La città veneta*, in "Bollettino del Centro Internazionale di Studi di Architettura Andrea Palladio", IV, 1962, p. 204.

[2] ROBERTO CESSI (edited by), *I diari di Girolamo Priuli*, in *Rerum Italicarum Scriptores*, edited by Ludovico Antonio Muratori (vol. XXV, part III), Città di Castello 1912, vol. IV, p. 50.

[3] Cited in JAMES S. ACKERMAN, *The Villa. Form and Ideology of Country Houses*, Princeton, p. 121.

[4] CAMILLO SEMENZATO (edited by), *Alvise Cornaro. Trattato di Architettura*, in *Pietro Cataneo, Giacomo Barozzi da Vignola, Trattati con l'aggiunta degli scritti di architettura di Alvise Cornaro...*, Milan 1985, p. 77.

[5] GIOVANNI ZAUPA, *Andrea Palladio e la sua committenza*, Rome 1990

[6] UGO SORAGNI, *Economia neo-feudale e dialettica del territorio nelle ville venete*, in "Bollettino del Centro Internazionale di Studi di Architettura Andrea Palladio", XXII, 1980, p. 137.

[7] Cfr. ANDREA PALLADIO, *Scritti sull'architettura (1554-1579)*, edited by Lionello Puppi, Vicenza 1988, p.101.

[8] *Ibid.*, p. 131.

[9] JOSEPH CONNORS, Introduction in *Francesco Borromini, Opus Architectonicum*, Milan 1998, p. XLVIII.

[10] KURT W. FORSTER, *Is Palladio's Rotonda an Architectural Novelty?* in KURT W. FORSTER and MARTIN KUBELIK (edited by), *Palladio: ein Symposium*, Rome 1980, p. 27. Obviously the reference to the Cuba and the Zisa in Palermo is as generic as the reference to many other buildings with two axes of orthogonal symmetry.

[11] Cfr. MARTIN KUBELIK, CHRISTIAN GOEDICKE and KLAUS SLUSALLEK, *La Rotonda di A. Palladio. Un mito oggetto di indagini obiettive*, Milan 2002.

[12] HUGO VON HOFMANNSTHAL, *Prosa*, II, Frankfurt 1951, p. 62.

[13] GIOVANNI COMISSO, *Veneto Felice*, Milan 1984.

[14] PIOVENE, *La città veneta* cit., p. 204-205.

[15] Cfr. letter by Rilke to a Russian reader reproduced in MAURICE BETZ, *Rilke in Frankreich, Erinnerung, Briefe, Dokumente*, Vienna 1938, p. 289, cited in MARTIN HEIDEGGER, *Off the Beaten Track*, Cambridge 2002.

[16] ANDRÈ CORBOZ, *Contributo all'urbanistica palladiana: la pianta di Hochelaga (1556) quale progetto del club Barbaro*, in FORSTER and KUBELIK (edited by), *Palladio: ein Symposium* cit., p. 57. Lionello Puppi also attributed it to Palladio.

CRENELLATION ON THE OUTER WALLS OF VILLA BADOER AT FRATTA POLESINE.

Villa Barbaro at Maser nestling on the green lawn, gracefully outlined against the woods in the background.

Indulged landscape The Palladian Landscape

THE MAIN HALL IN VILLA FOSCARI ALLA MALCONTENTA DIALOGUES WITH THE LANDSCAPE AND WITH THE SUNLIGHT FALLING ON ITS REAR FAÇADE.

The Palladian Landscape   Interior space projected into the countryside

Interior space projected into the countryside   The Palladian Landscape   245

Villa Foscari alla Malcontenta
from the banks of the Brenta.
Palladio often exploited nearby rivers to juxtapose
his buildings with the moving water.

In Palladian cupolas, the lantern has an unmistakable silhouette: often crowned with statues, with its simple lead-scovered volutes it seems to rise and flourish. The lanterns of the Duomo in Vicenza and San Giorgio Maggiore in Venice.

248   The Palladian Landscape   To draw against the sky

The lanterns of Il Redentore (Venice), of the Zitelle (Venice) and the chapel in Villa Barbaro at Maser.

To draw against the sky   The Palladian Landscape

The colonnade of the Teatro Olimpico (Vicenza).

250 The Palladian Landscape The theatre of the heavens

THE TYMPANUM OF SAN GIORGIO MAGGIORE (VENICE)
WITH ITS STATUES AND THE ANGEL ON THE BELFRY.

The theatre of the heavens   The Palladian Landscape

STEPS LEADING DOWN TO THE COUNTRYSIDE
IN VILLA CALDOGNO AT CALDOGNO
AND VILLA PISANI AT BAGNOLO.

252 The Palladian Landscape   Roots to the ground

THE BASE OF VILLA PISANI AT BAGNOLO, VILLA BADOER AT FRATTA POLESINE AND VILLA BARBARO AT MASER (DETAILS).

Roots to the ground   The Palladian Landscape

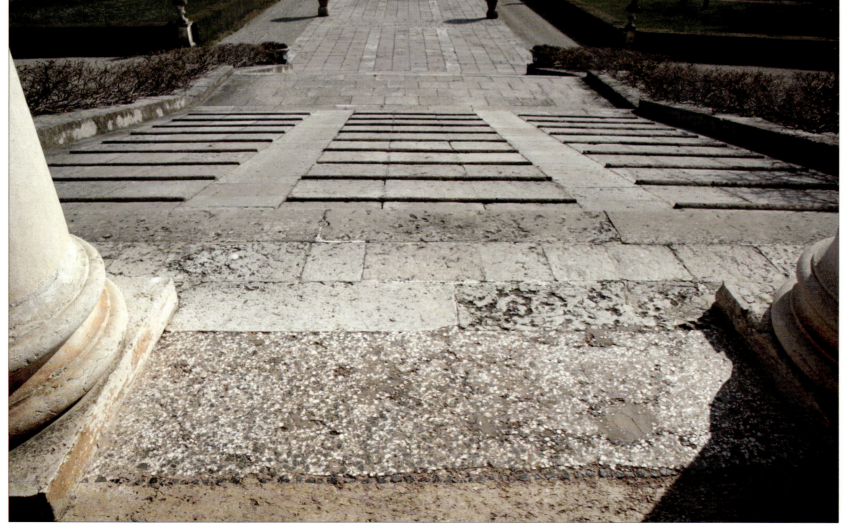

THE BASE OF PALAZZO CHIERICATI IN VICENZA
AND THE FLIGHT OF STEPS IN VILLA EMO CAPODILISTA AT FANZOLO.

254   The Palladian Landscape   The base, the flight of steps, the

THE STAIRS LEADING TO THE ENTRANCE
TO VILLA BADOER AT FRATTA POLESINE.

THE PEDIMENT, A TYPICAL ELEMENT IN PALLADIO'S VILLAS,
ANNOUNCES FROM A DISTANCE THE SACRED NATURE OF THE HOME
AND NESTLES IN THE LANDSCAPE WITH ITS SLIGHT UPWARD MOVEMENT,
ASSUMING THE TRAITS OF A HUMAN FACE.
VILLA POIANA AT POIANA MAGGIORE AND VILLA ZENO AT CESSALTO.

Bibliography

MONOGRAPHS AND SOURCES

ACKERMAN, JAMES S., *Palladio: The Architect and Society*, Harmondsworth 1966.

ID., *Palladio's Villas*, Glückstadt 1967.

ID., *Palladio*, Turin 1972.

BARBIERI, GIUSEPPE, *Andrea Palladio e la cultura veneta del Rinascimento*, Rome 1983.

BELTRAMINI, GUIDO and PADOAN, ANTONIO (edited by), *Andrea Palladio: atlante delle architetture*, introduction by H. Burns, Venice 2000.

BOUCHER, BRUCE, *Palladio*, Turin 1994.

ID., *Andrea Palladio: The Architect in his Time*, New York - London 1998.

BURGER, FRITZ, *Die Villen des Andrea Palladio*, Leipzig 1909.

BURNS, HOWARD, with FAIRBAIRN, LYNDA and BOUCHER, BRUCE, *Andrea Palladio 1508-1580: The Portico and the Farmyard*, London 1975.

BURNS, HOWARD and BELTRAMINI, GUIDO (edited by), *Andrea Palladio e la villa veneta. Da Petrarca a Carlo Scarpa*, exhibition catalogue, Venice 2005.

CAYE, PIERRE, *Le savoir de Palladio: architecture, métaphysique et politique dans la Venise du Cinquecento*, [Paris] 1995.

CHASTEL, ANDRÉ and CEVESE, RENATO (edited by), *Andrea Palladio: nuovi contributi*, 7th International Seminar of History of Architecture, Vicenza 1-7 September 1988, Milan 1990.

COSGROVE, DENIS, *The Palladian Landscape*, University Park, Penn. 1993.

DALLA POZZA, ANTONIO, *Andrea Palladio*, Vicenza 1943.

FORSSMAN, ERIK, *Palladios Lehrgebaude*, Stockholm 1964.

FROMMEL, CHRISTOPH LUITPOLD, *Roma e la formazione architettonica del Palladio: nuovi contributi*, Milan 1990.

HOLBERTON, PAUL, *Palladio's Villas: Life in the Renaissance Countryside*, London 1990.

IVANOFF, NICOLA, *Palladio*, Milan 1967.

JONES, INIGO, *Notes and Remarks of Inigo Jones upon the Plates of the Second Book of Palladio's Architecture: Taken from the Manuscript of the said Inigo Jones in the Library of Worcester College*, Oxford, June, 1741, in *The Architecture of A. Palladio in Four Books*, edited by G. Leoni, London 1742, pp. 70-72.

ID., *Inigo Jones on Palladio: Being the Notes by Inigo Jones in the Copy of "I Quattro libri dell'architettura di Andrea Palladio", 1601, in the Library of Worcester College*, Oxford, Newcastle upon Tyne 1970.

LEWIS, DOUGLAS, *The Drawings of Andrea Palladio*, New Orleans 2000 (first ed.: Washington, D.C. 1981).

MAGAGNATO, LICISCO and MARINI, PAOLA (edited by), *Palladio e Verona*, exhibition catalogue, Vicenza 1980.

MAGRINI, ANTONIO, *Memorie intorno la vita e le opere di Andrea Palladio*, Padova 1845.

MITROVIC, BRANKO, *Learning from Palladio*, New York 2004.

OLIVIERI, ACHILLE, *Palladio, le corti e le famiglie: simulazione e morte nella cultura architettonica del '500*, Vicenza 1981.

PANE, ROBERTO, *Andrea Palladio*, Turin 1961.

PÉE, HERBERT, *Die Palastbauten des Andrea Palladio*, Würzburg 1939.

PUPPI, LIONELLO, *Palladio*, Milan 1973.

ID. (edited by), *Palladio e Venezia*, Florence 1982.

ID., *Palladio. Corpus dei disegni al Museo Civico di Vicenza*, Milan 1989.

ID., *Andrea Palladio*, edited by D. Battilotti, Milan 1999.

ID., *Palladio: introduzione alle architetture e al pensiero teorico*, San Giovanni Lupatoto 2005.

TEMANZA, TOMMASO, *Vita di Andrea Palladio Vicentino egregio Architetto*, Venice 1762.

ID., *Vite dei più celebri architetti, e scultori veneziani*, Venice 1778.

TIMOFIEWITSCH, WLADIMIR, *Die sakrale Architektur Palladios*, Munich 1968.

TURRINI, GIANCARLO, *Aspetti costruttivi e strutturali nell'opera di Andrea Palladio. Nuovi contributi*, Milan 1988.

VASARI, GIORGIO, *Le vite de' più eccellenti pittori, scultori at architettori*, 3 vol., Florence 1568.

ZANELLA, GIACOMO, *Vita di Andrea Palladio*, Naples-Milan-Pisa 1880.

ZAUPA, GIOVANNI, *Andrea Palladio e la sua committenza: denaro e architettura nella Vicenza del Cinquecento*, Rome-Reggio Calabria 1990.

ZORZI, GIANGIORGIO, *I disegni delle antichità di Andrea Palladio*, Venice 1959.

ID., *Le opere pubbliche e i palazzi di Andrea Palladio*, [Venice] 1965.

ID., *Le chiese e i ponti di Andrea Palladio*, [Venice] 1966.

ID., *Le ville e i teatri di Andrea Palladio*, [Venice] 1969.

ESSAYS

ACKERMAN, JAMES S., *Palladio's lost Portico. Project for San Petronio in Bologna*, in *Essays in the History of Architecture Presented to Rudolf Wittkower*, London 1967, pp. 119-125.

ID., *Palladio e lo sviluppo della concezione della chiesa a Venezia*, in "Bollettino del Centro Internazionale di Studi di Architettura Andrea Palladio", XIX, 1977, pp. 9-26.

ID., *La villa. Forma e ideologia*, Turin 1990.

ID., *Disegni del Palladio per la facciata di San Petronio*, in *Una basilica per una città: sei secoli in San Petronio*, Conference Minutes, Bologna 1994, pp. 251-258.

ID., *Palladio: in che senso classico?*, in "Annali di architettura", 6, 1994, pp. 11-22.

ID., *Andrea Palladio. Villa Emo. Restrained Style and Noble Pleasures | Rigore e nobili piaceri*, in "Casabella", LXII, 662-663, 1998-1999, pp. 10-19.

ID., *Daniele Barbaro and Vitruvius*, in *Origins, Imitation, Conventions*, Cambridge (Mass.) 2002, pp. 217-234 (formerly published in *Architectural Studies in Memory of Richard Krautheimer*, edited by C. Stryker, Mainz 1996, pp. 1-5).

ALTMANN, LUDWIG, *Die venezianische Votivkirche Il Redentore: ein Beitrag zur Interpretation von Architektur*, in "Das Müster", 30, 1977, pp. 151-154.

ARGAN, GIULIO CARLO, *Andrea Palladio e la critica neoclassica*, in "L'Arte", 1930, pp. 327-346.

ID., *Palladio e palladianesimo*, in *Architettura e utopia nella Venezia del Cinquecento*, edited by L. Puppi, Milan 1980, pp. 11-15.

ID., *Palladio e il Manierismo veneto*, in "Bollettino del Centro Internazionale di Studi di Architettura Andrea Palladio", XXIII, 1980, pp. 1-15.

ASQUINI, LICIA, *Sul lavoro di Andrea Palladio in Palazzo Antonini*, in "Arte/Documento", 9, 1996, pp. 75-79.

ASQUINI, MASSIMO, *Palladio e i Canonici regolari lateranensi: per una ricerca sul Convento della Carità a Venezia*, in "Arte/Documento", 6, 1992, pp. 231-237.

ASSUNTO, ROSARIO, *Introduzione all'estetica del Palladio*, in "Bollettino del Centro Internazionale di Studi di Architettura Andrea Palladio", XIV, 1972, pp. 9-26.

ID., *La Rotonda e il paesaggio: architettura nella natura e architettura della natura*, in *La Rotonda*, Milan 1988, pp. 9-19.

AVAGNINA, MARIA ELISA, *Le statue dell'Olimpico, ovvero la "messa in pietra" degli Accademici fondatori del teatro*, in L. MAGAGNATO, *Il teatro Olimpico*, notes and editing by L. Puppi, Milan 1992, pp. 85-127.

AZZI VISENTINI, MARGHERITA, *Il ponte di Bassano. Il ponte fino al 1567. Il ponte dalla fine del sec. XVI ai giorni nostri*, in *I ponti di Palladio*, exhibition catalogue, edited by F. Rigon, Milan 1980, pp. 21-24, 29-31.

ID., *Daniele Barbaro e il giardino: dall'Orto Botanico di Padova a Villa Barbaro a Maser*, in *Una famiglia veneziana nella storia: i Barbaro*, Acts of the Conference held to mark to 5th hundred anniversary of the death of the Humanist Hermolao Barbaro (Venice, 4-6 November, 1993), edited by M. Marangoni and M. Pastore Stocchi, Venice 1996, pp. 397-434.

BARBIERI, FRANCO, *Il Palazzo Chiericati sede del Museo Civico di Vicenza*, in *Il Museo Civico di Vicenza*, vol. I, Vicenza 1962, pp. 9-62.

ID., *Il primo Palladio*, in "Bollettino del Centro Internazionale di Studi di Architettura Andrea Palladio", IX, 1967, pp. 24-36.

ID., *La Basilica Palladiana*, in "Corpus Palladianum", vol. II, Vicenza 1968.

ID., *Palladio in villa negli anni quaranta: da Lonedo a Bagnolo*, in "Arte Veneta", 24, 1970, pp. 63-79.

ID., *Giangiorgio Trissino e Andrea Palladio*, in Acts of the Conference on Giangiorgio Trissino, Vicenza, 31 March - 1 April 1979, edited by N. Pozza, Vicenza 1980, pp. 191-211.

ID., *Vicenza città di palazzi*, Vicenza 1987.

ID., *Interventi su architetture palladiane...*, in *Vincenzo Scamozzi 1548-1616*, exhibition catalogue, edited by F. Barbieri and G. Beltramini, Venice 2003, pp. 197-198.

BASSI, ELENA, *Il Convento della Carità*, in "Corpus Palladianum", vol. VI, Vicenza 1971.

ID., *Il complesso palladiano della Carità*, Milan 1980.

BATTILOTTI, DONATA, *Nuovi contributi archivistici per Palladio*, in "Atti dell'Istituto Veneto di Scienze, Lettere e Arti", 138, 1979-1980, pp. 199-218.

ID., *Vicenza al tempo di Andrea Palladio attraverso i libri d'estimo del 1563-1564*, Vicenza 1980.

ID., *Per il palazzo di Iseppo da Porto del Palladio: un documento inedito e una nota*, in "Antichità viva", 20, 1, 1981, pp. 40-44.

ID., *Villa Barbaro a Maser: un difficile cantiere*, in "Storia dell'arte", 53, 1985, pp. 33-48.

BATTISTI, EUGENIO, *Un tentativo di analisi strutturale del Palladio tramite le teorie musicali del Cinquecento e l'impiego di figure rettoriche*, in "Bollettino del Centro di Studi di Architettura Andrea Palladio", XV, 1973, pp. 211-232.

BIASUTTI, GUGLIELMO, *Storia e guida del Palazzo Arcivescovile di Udine*, Udine 1958.

BOUCHER, BRUCE, *Nature and the Antique in the Work of Andrea Palladio*, in "Journal of the Society of Architectural Historians", 59, 2000, pp. 296-311.

BRANDI, CESARE, *Perché Palladio non fu neoclassico*, in *Essays in History of Architecture Presented to Rudolf Wittkower*, edited by D. Fraser, H. Hibbard and M. J. Levine, London 1967, pp. 116-121.

BRUSCHI, ARNALDO, *Roma antica e l'ambiente romano nella formazione di Palladio*, in "Bollettino del Centro Internazionale di Studi di Architettura Andrea Palladio", XX, 1978, pp. 9-26.

ID., *Palladio architetto a Roma e la sua attività per l'ospedale di Santo Spirito*, in *Studi in onore di Renato Cevese*, edited by G. Beltramini, A. Ghisetti Giavarina and P. Marini, Vicenza 2000, pp. 61-82.

BURNS, HOWARD, *I disegni del Palladio*, in "Bollettino del Centro Internazionale di Studi di Architettura Andrea Palladio", XV, 1973, p. 169.

ID., *Le opere minori del Palladio*, in "Bollettino del Centro Internazionale di Studi di Architettura Andrea Palladio", XXI, 1979, pp. 9-34.

ID., *Suggerimenti per l'identificazione di alcuni progetti e schizzi palladiani*, in "Bollettino del Centro Internazionale di Studi di Architettura Andrea Palladio", XXI, 1979, pp. 113-140.

ID., "A Tomb Designed by Andrea Palladio and an Early Sentimental Attachment of Daniele Barbaro". Talk given at College Art Association Annual Meeting, 12-14 February 1987, abstract published in *Abstracts of the 75th Annual Meeting of the College Art Association of America*, New York 1987.

ID., *Building and Construction in Palladio's Vicenza*, in *Les Chantiers de la Renaissance*, Conference Minutes, Tours 1983-1984, edited by J. Guillaume, Paris 1991, pp. 191-226.

BURROUGHS, CHARLES, *Palladio and Fortune: Notes on the Sources and Meaning of the Villa Rotonda*, in "Architettura", 18, 1988, pp. 59-91.

CALABI, DONATELLA and MORACHIELLO, PAOLO, *Rialto: le fabbriche e il ponte, 1514-1591*, Turin 1987.

CALABI, DONATELLA, *Le chiese di Palladio*, in *Storia dell'architettura italiana. 4. Il secondo Cinquecento*, edited by C. Conforti and R. Tuttle, Milan 2001, pp. 436-453.

CARPEGGIANI, PAOLO, *Testimonianze mantovane per Palladio e la Venezia del tardo Cinquecento*, in *Palladio a Venezia*, edited by L. Puppi, Florence 1982, pp. 139-154.

CARTAGO SCATTAGLIA, GABRIELLA, *Palladio e Bernini scrittori*, in "Bollettino del Centro Internazionale di Studi di Architettura Andrea Palladio", XXIII, 1981, pp. 203-222.

CARUNCHIO, TANCREDI, *Indagini conoscitive sul teatro Olimpico di Vicenza*, in LICISCO MAGAGNATO, *Il teatro Olimpico*, notes and editing by L. Puppi, Milan 1992, pp. 129-138.

CAVAGGIONI, ILARIA and DEL ZOPPO, CINZIA, *Villa Saraceno a Finale di Agugliaro attraverso i documenti e la cartografia*, in "Arte Veneta", 43, 1989-1990, pp. 142-152.

CAVAZZANA ROMANELLI, FRANCESCA, *Palladio ai Frari. Una perizia inedita dall'archivio della Scuola grande di S. Rocco*, in "Bollettino dei civici musei veneziani", XXXII, 174, 1988, pp. 42-47.

CELLAURO, LOUIS, *Palladio e le illustrazioni delle edizioni del 1556 e del 1567 di Vitruvio*, in "Saggi e memorie di storia dell'arte", 22, 1998, pp. 58-128.

ID., *Disegni di Palladio e di Daniele Barbaro nei manoscritti preparatori delle edizioni del 1556 e del 1567 di Vitruvio*, in "Arte Veneta", 56, 2000, pp. 52-63.

ID., *La biblioteca di un architetto del Rinascimento: la raccolta di libri di Giovanni Antonio Rusconi*, in "Arte Veneta", 58, 2003, pp. 224-236.

CEVESE, RENATO, *Appunti palladiani*, in "Bollettino del Centro Internazionale di Studi di Architettura Andrea Palladio", VII, 1965, pp. 305-315.

ID., *L'opera del Palladio*, in *Palladio*, exhibition catalogue, Milan 1980.

ID., *I restauri del 1869 compiuti nella Rotonda*, in "Bollettino del Centro Internazionale di Studi di Architettura Andrea Palladio", XXIV, 1982-1987, pp. 139-143.

ID., *Contributi palladiani*, in "Annali di architettura", 14, 2002, pp. 163-170.

CHASTEL ANDRÉ, *Palladio et l'art des fêtes*, in "Bollettino del Centro Internazionale di Studi di Architettura Andrea Palladio", II/2, 1960, pp. 29-33.

ID., *Palladio et l'éscalier*, in "Bollettino del Centro Internazionale di Studi di Architettura Andrea Palladio", VII/1, 1965, pp. 11-12.

ID., *Le nu de Palladio*, in "Bollettino del Centro Internazionale di Studi di Architettura Andrea Palladio", XXII, 1980, pp. 33-46.

CHIAPPINI DI SORIO, ILEANA, *Palladio e la "Vigna" Pisani del Lido*, in "Notizie da Palazzo Albani", 17/2, 1988, pp. 49-54.

CHOJNACKA, MONICA, *Women, Charity and Community in Early Modern Venice: The Casa delle Zitelle*, in "Renaissance Quaterly", 51, 1998, pp. 68-91.

CICOGNARA, LEOPOLDO, DIEDO, ANTONIO and SELVA, GIANANTONIO, *Le fabbriche e i monumenti più cospicui di Venezia*, edited by F. Zanotto, 2 voll., Venice 1858.

COCKE, RICHARD A., *Barbaro and the Decoration of the Villa Barbaro at Maser*, in "Journal of the Warburg and Courtald Institutes", 35, 1972, pp. 225-246.

CONFORTI, GIUSEPPE, *Miti familiari a autoglorificazione dinastica: Marcantonio Serego, Palladio e la villa di Santa Sofia*, in "Studi Storici Luigi Simenoni", 48, 1998, pp. 43-66.

ID., *Villa Serego a Santa Sofia, Palladio, l'opera rustica e il committente*, in "Arte/Documento", 14, 2000, pp. 95-103.

COOPER, TRACY E., *The History and Decoration of the*

Church of San Giorgio Maggiore in Venice, Ph.D. dissertation, Princeton University 1990, Ann Arbor (Mich.) 1990.

ID., "Locus Meditandi et orandi": Architecture, Liturgy and Identity at San Giorgio Maggiore, in Musica, scienza e idee nella Serenissima durante il Seicento, edited by F. Passadore and F. Rossi, Venice 1996, pp. 79-105.

CORBOZ, ANDRÉ, Per un'analisi psicologica della villa palladiana, in "Bollettino del Centro Internazionale di Studi di Architettura Andrea Palladio", XV, 1973, p. 253.

ID., Contributo all'urbanistica palladiana: la pianta di Hochelaga (1556) quale progetto del club Barbaro, in Palladio: ein Symposium, edited by K. Forster and M. Kubelik, Rome 1980, pp. 57-70.

CORSINI, LOREDANA, Villa Zeno di Palladio a Cessalto, in "Atti dell'Istituto Veneto di Scienze, Lettere e Arti", 155, 1996-1997, pp. 117-159.

DALLA POZZA, ANTONIO, Elementi e motivi ricorrenti in A. Palladio, in "Bollettino del Centro Internazionale di Studi di Architettura Andrea Palladio", VII, 1965, pp. 43-58.

DAMERINI, GINO, L'isola e il cenobio di San Giorgio Maggiore, Venice 1956.

DE ANGELIS D'OSSAT, GUGLIELMO, Un palazzo veneziano progettato da Palladio, in "Palladio", 4, 1956, pp. 158-161.

ID., Bramante e Palladio, in "Bollettino del Centro Internazionale di Studi di Architettura Andrea Palladio", VIII/2, 1966, pp. 34-42.

ID., I Sangallo e Palladio, in "Bollettino del Centro Internazionale di Studi di Architettura Andrea Palladio", VIII/2, 1966, pp. 43-51.

ID., Palladio rivisitato, in "Bollettino del Centro Internazionale di Studi di Architettura Andrea Palladio", XXII, 1985, pp. 9-32.

DE GREGORIO, M. L., Finale di Agugliaro, villa Saraceno e terre di proprietà del conte Angelo Caldogno (entry no. 3); Caldogno, case e terre del conte Girolamo Caldogno (entry no. 10), in L'immagine del Veneto. Il territorio nella cartografia di ieri e di oggi, edited by P. L. Fantelli, Padua 1994, pp. 96-110.

D'EVELYN, MARGARET, Venice and Vitruvio's City in Daniele Barbaro's Commentaries, in "Studi veneziani", 32, 1996, pp. 83-104.

FAGIOLO, MARCELLO, Il contributo all'interpretazione dell'ermetismo in Palladio, in "Bollettino del Centro Internazionale di Studi di Architettura Andrea Palladio", XIV, 1972, pp. 357-380.

FANCELLI, PAOLO, Palladio e Preneste. Archeologia, modelli, progettazione, Rome 1974.

FEINSTEIN, DIEGO HORACIO, Palladio und das Problem der musikalischen Proportionen in Architektur, in Aureger durch Vier Jahrunderte: Palladio, in "Freiburger Universitätblätter", 1988, pp. 39-52.

FIOCCO, GIUSEPPE, Andrea Palladio padovano, in "Annuario dell'Università di Padova", 1932-1933, pp. 31-39.

ID., L'esposizione dei disegni di A. Palladio, in "Arte Veneta", 1949, p. 184.

FORSSMAN, ERIK, Palladio and Daniele Barbaro, in "Bollettino del Centro Internazionale di Studi di Architettura Andrea Palladio", VIII/2, 1966, pp. 68-81.

ID., Falconetto e Palladio, in "Bollettino del Centro Internazionale di Studi di Architettura Andrea Palladio", VIII/2, 1966, pp. 52-67.

ID., Il palazzo da Porto-Festa di Vicenza, in "Corpus Palladianum", vol. VIII, Vicenza 1973.

ID., Visible Harmony: Palladio's Villa Foscari at Malcontenta, [Stockholm] 1973.

FORSTER, KURT W., Is Palladio's Rotonda an Architectural Novelty?, in Palladio: ein Symposium, edited by K. W. Forster and M. Kubelik, Rome 1980.

FOSCARI, ANTONIO, Per Palladio: note sul Redentore a San Vidal e sulle Zitelle, in "Antichità viva", 14, 1975, pp. 44-56.

ID., Ricerche sugli "Accesi" e su "questo benedetto theatro" costruito da Palladio in Venezia nel 1565, in "Notizie da Palazzo Albani", 8, 1979, pp. 68-83.

ID., Palladio a Feltre: "Accordo per la facciata di S. Pietro di Castello in Venezia". Tre appunti veneziani per Palladio, in Contributi su Andrea Palladio nel quarto centenario della morte (1580-1980), Venice 1982, pp. 57-78.

FOSCARI, ANTONIO and TAFURI, MANFREDO, L'armonia e i conflitti: la chiesa di San Francesco della Vigna nella Venezia del '500, Turin 1983.

FOSCARI, ANTONIO, Un dibattito sul foro marciano allo scadere del 1577 e il progetto di Andrea Palladio per il Palazzo Ducale di Venezia, in Saggi in onore di Guglielmo De Angelis d'Ossat, in "Quaderni dell'Istituto di storia dell'architettura", n.s., 1/10, 1983-1987, pp. 323-332.

FRANK, MARTINA, Il luogo delle Zitelle: segni e forme di un pensiero palladiano, in Le Zitelle: architettura, arte e storia di un'istituzione veneziana, edited by L. Puppi, Venice 1992, pp. 97-128.

ID., Un committente ungherese di Andrea Palladio, in "Il Veltro", 37, 1-2, 1993, pp. 27-34.

FROMMEL, CHRISTOPH, Palladio e la chiesa di San Pietro a Roma, in "Bollettino del Centro Internazionale di Studi di Architettura Andrea Palladio", XIX, 1977, pp. 107-124.

GABOR, HAJNOCZI, Palladio e San Carlo Borromeo, in "Bollettino del Centro Internazionale di Studi di Architettura Andrea Palladio", XXII, 1980, pp. 205-211.

GARDANI, DANTE, La chiesa di S. Maria della Presentazione (delle Zitelle) a Venezia, Venice 1961.

GHISETTI GIAVARINA, ADRIANO, Palladio "minore"? La casa del notaio Cogollo a Vicenza, in "Opus". Quaderno di Storia dell'architettura e Restauro dell'Università di Chieti, 2, 1990, pp. 71-76.

ID., Andrea Palladio e le antichità della Campania, in "Napoli Nobilissima", 36, 1997, pp. 207-214.

GLOTON, JEAN-JACQUES, Vignola et Palladio, in "Bollettino del Centro Internazionale di Studi di Architettura Andrea Palladio", VIII, 1966, pp. 82-100.

GOEDICKE, CHRISTIAN, SLUSALLEK, KLAUS and KUBELIK, MARTIN, Primi risultati sulla datazione di alcune ville palladiane grazie alla termoluminescenza, in "Bollettino del Centro Internazionale di Studi di Architettura Andrea Palladio", XXII/1, 1980, pp. 97-118.

GROS, PIERRE and BELTRAMINI, GUIDO, Il ponte di Cesare sul Reno, in John Soane e i ponti in legni svizzeri. Architettura e cultura tecnica da Palladio ai Grubenmann, exhibition catalogue, Mendrisio-Vicenza 2002, pp. 162-189.

GUALDO, PAOLO, Vita di Andrea Palladio, edited by G. Zorzi, in "Saggi e memoria di storia dell'arte", 2, 1958-1959, pp. 93-104.

GUERRA, ANDREA, Quel che resta di Palladio. Eredità e dispersione dei progetti per la chiesa di San Giorgio Maggiore a Venezia, in "Annali di architettura", 13, 2001, pp. 93-110.

ID., Movable Façades: Palladio's Plan for the Church of San Giorgio Maggiore in Venice and Its Successive Vicissitudes, in "Journal of the Society of Architectural Historians", 61, 2002, pp. 276-295.

GUIOTTO, MARIO, Recenti restauri di edifici palladiani, in "Bollettino del Centro Internazionale di Studi di Architettura Andrea Palladio», IV, 1964, pp. 70-88.

HALE, JOHN R. (edited by), Renaissance Venice, London 1973.

ID., Andrea Palladio. Polybius and Julius Caesar, in "Journal of the Warburg and Courtauld Institute", 40, 1977, pp. 240-255.

HARRIS, J., Three Unrecorded Palladio Designs from Inigo Jones' Collection, in "The Burlington Magazine", 1971, pp. 34-37.

HOFER, PAUL, Palladios Erstling: Die Villa Godi Valmarana in Lonedo bei Vicenza, Basel-Stockholm 1969.

HOWARD, DEBORAH and LONGAIR, MALCOM, Harmonic Proportion in Palladio's Quattro Libri, in

"Journal of the Society of Architectural Historians", 41, 4, 1982, pp. 116/143.

HOWARD, DEBORAH, *La Scuola Grande della Misericordia di Venezia e appendice documentaria*, in *La Scuola Grande della Misericordia di Venezia: storia e progetto*, edited by G. Fabbri, with P. Piffaretti, Milan 1999, pp. 13/70.

ID., *Venice between East and West: Marc'Antonio Barbaro and Palladio's Church of the Redentore*, in "Journal of the Society of Architectural Historians", 62, 2003, pp. 306/325.

HUSE, NORBERT, *Palladio und die Villa Barbaro in Maser: Bemerkungen zum Problem der Autorschaft*, in "Arte Veneta", 28, 1974, pp. 106/122.

ID., *Palladio am Grand Canal*, in "Städel Jahrbuch", 7, 1979, pp. 61/99.

INGLOTT, PETER, *Appunti sulla chiesa palladiana: il rapporto tra stile, simbolismo e funzionalità*, in "Arte cristiana", 70, 1980, pp. 153/168.

ISERMEYER, CHRISTIAN-ADOLF, *Le chiese di Palladio in rapporto al culto*, in "Bollettino del Centro Internazionale di Studi di Architettura Andrea Palladio", X, 1968, pp. 42/58.

ID., *La concezione degli edifici sacri palladiani*, in "Bollettino del Centro Internazionale di Studi di Architettura Andrea Palladio", XIV, 1972, pp. 105/135.

ID., *I commentari di G. Cesare nell'edizione palladiana del 1575 e i suoi precedenti*, in "Bollettino del Centro Internazionale di Studi di Architettura Andrea Palladio", XXI, 1979, pp. 253/272.

ID., *Il primo progetto del Palladio per S. Giorgio secondo il modello del 1565*, in "Bollettino del Centro Internazionale di Studi di Architettura Andrea Palladio", XXII, 1980, pp. 259/268.

KOLB, CAROLYN, *New Evidence for the Villa Pisani at Montagnana*, in *Interpretazioni veneziane: studi di storia dell'arte in memoria di Michelangelo Muraro*, edited by D. Rosand, Venice 1984, 227/239.

KUBELIK, MARTIN, *Per una lettura del secondo libro di Andrea Palladio*, in "Bollettino del Centro Internazionale di Studi di Architettura Andrea Palladio", XXI, 1979, pp. 177/197.

ID., *The Basilica Palladiana and the Loggia del Capitaniato: An Architectural and Socio-historical Confrontation*, in *Palladio: ein Symposium*, edited by K. Forster and M. Kubelik, Rome 1980, pp. 47/56.

ID., *Palladio's Villas in the Tradition of the Veneto Farm*, in "Assemblage", October, 1986, pp. 91/115.

LEHMANN JACOBSEN, MAJA, *Das Bildprogramm der Villa Godi in Lonedo di Lugo*, Cologne 1996.

LEONARDI, M., *Nuovi documenti sulla demolita chiesa di Santa Lucia a Venezia*, in "Atti dell'Istituto Veneto di Scienze, Lettere e Arti", 145, 1985/1986, pp. 165/172.

LEWIS, DOUGLAS, *La datazione della villa Corner a Piombino Dese*, in "Bollettino del Centro Internazionale di Studi di Architettura Andrea Palladio", XIV, 1972, pp. 381/393.

ID., *Disegni autografi del Palladio non pubblicati: le piante per Caldogno e Maser, 1548/1549*, in "Bollettino del Centro Internazionale di Studi di Architettura Andrea Palladio", XV, 1973, pp. 369/379.

ID., *A New Book of Drawings by Francesco Muttoni*, in "Arte Veneta", 30, 1976, pp. 132/146.

ID., *Il significato della decorazione plastica e pittorica a Maser*, in "Bollettino del Centro Internazionale di Studi di Architettura Andrea Palladio", XXII, 1980, pp. 203/213.

ID., *Palladio's Painted Architecture*, in *Vierhundert Andrea Palladio* [lecture in Wuppertal, 1980], Heidelberg 1982, pp. 59/74.

LOTZ, WOLFGANG, *Riflessioni sul tema "Palladio urbanista"*, in "Bollettino del Centro Internazionale di Studi di Architettura Andrea Palladio", VIII, 1966, pp. 123/127.

ID., *Palladio e Sansovino*, in "Bollettino del Centro Internazionale di Studi di Architettura Andrea Palladio", IX, 1967, pp. 13/23.

ID., *Ricostruzioni dei teatri antichi nei disegni del Cinquecento*, in *L'architettura teatrale dall'epoca greca a Palladio*, in "Bollettino del Centro Internazionale di Studi di Architettura Andrea Palladio", XVI, 1974, pp. 9/34, 139/140.

ID., *Architecture in Italy, 1500/1600*, introduction by D. Howard, New Haven/London 1995, revised edition.

LUNARDON, SILVIA, *Ancora ipotesi sull'altare palladiano dell'Ospedaletto*, in *Per l'arte da Venezia all'Europa*, Venice 2001, pp. 203/212.

MAGAGNATO, LICISCO, *Il teatro Olimpico*, notes and editing by L. Puppi, Milan 1992.

MAGRINI, ANTONIO, *Il palazzo del Museo Civico di Vicenza descritto ed illustrato*, Vicenza 1855.

MANNO, ANTONIO, *Un magazzino di Andrea Palladio nell'Arsenale di Venezia*, in "Casabella", 49, 514, 1985, pp. 30/33.

MANTESE, GIOVANNI, *Montano IV Barbarano committente del palladiano palazzo Barbaran da Porto*, in "Bollettino del Centro Internazionale di Studi di Architettura Andrea Palladio", XXII/1, 1980, pp. 147/157.

ID., *Paolo Almerico committente della Rotonda*, in *La Rotonda*, Milan 1988, pp. 33/36.

MARCADELLA, GIOVANNI, *Caldogno, palazzo dei conti Vincenzo e Angelo Caldogno* (entry no. 11), in *L'immagine del Veneto. Il territorio nella cartografia di ieri e di oggi*, edited by P. L. Fantelli, Padua 1994, p. 112.

MAROTTI, FERRUCCIO, *Teoria e tecnica dello spazio scenico dal Serlio al Palladio nella trattatistica rinascimentale*, in *L'architettura teatrale dall'epoca greca a Palladio*, in "Bollettino del Centro Internazionale di Studi di Architettura Andrea Palladio", XVI, 1974, pp. 257/270.

MASELLI CAMPAGNA, MARCELLA, *Villa Chiericati a Vancimuglio*, in "Opus". Quaderno di Storia dell'architettura e Restauro dell'Università di Chieti, 6, 1999, pp. 83/128.

MAZZONI, STEFANO, *L'Olimpico di Vicenza: un teatro e la sua "perpetua memoria"*, Florence 1998.

ID., *Fonti e metodi per la storia del Teatro Olimpico di Vicenza e dello "Stanzone delle Commedie" di Livorno*, in *Omaggio a Lionello Puppi*, II, in "Venezia Cinquecento", 11, 22, July-December 2001, pp. 89/100.

MITROVIC, BRANKO, *Palladio's Theory of Proportions and Second Book of the "Quattro libri dell'Architettura"*, in "Journal of the Society of Architectural Historians", 49, 1990, pp. 279/292.

ID., *Paduan Aristotelism and Daniele Barbaro's Commentary on Vitruvius "De Architectura"*, in "Sixteenth Century Journal", 29, 3, 1998, pp. 667/688.

MONTENARI, GIOVANNI, *Del Teatro Olimpico di Andrea Palladio in Vicenza*, Padua 1749.

MURARO, MICHELANGELO, *Palazzo Chiericati "villa marittima"*, in "Arte Veneta", 32, 1978, pp. 187/194.

ID., *La villa palladiana dei Repeta a Campiglia dei Berici*, in G. MARASCO and M. MURARO, *Campiglia dei Berici*, Campiglia dei Berici 1981.

MURRAY, PETER, *Palladio's Churches*, in *Arte in Europa: scritti di storia dell'arte in onore di Edoardo Arslan*, edited by G. C. Argan et al., Milan 1966, vol. I, pp. 597/608.

MUTTONI, FRANCESCO ANTONIO, *Architettura di Andrea Palladio ... di nuovo ristampata. E di figure in rame ...arricchita ...con le osservazioni dell'Architetto N. N.*, 8 volumes in IV, Venice, 1740/1748.

NIERO, ANTONIO, *I templi del Redentore e della Salute: motivazioni teologiche*, in *Venezia e la peste, 1348/1797*, exhibition catalogue, Venice 1979, pp. 294/298.

ID., *Spiritualità popolare e dotta*, in *La Chiesa di Venezia nel Seicento, Contributi alla storia della chiesa di Venezia 5*, edited by B. Bertoli, Venice 1992, pp. 253/290.

OECHSLIN, WERNER, *"C'est du Palladio": un avvicinamento al fenomeno del palladianesimo*, in *Palladio nel Nord Europa*, exhibition catalogue, Milan 1999, pp. 64/91.

PALLUCCHINI, RODOLFO, *Andrea Palladio e Giulio Romano*, in "Bollettino del Centro Internazionale di Studi di Architettura Andrea Palladio", I, 1959, pp. 38/44.

PAVAN, GIANFRANCO, *La Rocchetta di Vicenza in un*

disegno del Palladio e in un suo recente rilievo, in "Castellum", 31, 1981, pp. 51-55.

PERESWET SOLTAN, ANDRZEI, *Il restauro di villa Pisani, ora Ferri, a Bagnolo*, in "Bollettino del Centro Internazionale di Studi di Architettura Andrea Palladio", XX, 1978, pp. 283-296.

PIANA, MARIO, *Il convento della Carità: materiali, tecniche, strutture*, in "Annali di architettura", 10-11, 1998-1999, pp. 310-321.

PIEPER, JAN, *Palladiobrücken / Palladian Bridges*, in "Daidalos", 57, 1995, pp. 89-93.

PIOVENE, GUIDO, *Trissino e Palladio nell'Umanesimo vicentino*, in "Bollettino del Centro Internazionale di Studi di Architettura Andrea Palladio", V, 1963, pp. 13-23.

PIZZIGONI, VITTORIO, *I tre progetti di Palladio per il Redentore*, in "Annali di architettura", 15, 2003, pp. 165-177.

POGGENDORF, GABRIELE, *Palladios Villa Emo in Fanzolo. Hemorum Origo. Zur Ikonographie der Fresken von Giambattista Zelotti*, Berlin 1995.

PUPPI, LIONELLO, *Il Teatro Olimpico*, Vicenza 1963.

ID., *La Villa Badoer a Fratta Polesine*, in "Corpus Palladianum", vol. VII, Vicenza 1972.

ID. (edited by), *Architettura e utopia nella Venezia del Cinquecento*, Milan 1980.

ID., *Palladio e il Palladianesimo*, in "Bollettino del Centro Internazionale di Studi di Architettura Andrea Palladio", XXVII, 1980, pp. 67-75.

ID., *Palladio in cantiere*, in *Palladio: ein Symposium*, edited by K. Forster and M. Kubelik, Rome 1980, pp. 13-26.

ID. (edited by), *Le Venezie possibili*, Milan 1985.

ID., *Modelli di Palladio, modelli palladiani*, in "Rassegna", 32, 1987, pp. 20-28.

ID., *Palladio e Leonardo Mocenigo. Un palazzo a Padova. Una villa "per un ...sito sopra la Brenta"; e una questione di metodo*, in *Klassizismus, Epoche e Problemi. Festschrift für Erik Forssman zum 70. Geburtstag*, edited by J. Meyer zur Capellen and G. Oberreuter-Kronabel, Hildesheim-Zurich-New York 1987, pp. 336-362.

ID., *Palladio teorico giudica Tibaldi*, in "Arte lombarda", 94-95, 1990, pp. 100-104.

ID., *Le Zitelle: architettura, arte e storia di un'istituzione veneziana*, Venice 1992.

ID., *"Presso a Bassano... ho ordinato il ponte di legnale". Vera gloria e un'ambiguità di Andrea Palladio?*, in *Il ponte di Bassano*, Vicenza 1993, pp. 35-63.

ID., *Palladio e il "cavalier Lione"*, in *Leone Leoni tra Lombardia e Spagna*, Conference Minutes, edited by M. L. Gatti Perer, Milan 1994, pp. 69-74.

ID., *Palladio e Pirro Ligorio*, in *Napoli, l'Europa. Ricerche di storia dell'arte in onore di Ferdinando Bologna*, edited by F. Abbate and F. Sricchia Santoro, Catanzaro 1995, pp. 169-175.

ID., *Il Teatro Olimpico come architettura tragica. Un'ipotesi di metodo*, in "Arte/Documento", 13, 1999, pp. 243-253.

ID., *Lo stemma di Palladio*, in *Per l'arte da Venezia all'Europa*, Venice 2001, pp. 197-202.

RAY, STEFANO, *Integrità e ambiguità: note per una critica palladiana*, in *Palladio: ein Symposium*, edited by K. Forster and M. Kubelik, Rome 1980, pp. 35-46.

ID., *Palladio e le radici del Rinascimento nel Veneto*, in ID., *Lo specchio del cosmo. Da Brunelleschi a Palladio: itinerario dell'architettura nel Rinascimento*, Rome 1991, pp. 137-147.

RINALDI, ALESSANDRO, *Tra "locus" e testo: villa Badoer nei "Quattro Libri" di Andrea Palladio*, in "Qasar", 1, 1989, pp. 23-30.

RIGON, FERNANDO (edited by), *I ponti di Palladio*, Milan 1980.

ROSE, PAUL, *Jacomo Contarini (1536-1595): A Venetian Patron and Collector of Mathematical Instruments and Books*, in "Physis", 18, 1976, pp. 117-130.

RYKWERT, JOSEPH, *Palladio chiese veneziane / Venetian Church Façades*, in "Domus", 609, 1980, pp. 28-31.

SACCARDO, MARIO, *Il perfezionamento della Rotonda promosso da Odorico e Mario Capra (1591-1619)*, in "Bollettino del Centro Internazionale di Studi di Architettura Andrea Palladio", XXIV, 1982-1987, pp. 161-209.

SALMON, FRANK, *Eighteenth-Century Alterations in Palladio's Villa Rotonda*, in "Annali di architettura", 7, 1995, pp. 177-181.

SANSOVINO, FRANCESCO, *Venetia città nobilissima et singolare*, edited by L. Moretti, Venice 1968 (first edition, Venice 1581).

SARTORI, M., *Il viaggio a Trento di Andrea Palladio*, in *I Madruzzo e l'Europa 1539-1658. I principi vescovi di Trento tra Papato e Impero*, edited by L. Dal Prà, Florence 1993, pp. 523-519.

SCHMIED-HARTMANN, PETRA, *Die Dekoration von Palladios Villa Poiana*, Munich 1997.

SELVATICO, PIETRO, *Vicenza. Palazzo della Ragione detto la Basilica*, in *Monumenti artistici e storici delle Province Venete...*, Milan 1859.

SEMENZATO, CAMILLO, *La Rotonda di Vicenza*, Vicenza 1968.

SGARBI, VITTORIO, *Palladio e la Maniera*, exhibition catalogue, Milan 1980.

SICCA, CINZIA MARIA, *La fortuna della Rotonda*, in *La Rotonda*, Milan 1988, pp. 169-204.

SINDING-LARSEN, STAALE, *Palladio's Redentore: A Compromise in Composition*, in "Art Bulletin", 47, 1965, pp. 419-437.

SPIELMANN, HEINZ, *Andrea Palladio und die Antike*, Munich-Berlin 1966.

SVEDEBORG, J. J., *Palladio, matematiken och instrumenten*, in "Konsthistorisk tidskrift", 52, 1983, pp. 7-14.

TAFURI, MANFREDO, *Committenza e tipologia delle ville palladiane*, in "Bollettino del Centro Internazionale di Studi di Architettura Andrea Palladio", XI, 1969, pp. 120-136.

ID., *Venezia e il Rinascimento. Religione, scienza, architettura*, Turin 1985.

TESSAROLO, ANNALISA, *Socrate, Alvise Cornaro, Andrea Palladio... virtù dell'agricoltura nella tradizione economica*, in "Studi Veneziani", n.s., 30, 1995, pp. 153-165.

TESSAROLO ROSSI, ANNALISA, *Battista Zelotti: Concordia maritale ed Economia a Villa Emo a Fanzolo*, in "Arte/Documento", 11, 1997, pp. 98-101.

TIMOFIEWITSCH, WLADIMIR, *Eine Zeichnung Andrea Palladios für Klosteranlage von S. Giorgio Maggiore*, in "Arte Veneta", 16, 1962, pp. 160-163.

ID., *Eine neuerbautrag zu der Baugeschicte von San Giorgio Maggiore*, in "Bollettino del Centro Internazionale di Studi di Architettura Andrea Palladio", V, 1963, pp. 330-339.

ID., *La Chiesa del Redentore*, in "Corpus Palladianum", vol. III, Vicenza 1969.

ID., *Delle chiese palladiane: alcune osservazioni in rapporto alle facciate*, in "Bollettino del Centro Internazionale di Studi di Architettura Andrea Palladio", XXII, 1980, pp. 237-246.

TOMMASI, F., *Antichi e recenti interventi edilizi di restauro in villa Serego a Santa Sofia di Pedemonte*, in "Annuario Storico della Valpolicella", 1999-2000, pp. 81-108.

ID., *Il progetto di Andrea Palladio per villa Serego di Santa Sofia di Pedemonte*, in "Annuario Storico della Valpolicella", 1999-2000, pp. 125-148.

VALENTINO, D. A., *Palazzo Pretorio: edificio palladiano di Cividale*, in "Forum Julii", 14, 1990, pp. 25-29.

VAN DER SMAN, GERT JAN, *L'iconologia nella villa veneta del Cinquecento: l'esempio di Villa Emo*, in "Storia dell'Arte", 71, 1991, pp. 37-58.

VERLATO, A., *Progetti per Villa Arnaldi a Meleto*, in *Decimo e undicesimo incontro in ricordo di Michelangelo Muraro*, 15 May 2001 and 2002, edited by G. Menin Muraro and D. Puppulin, Sossano 2003, pp. 81-90.

WITTKOWER, RUDOLF, *L'influenza del Palladio sullo sviluppo dell'architettura veneziana del Seicento*, in "Bollettino del Centro Internazionale di Studi di Architettura Andrea Palladio", V, 1963, pp. 61-72.

ID., *Principi architettonici nell'età dell'Umanesimo*, Turin 1964.

WOLTERS, WOLFGANG, *Andrea Palladio e la decorazione*

dei suoi edifici, in "Bollettino del Centro Internazionale di Studi di Architettura Andrea Palladio", X, 1968, pp. 255-267.

ID., *Le architetture erette al Lido per l'ingresso a Venezia di Enrico II nel 1574*, in "Bollettino del Centro Internazionale di Studi di Architettura Andrea Palladio", XXI, 1979, pp. 273-289.

ID., *Le perizie sulla ricostruzione del Palazzo dopo l'incendio del 20 dicembre 1577*, in *Palazzo Ducale: storia e restauri*, edited by G. Romanelli, Verona 2004, pp. 193-204.

ZAUPA, GIOVANNI, *Origine e scomparsa del Palazzo Piovene all'Isola di Vicenza*, in "Odeo Olimpico", 17-18, 1981-1982, pp. 79-113.

ID., *I committenti vicentini di Andrea Palladio*, in *Storia di Vicenza*, edited by F. Barbieri and P. Preto, Vicenza 1990, vol. III/2, pp. 311-325.

ID., *L'origine del "Palladio". Andrea di Pietro della Gondola da Padova a Vicenza e il Rinascimento Veneto*, Padua 1990.

ZAVATTA, GIULIO, *La perizia di demolizione di villa Serego alla Miega*, in "Annali di architettura", 16, 2004, pp. 153-168.

ZEVI, BRUNO, *Palladio*, in *Enciclopedia Universale dell'Arte*, vol. X, Rome 1963, cll. 438-458.

ID., *Michelangelo e Palladio*, in "Bollettino del Centro Internazionale di Studi di Architettura Andrea Palladio", VI, 1964, pp. 13-28.

ZOCCA, MARIO, *Le concezioni urbanistiche di Palladio*, in "Palladio", 1960, pp. 67-83.

ZOCCONI, MARIO, *Il Palladio nel processo produttivo del Cinquecento veneto*, in "Bollettino del Centro Internazionale di Studi di Architettura Andrea Palladio", XX, 1978, pp. 171-201.

ZORZI, GIANGIORGIO, *Nuove rivelazioni sulla ricostruzione delle sale del piano nobile del Palazzo Ducale di Venezia dopo l'incendio del maggio 1574*, in "Arte Veneta", 7, 1953, pp. 123-151.

ID., *Progetti giovanili di Andrea Palladio per palazzo e case in Venezia e terraferma*, in "Palladio", n.s., 4, 1954, pp. 105-121.

ID., *Il contributo di Andrea Palladio e Francesco Zamberlan al restauro di Palazzo Ducale di Venezia dopo l'incendio del 20 dicembre 1577*, in "Atti dell'Istituto Veneto di Scienze, Lettere e Arti", 115, 1956-1957, pp. 10-68.

ID., *L'abside della cattedrale Vicenza e il contributo di Andrea Palladio al suo compimento*, in *Studi in onore di Federico M. Mistrorigo*, Vicenza 1958, pp. 271-310.

ID., *La famiglia di Palladio secondo nuovi documenti*, in "Archivio veneto", s. 5, 70, 1962, pp. 15-54.

ID., *Domenico Groppino di Musso. Un altro architetto lombardo vicentino imitatore del Palladio*, in "Arte lombarda", 2, 1963, pp. 114-146.

ID., *Quattro monumenti sepolcrali disegnati da Andrea Palladio*, in "Arte Veneta", 27, 1963, pp. 96-103.

ID., *Urbanistica palladiana*, in "Bollettino del Centro Internazionale di Studi di Architettura Andrea Palladio", IX, 1967, pp. 168-184.

ID., *La datazione delle ville palladiane*, in "Bollettino del Centro Internazionale di Studi di Architettura Andrea Palladio", XI, 1969, pp. 137-162.

BOOKS BY ANDREA PALLADIO

L'antichità di Roma, Rome 1554.

Descritione de le Chiese, Stationi, Indulgenze & Reliquie de Corpi Sancti, che sonno in la Citta de Roma, Rome 1554.

Le Chiese di Roma (1554), introduction and indexes edited by L. Puppi, Vicenza 2000.

L'antichità di Roma, Venice 1555.

I quattro libri di architettura di Andrea Palladio. Ne' quali, dopo un breue trattato de' cinque ordini, & di quelli auertimenti, che sono piu necessarij nel fabricare, in Venetia, appresso a Dominico de' Franceschi, 1570.

I Commentari di C. Giulio Cesare, con le figure in rame de gli Allogiamenti, de' fatti d'arme, delle circonvallatione delle città, & di molte altre cose notabili scritte in essi, Venice 1574.

BERTOTTI SCAMOZZI, OTTAVIO, *Le terme dei Romani disegnate da Andrea Palladio: e ripublicate con la giunta di alcune osservazioni di Ottavio Bertotti Scamozzi, giusta l'esemplare del lord co. di Burlingthon impresso in Londra l'anno 1732*, Vicenza 1785.

ID., *Le fabbriche e i disegni di Andrea Palladio: raccolti ed illustrati da Ottavio Bertotti Scamozzi*, 4 volumes in I, Vicenza 1786.

The Four Books of Architecture, introduction by A. Placzek, New York 1965 (first edition London, 1738).

I Quattro Libri dell'architettura [1570], Trattati di architettura 6, "Classici italiani di scienze tecniche e arti", edited by L. Magagnato and P. Marini, Milan 1980.

Andrea Palladio: scritti sull'architettura (1554-1579), edited by L. Puppi, Vicenza 1988.

The Four Books on Architecture, translation by R. Tavernor and R. Schofield, Cambridge (Mass.) 1997.

VITRUVIUS POLLIO, MARCUS, *I dieci libri dell'architettura di M. Vitruvio, tradotti et commentati da Monsignor Barbaro eletto patriarca d'Aquileggia*, Venice 1556 (illustrations by Andrea Palladio).

ID., *De architectura libri decem, cum commentariis Danielis Barbari, electi Patriarchae Aquileiensis, multis aedificiorum, horologiorum, et machinarum descriptionibus, et figuris*, Venice 1567.

ID., *I dieci libri dell'architettura di M. Vitruvio, tradotti et commentati da Daniele Barbaro 1567*, with an essay by Manfredo Tafuri and a study by Manuela Morresi, Milan 1987.

Index of names

The numbers correspond to the pages, the letter n to the notes and the italics to the captions.

Ackerman, James S. 8, 17, 145, 160n, 240n.
Alberti, Leandro 233.
Alberti, Leon Battista 96, 116, 155, 177, 206, 225, 230, 239.
Alidosio, Francesco 227.
Alidosio, Rizzardo 9, 227.
Allegradonna (Maragon) 9, 14.
Almerico, Paolo 13, 96, 233.
Angarano, family 17, 227.
Angarano, Giacomo 13.
Apelles of Kos 11.
Appio Claudio Crasso 18.
Argan, Giulio Carlo 8, 89, 233.
Aristotle 26, 35, 115.
Arnaldi, family 227.
Arnaldi, Vincenzo 13, 155.
Assunto, Rosario 8, 96, 96n.
Bach, Johann Sebastian 160.
Barbarano, family 21.
Barbaro, brothers 12, 151.
Barbaro, Daniele 11, 12, 13, 23, 27, 28, 92, 95, 113, 115, 149, *152*, 155, 159, 177, 183, *238*, 239.
Barbaro, Marcantonio 12, 26, 27, 123, 148.
Barbieri, Franco 8.
Bassano, brothers 17.
Bassi, Martino 23.
Battilotti, Donata 160n.
Battisti, Eugenio 179, 184n.
Beazzano, Agostino 151.
Beccanuvoli, Lucrezio 10.
Belli, Silvio 179, 184n.
Bernini, Gian Lorenzo 28, 31, 91, 154, 160.
Bertotti Scamozzi, Ottavio 39, 40n, *118*, *123*, 151, *152*, 155, 159, 179.
Betz, Maurice 240n.
Bilodeau, Denis 40n.
Borromeo, Carlo 23, 27, 40n.
Borromini, Francesco Castelli *called* 7, 28, 38, 154, 201, 230.
Boucher, Brucer 96, 96n.
Boullée, Étienne-Luois 26, 145, 201.
Bramante, Donato di Pascuccio di Antonio *called* 11, 21, 34, 35, 89, 90, 115, 116, 123, 145, 201, 202, 207.
Brandi, Cesare 113.
Briseux, Charles-Étienne *182*, 183.
Burns, Howard 8, 31, *39*, 40n.
Caesar, Gaius Julius 14, 39, 201.
Calabi, Donatella 27, 40n.
Caldogno, family 17.
Camera, Alessandro 13.
Canaletto, Giovanni Antonio Canal *called* il 28, *231*.
Canera, Anselmo 151.

Capra, Antonio Giovanni 35.
Capra, family 21, 227.
Caramuel, Juan *238*.
Cavazza, Bartolomeo 9.
Ceredi, Giuseppe 13.
Cessi, Roberto 240n.
Cevese, Renato 8, 128n, 202, 208n.
Chastel, André 145, 160n, 208.
Chiappini, Paolo 155.
Chiericati, family 11, 227.
Cicero, Marcus Tullius 225.
Civena, family 227.
Comisso, Giovanni 235, 240n.
Connors, Joseph 230, 240n.
Contarini, Jacopo 13.
Corboz, Andrè 17, 19, 40n, *237*, *238*, 240, 240n.
Cornaro, Alvise 10, 225.
Countess Foscari, Barbara Del Vicario *called* 202.
Curio, Gaius Scribonius 159.
Da Porto, Iseppo, family 21.
Dalla Fede, Giambattista 12.
Dalla Pozza, Antonio Marco 8.
De Angelis d'Ossat, Guglielmo 8, 96n.
De' Franceschi, Domenico 13, 14.
De Monte, Count 155.
De Poli, Dino 8.
Del Moro, Battista 151.
Della Gondola, Pietro *called* 9, 177.
Di Giorgio, Francesco 116, 230.
Di Pepolli, Giovan 154, 177.
Diedo, Vincenzo 230.
Donatello, Donato di Niccolò di Betto Bardi *called* 123.
Doni, Anton Francesco 13.
Dortelata, Neri 115.
Durand, Jean-Nicolas-Louis 35.
Eliot, Thomas Stearns 8.
Emanuele Filiberto of Savoy 11, 13.
Ercadi, Maria 8.
Fagiolo, Marcello 8, 17, 148, 160n, 233.
Ficino, Marsilio 115, 116, 128n.
Filippini, family 154.
Fiocco, Giuseppe 124, 128n.
Forster, Kurt W. 240n.
Foscari, Tonci 8, 202.
Francis I of France, King 207.
Franco, Battista 149.
Frommel, Christoph Luitpold 8, 33, 96, 96n.
Frommel, Sabine 8.
Gallo, Agostino 18, 40n.
Gaudet, Julien 180.
Gazzotti, family 17, 227.
Gazzotti, Taddeo 9.

Gesualdo da Venosa, Carlo 179.
Giallo Fiorentino 149.
Gibbs, James 28.
Giedion, Sigfried 113, 128n.
Gilly, Friedrich 145.
Giovanni di san Bonaventura, Brother 201.
Giovanni di Giacomo da Porlezza 9, 11.
Godi, family 11, 17, 227, 239.
Godi, Ludovico 9.
Goedicke, Christian 240n.
Goethe, Johann Wolfgang 9, 12, 15, 147, 160n, 209.
Grandi, Vincenzo 9.
Gualdo, family 227.
Gualdo, Paolo 10, 11, 201.
Harris, John 128, 128n.
Heidegger, Martin 235, 240n.
Henry III of France (Orleans), King 14, 28, 154.
Hesse, Herman 90.
Hofer, Paul 180, 184n.
Horace, Quintus Flaccus 225.
Howard, Deborah 179, 184n.
Indemio, Giovanni 151.
India, Bernardino 39, 151, *193*.
Jefferson, Thomas 230.
Jones, Inigo 28.
Kahn, Louis 205.
Kent, William 28.
Kubelik, Martin 240n.
Laugier, Marc-Antoine 145.
Le Corbusier, Charles-Édouard Jeanneret *called* 30.
Ledoux, Claude-Nicolas 26.
Lefaivre, Liane 40n.
Leonardo Da Vinci 125, 207.
Lewis, Douglas 17 37, 38, 40n, 123, *146*, 148, 160n.
Logorio, Pirro 92, 151.
Lombardo, Pietro 92.
Longair, Malcom 179, 184n.
Longhena, Baldassarre 7.
Lord Burlington, Richard Boyle III *called* 37, *94*.
Lucrino, Vincenzo 11.
Luther, Martin 23.
Madruzzo, Cristoforo, Cardinal 11.
Magagnato, Licisco 8, 15n.
Magagnò, Gian Battista Maganza *called* 9, 13, 41, *88*, 151, 160, 227.
March, Lionel 177, 179, 184n, 233.
Marcolini, Francesco 9, 159.
Marini, Paola 15n.
Mascherino, Ottavio (Ottaviano) 21.
Michelangelo Buonarroti, 11, 34, 115, 152.
Milizia, Francesco 151.
Mitrovic, Branko 113, 115, 128n, 179, 180, 184n.

263

Monza, Alberto 9, 227.
Morachiello, Paolo 27, 40n.
Muraro, Bartolomeo 35.
Muratori, Ludovico Antonio 240n.
Muttoni, Francesco Antonio 24, 28, *93*, *119*.
Muzio, Giovanni 145.
Navagero, Andrea 151.
Nervi, Pier Luigi 205.
Nettesheim, Agrippa von 177.
Orlando di Lasso, Roland de Lassus *called* 179.
Padovano, Gualtiero 151.
Pagello, Antenore 9.
Pagello, Giacomo 9, 227.
Palladio, Leonida 9, 13, 14, 39.
Palladio, Marcantonio 9, 39, *156*.
Palladio, Orazio 13, 14, 39.
Palladio, Silla (Sulla) 9, 12, 15, 33, 39, 159.
Palladio, Zenobia 9, 12.
Pane, Roberto 113, 117, 128n, 152, *232*.
Paul III, Alessandro Farnese, Pope 11.
Pausanias 148, 151.
Perrault, Claude 184.
Perret, Auguste 145.
Peruzzi, Baldassarre 11, 34, 91, 96, 116.
Piacentini, Marcello 145.
Piccolomini, Alessandro 155.
Piovene, family 227.
Piovene, Giuliano 123.
Piovene, Guido 17, 123, *177*, 225, 235, 240n.
Pirandello, Luigi 160.
Pisani, family 227.
Pisani, Francesco 13.
Pius IV, Giovanni Angelo Medici di Marignano, Pope 92.
Plato 115.
Poiana, Angela 9.
Poiana, Bonifacio 9.
Pomponazzi, family 227.
Praxiteles of Athens 11.
Priuli, Girolamo 225.
Ptolemy, Claudius Ptolemaeus *178*.
Puppi, Lionello 8, 13, 15n, 37, 38, 40n, 117, 123, 128n, 160n, 184n, 240n.
Raphael, Sanzio 10, 21, 35, 115, 123, 147, 151.
Ramusio, Giovan Battista *238*, 240.
Repeta, family 227.
Ridolfi, Niccolò 10.
Rilke, Rainer Maria 235, 240n.
Romano, Giulio 10, 11, 21, 37, 159.
Rupprecht, Bernhard 17, 18, 40n.
Sangallo, Antonio da 11, 34, 91, 119.
Sangallo, Giuliano da 205.

Sanmicheli, Michele 10, 11, 21.
Sansovino, Jacopo Tatti *called* 11, 12, 13, 31.
Saraceno, family 17, 227.
Scamozzi, Vincenzo 10, 15, 21, 34, 233.
Scharoun, Hans 233.
Schinkel Karl Friedrich 26, 28.
Scipio Africanus, Publius Cornelius *called* 18.
Semenzato, Camillo 8, 240n.
Semper, Gottfried 28.
Serego, family 13, 37, 239.
Serlio, Sebastiano 9, 10, 11, 19, 37, 89, 155.
Slusallek, Klaus 240n.
Smeraldi, Francesco 117.
Soane, John 28, 145.
Soragni, Ugo 227, 240n.
Speroni, Sperone 225.
Tafuri, Manfredo 8, 95, 96, 96n.
Temanza, Tomaso 119, 147.
Terragni, Giuseppe 145.
Terzo, Antonio 227.
Thiene, family 227.
Thiene, Marco 11.
Titian, Tiziano Vecellio *called* 17.
Tolstoy, Lev Nikolayevich 30.
Trento, Francesco 206.
Trissino, family 227.
Trissino, Giangiorgio 10, 11, 14, *37*, 39, 155, 177.
Turrini, Giancarlo 207, 208n.
Tzonis, Alexander 40n.
Valadier, Giuseppe 28.
Valery, Paul 28.
Valmarana, family 11, 21, 227.
Varro, Marcus Terentius 225.
Vasari, Giorgio 9, 13, 154.
Veronese, Paolo Caliari (or Cagliari) *called* il 17, 39, 148, 149, 151, *200*.
Vignola, Jacopo (or Giacomo) Barozzi (or Barocchio) *called* 31, 31, 113, 207.
Virginia 18.
Vitruvius Pollio, Marcus 10, 17, 18, 21, 31, 35, 91, 95, 113, 115, 123, 124, 147, 155, 159, 177, 183, 206, 229, 230, *238*.
Vittoria, Alessandro 151.
Volpe, Brunoro 31.
von Hofmannsthal, Hugo 235, 240n.
Wenders, Wim 124.
Wittkower, Rudolf 8, 17, *18*, 27, 115, 116, 117, 128n, 177, 179, 180, 183, 184n, 207.
Wren, Christopher 28.
Zamberlan, Francesco 39.
Zarlino, Gioseffo *178*, 179.
Zaupa, Giovanni 202, 208n, 227, 240n.

Zelotti, Giovanni Battista 18, 149, 151.
Zevi, Bruno 151.
Zorzi, Giangiorgio 15n, 39, 40n, 123, 128n, 159, 160n.
Zota, Maria *called* la 9.
Zuccari, Federico 39.

Index of places

The numbers correspond to the pages, the letter n to the notes.
The buildings designed, built or altered by Palladio are in bold,
the references to the illustrations in italics.

ANCONA
Arch 116.

AQUILEIA (UDINE) 11.

ATHENS (GREECE) 10.

BAGNOLO DI LONIGO (VICENZA)
Villa Pisani 10, 17, 31, 34, 37, 42, 44, 72, 79, 89, 90, 91, 92, 99, *100*, 139, *146*, 167, *186*, *189*, 208, 212, 223, *237*, *252*, *253*.

BASSANO DEL GRAPPA (VICENZA)
Bridge 13.
Villa Angarano 17.

BELLUNO 14.

BERLIN (GERMANY)
Philharmonic Hall 233.

BERTESINA (VICENZA)
Villa Gazzotti 10, 31, 42, 89, 92.

BOLOGNA
San Petronio 14, *123*, 127, 154, 229.

BRESCIA
Basilica 177, 201.
Cathedral 23.
Tosio-Martinengo gallery 152.
Town Hall *35*, 39.

BUDAPEST (HUNGARY)
Museum of Beaux-Arts 38.

CALDOGNO (VICENZA)
Villa Caldogno 31, 37, 39, 43, 44, 48, 79, 80, 82, 83, 84, 239, *252*.
Villa Saraceno 10.

CAMPELLO SUL CLITUNNO (PERUGIA)
Temple 113, *114*.

CAMPIGLIA DEI BERICI (VICENZA)
Villa Repeta 12, 17, *237*, 239.

CANADA *238*.

CAPRANICA (VITERBO)
Cupola by Bramante 145.

CARPI (MODENA)
Church 116.

CHAMBORD (FRANCE)
Castle 207, *207*.

CICOGNA DI VILLAFRANCA PADOVANA (PADUA)
Villa Thiene 17, *20*, 239.

CIVIDALE DEL FRIULI (UDINE)
Palazzo Pretorio 13.
Town Hall *139*.

CRICOLI DI VICENZA (VICENZA)
Villa Cricoli 10.
Villa Trissino 7, 17, 230.

DOLO (VENICE)
Villa Mocenigo 17.

DONEGAL DI CESSALTO (TREVISO)
Villa Zeno 13, 17, 46, 147, *164*, *256*.

FANO (PESARO AND URBINO)
Basilica 124.

FANZOLO DI VEDELAGO (TREVISO)
Villa Emo Capodilista 13, 17, 18, 32, 33, 46, 92, *101*, 149, *161*, 239, *254*.

FINALE DI AGUGLIARO (VICENZA)
Villa Saraceno 11, 17, 42, *48*, 89, 239.

FLORENCE
Santa Maria Novella 116.

FRATTA POLESINE (ROVIGO)
Villa Badoer, called La Badoera 12, 17, *19*, 32, 33, *43*, *48*, *51*, 72, 92, *101*, 210, 239, *241*, *253*, *255*.

GENAZZANO (ROME)
Nymphaeum 145.

GENOA 10.

GHIZZOLE DI MONTEGALDELLA (VICENZA)
Villa Ragona 12, 17, 207, 239.

HOCHELAGA (CANADA) *238*, 239.

INNSBRUCK (AUSTRIA) 11.

ITALY 10, 11, 12, 15, 28, 90, 233.

LABADEIA (GREECE)
Sanctuary of Trophonius 148.

LEIPZIG (GERMANY) 160.

LEPANTO 152.

LISIERA DI BOLZANO VICENTINO (VICENZA)
Villa Valmarana 13, 92.

LONDON (UK)
Globe Theatre 155.
Royal Institute of British Architects (RIBA) 20, *20*, 21, 22, 24, 27, *30*, 33, *35*, 37, *37*, 38, *39*, *39*, 40, 89, *90*, 94, 113, *114*, *115*, 116, *118*, *119*, 123, *126*, 127, 145, *146*, 148, *156*, *202*.

LONEDO DI LUGO (VICENZA)
Villa Godi Valmarana 9, 39, 42, 79, *84*, *85*, 89, 145, 149, *151*, *166*, *180*, *211*, *218*, 239.
Villa Piovene 46.

LONGARE DI COSTOZZA (VICENZA)
Villa Trento, called Eolia 206.

MALCONTENTA DI MIRA (VENICE)
Villa Foscari, called La Malcontenta 7, 12, 17, 32, 45, 52, 68, 92, *108*, 167, *168*, *169*, 181, *190*, 202, 210, 214, 219, 222, *236*, 239, *244*, *246*.

MANTUA 37.

MAROCCO DI MOGLIANO (TREVISO)
Villa Mocenigo 17, *20*, 39, 92, *183*.

MASER (TREVISO)
Villa Barbaro 15, 17, 39, 40, 46, 48, 49, 66, 69, 78, 109, 110, 148, 149, 151, 154, *164*, 170, 171, 174, 181, *188*, 200, 208, *243*, *249*, *253*.

MELEDO DI SAREGO (VICENZA)
Villa Trissino 13, 17, *43*, 207, *228*, 230.

MIEGA DI COLOGNA VENETA (VERONA)
Villa Sarego 17.

MILAN
Cathedral 23.

MONTAGNANA (PADUA) 13.
Villa Pisani 12, 17, 31, 32, 33, 37, *45*, 89, 92, 147, 181, 183, *210*, 239.

MONTE BERICO (VICENZA) 10, 14.

MONTECCHIO PRECALCINO (VICENZA)
Villa Forni-Cerato 89.

MONTICELLO (VIRGINIA, USA) 230.

NAPLES
Chapel of San Giacomo degli Spagnoli 119.

NIMES (FRANCE) 13.

ORANGE (FRANCE)
Arch 151.

ORIAGO DI MIRA (VENICE)
Villa Mocenigo on the Brenta 13, 17, 92, 20.

PADUA
Palazzo della Ragione 9, 10, 11, 90, 155.

PALERMO
Palace of the Cuba 233, 240n.
Palace of the Zisa 233, 240n.

PALESTRINA (ROME)
Sanctuary of Fortuna Primigenia 9, *33*.

PARIS (FRANCE)
Ecole des Beaux-Arts 35.
Louvre 31, 154.

PESARO
Port *37*.

PIEDMONT 11, 13.

PIOMBINO DESE (PADUA)
Villa Cornaro 7, 12, 17, 28, 32, 35, *43*, *50*, 73, *83*, 92, *109*, 110, 147, 183, 187, *189*, 219, 235.

POGGIO A CAIANO (PRATO)
Villa Medicea 90.

POIANA MAGGIORE (VICENZA)
Villa Poiana 9, 11, 17, 31, 33, 34, *42*, 68, *69*, 89, 123, 145, 149, *163*, 164, *168*, *192*, *193*, *209*, 217, 239, *256*.

POLA (CROATIA)
Theatre of Mount Zaro 155.

POMPEII (NAPLES) 183.

PROVENCE (FRANCE) 11, 13.

QUINTO VICENTINO (VICENZA)
Villa Thiene 11, 17, *20*, *44*, 183, *213*.

RAVENNA
Porta Aurea 29.

ROCCAVERANO (ASTI)
Church 116.

ROME - VATICAN
Arch of Constantine *29*, *33*.
Arch of Settimio Severo 151.
Balbi crypt 21, *202*, 205.
Belvedere Courtyard 89, *90*, 201, 208.
Campo Marzio 11.
Church of San Carlino 7.
Church of Sant'Eligio degli Orefici 239.
Church of Sant'Ivo 7.
Church of Santo Spirito in Sassia 11.
Church of St. Paul outside the Walls 7, 19, 154.
Church of St. Peter (San Pietro) 11, 127, 152.
Colosseum *30*, 31.
Farnesina ai Baullari 32.
Forum of Nerva 33, 124, 160.
Palazzetto Le Roy 91.
Palazzo dei Conservatori 152.
Palazzo dei Massimi 201.
Palazzo dei Tribunali 21.
Palazzo del Quirinale 21.
Palazzo Falconieri 7.
Pantheon 11, 27, 123, *123*, 128.
Porta Maggiore 35.
Porta Santo Spirito 201.
Portico of the Celio 35.
Quirinale Hill 38.
Santo Spirito Hospital, altar 11.
Temple by Bramante, in San Pietro in Vincoli court 201.
Temple of Mars Ultor 39.
Temple of Romulus 27.
Temple of Serapidis 38.
Temples of Portunus 32.
Trajan's Market 145.
Vallicelliana Library 7.

Via Appia 239.
Via Giulia 21.
Via Prenestina *33*, 145.
Villa Giulia 32.

RONCADE (TREVISO)
Villa Giustiniani 92, 96.

SANTA SOFIA DI PEDEMONTE (VERONA)
Villa Serego 17, *19*, 32, 37, *45*, *47*, *72*, *138*, *139*, 239.

SIRMIONE (BRESCIA) 11.

SPOLETO (PERUGIA)
Roman Tomb 30.

TIVOLI (ROME)
Garden of the Esperidi 151.
Temple of Hercules 37.
Temple of Vesta 33.
Villa d'Este 151.

TRENTO 11.

UDINE
Palazzo Antonini 12, 17, 32, 79, 92, *139*, 183.

VANCIMUGLIO (VICENZA)
Villa Chiericati 12, 32, 39, *43*, *45*, *84*, 92, *105*, 106, *109*.

VENETO 14, 205, 206, *226*.

VENICE
Carampane 147.
Church and Convent of Charity 12, 15, *60*, *61*, *86*, 147, 167, 183, 207, 213, 220.
Church of Il Redentore at the Giudecca 14, 15, 24, *24*, 26, *64*, 71, 74, 113, 117, 119, *119*, 124, 125, 127, 128, 131, *132*, 134, *136*, 144, *198*, 239, *249*.
Church of Saint Mark 119.
Church of San Francesco della Vigna 29, 34, 38, *62*, *69*, 115, 116, 117, 129, *130*, 239.
Church of San Giorgio Maggiore 21, 23, 24, *58*, *59*, *62*, *64*, 74, *76*, *78*, 118, 119, 127, 128, 130, 132, 133, 134, 152, 201, 239, *248*, *251*.
Church of San Pietro di Castello 12, 34, 117, 119, 127.
Church of Santa Lucia 12.
Church of Santa Maria della Salute 7.
Church of Santa Maria di Castello *130*.
Church of the Le Zitelle *78*, *130*, 239, *249*.
Grand Canal 28, 147.

Marciana Library 31.
Nicolini Chapel in Santa Croce 38.
Palazzo Capra 183.
Palazzo Ducale 12, 14, 39, *79*.
Palazzo Foscari in Santa Croce 13.
Rialto bridge 12, *25*, *27*, *28*, 38, *206*, *231*, *232*.
Rio terà of Sant'Agnese 147.

VENOSA (POTENZA) 179.

VERONA
Arch of Jupiter Ammon 127.
Gavi arch 31.
Palazzo Dalla Torre 12, 13, 17, 92, 183, 207.
Roman theatre *33*, *202*.
Villa della Torre 17.

VERONELLA (VERONA)
Villa Cucca 13.

VICENZA
Accademia Olimpica 12, 155.
Basilica 90, *93*, *103*, *111*, *140*.
Berga theatre 155.
Casa Cogollo 12, 54, *141*.
Cathedral (Basilica of Santa Maria Maggiore) 7, 12, 13, *72*, *87*, 90, *130*, 154, 201.
Church of San Lorenzo 31.
Church of Santa Corona 14, 15, *82*.
Church of Santa Maria dei Servi 9.
Church of Santa Maria Nova 14, 23, 115, *130*.
Civic Museum *25*, *27*, *29*, *33*, 37, 38, *226*.
Convent of San Michele 9.
Corso Palladio 35.
Duomo *248*.
House of the Filippini 7, 154.
Loggia del Capitanio 13, 15, 21, 28, 32, 33, *70*, *72*, 91, 148, 151, *151*, 152, 154, *172*, *174*, 205, *212*, *217*.
Palazzo Angarano 13, 19.
Palazzo Barbaran(o) 13, 21, 32, 34, 39, 54, 141, *141*, 148, *172*, 183, *194*.
Palazzo Chiericati 11, 21, 30, 31, 32, 33, *56*, *72*, *79*, 89, 90, 91, *94*, *97*, *98*, *99*, 112, 148, 151, 154, 181, *186*, *192*, *193*, *216*, *222*, *254*, 239.
Palazzo Civena 10, *27*, 37, *139*, *171*.
Palazzo Cividale 37.
Palazzo Colleoni Porto 9.
Palazzo Da Monte *27*, 38, 123.
Palazzo di Antonio Giovanni Capra 35.
Palazzo Garzadori 92.
Palazzo Iseppo da Porto 7, 11, 21, *22*, 31, 34, *54*, *56*, *70*, *79*, *84*, *86*, 147, 148, 149, 154, *171*, 183, 205, *205*, 239.
Palazzo Poiana 12, *139*.
Palazzo Porto-Breganze 14, 21, 34, *55*, *70*, 123, 152, 154, *172*.
Palazzo Schio 13, 37, *84*, *138*.
Palazzo Thiene 10, 19, 21, 34, 35, 37, *55*, *57*, *86*, *138*, *139*, 154, 159, 181, *188*, 205, *212*, *213*, *224*, 239.
Palazzo Bonin Thiene 21, *70*.
Palazzo Trissino 12, 19, 92.
Palazzo Valmarana 13, 32, 33, 34, 37, *87*, 123, 124, *126*, *127*, *141*, 151, 152, *182*, 183.
Piazza dei Latini 21.
Piazza del Castello 35.
Piazza dell'Isola 91.
Piazza delle Erbe 11.
Piazza Maggiore 12.
Roman Theatre 159.
Teatro Olimpico 15, 33, 39, *70*, *72*, *78*, *143*, 151, 152, 155, *155*, *156*, 159, 160, *173*, *176*, 203, *217*, *250*.
Town Hall 90.
Valmarana Chapel at Santa Corona 14, *82*.
Via del Monte 152.
Villa Almerico, called La Rotonda 13, 15, 17, 19, 32, *33*, 35, *46*, 92, 96, 151, *110*, 154, 181, *185*, *196*, 205, 206, *210*, *211*, *216*, *217*, *221*, 230, *233*, *235*.
Villa Garzadori 17, 92.
Villa Montano Barbarano 154.
Villa Valmarana ai Nani *41*, *88*.

VIGARDOLO DI MONTICELLO (VICENZA)
Villa Valmarana 10, *42*, *82*, *146*, 148, *192*.

WASHINGTON (D.C., USA) 37.

WINDSOR (UK)
Windsor Castle 231.

WORCESTER (UK)
College *123*, 128.

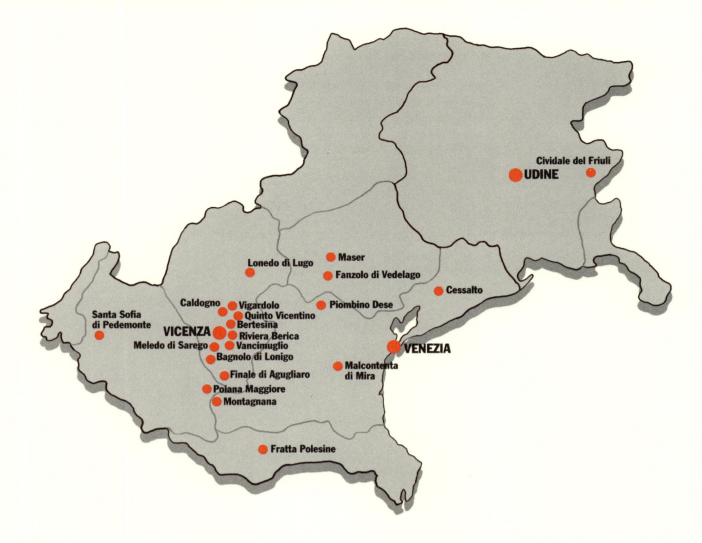

List of Palladian buildings illustrated in the book

BAGNOLO DI LONIGO (VICENZA)
Villa Pisani

BERTESINA (VICENZA)
Villa Gazzotti

CALDOGNO (VICENZA)
Villa Caldogno

CESSALTO (TREVISO)
Villa Zeno

CIVIDALE DEL FRIULI (UDINE)
Palazzo Pretorio

FANZOLO DI VEDELAGO (TREVISO)
Villa Emo Capodilista

FINALE DI AGUGLIARO (VICENZA)
Villa Saraceno

FRATTA POLESINE (ROVIGO)
Villa Badoer

LONEDO DI LUGO (VICENZA)
Villa Godi
Villa Piovene

MALCONTENTA DI MIRA (VENICE)
Villa Foscari

MASER (TREVISO)
Villa Barbaro

MELEDO DI SAREGO (VICENZA)
Villa Trissino

MONTAGNANA (PADUA)
Villa Pisani

PIOMBINO DESE (PADUA)
Villa Cornaro

POIANA MAGGIORE (VICENZA)
Villa Poiana

QUINTO VICENTINO (PADUA)
Villa Thiene

RIVIERA BERICA (VICENZA)
Villa Almerico called La Rotonda

SANTA SOFIA DI PEDEMONTE (VERONA)
Villa Serego

UDINE
Palazzo Antonini

VANCIMUGLIO (VICENZA)
Villa Chiericati

VENICE
Church of Il Redentore
Church of Le Zitelle
Church of San Francesco della Vigna
Church of San Giorgio Maggiore
Church of Santa Maria di Castello
Convent of Charity
Convent of San Giorgio Maggiore
Palazzo Ducale (The Doge's Palace)

VICENZA
Basilica
The Valmarana Chapel
Casa Cogollo
Church of Santa Maria Nova
Cathedral Basilica of St. Mary Major
The Loggia del Capitanio
Palazzo Barbaran(o)
Palazzo Bonin Thiene
Palazzo Chiericati
Palazzo Civena
Palazzo Iseppo da Porto
Palazzo Poiana
Palazzo Porto-Breganze
Palazzo Schio
Palazzo Thiene
Teatro Olimpico
Villa Valmarana ai Nani

VIGARDOLO DI MONTICELLO (VICENZA)
Villa Valmarana

© 2008 UMBERTO ALLEMANDI & C., TURIN
EDITORIAL COORDINATION LINA OCARINO
DESKTOP PUBLISHING ELISABETTA PADUANO
PHOTOLITHOGRAPHY FOTOMEC, TURIN
PRINTED IN THE MONTH OF SEPTEMBER 2008
BY TIPO STAMPA, MONCALIERI (TURIN)